# A Perth Camera

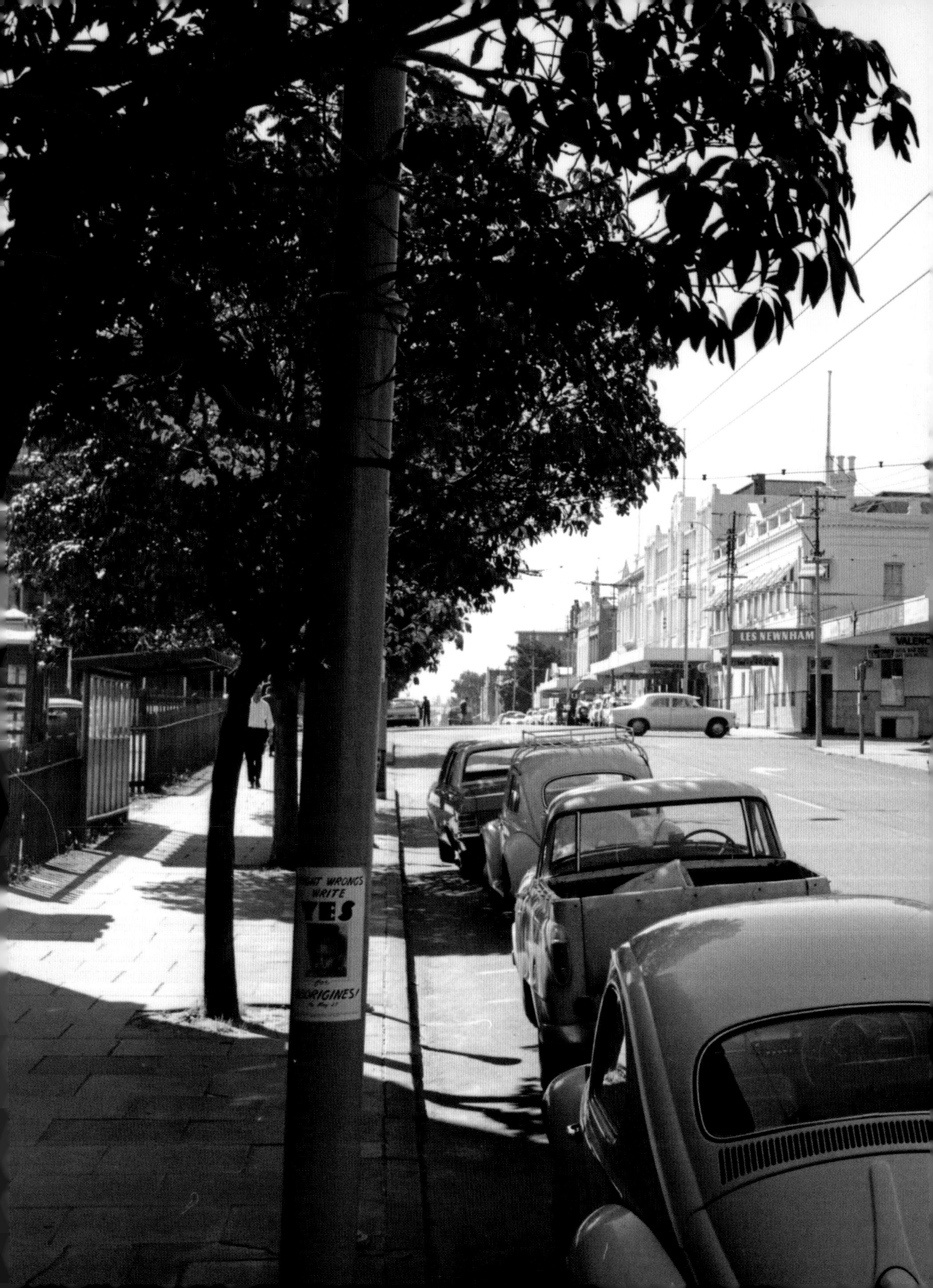
WRONGS
WRITE
YES
LES NEWNHAM

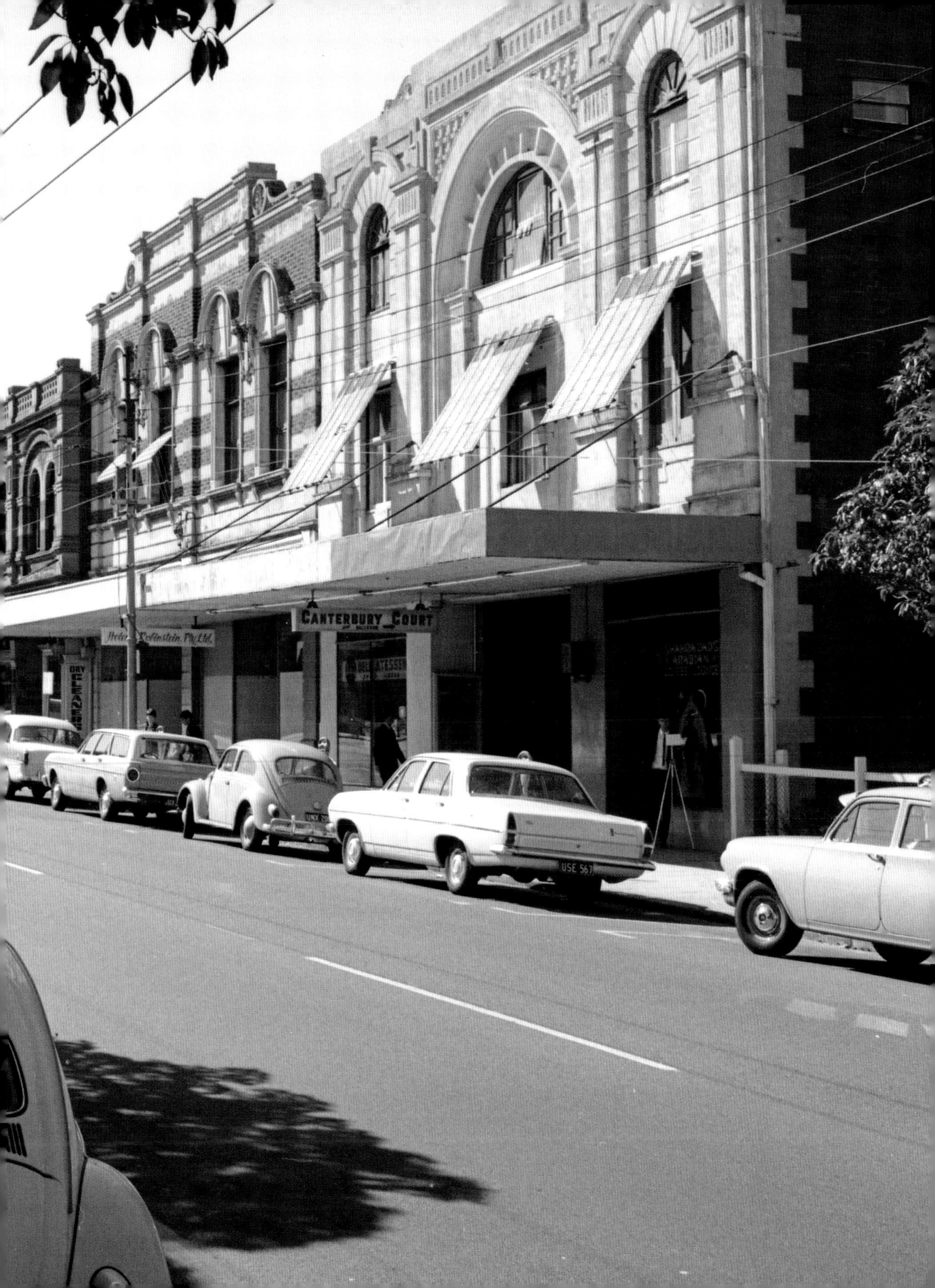
CANTERBURY COURT
Helena Rubinstein Pty. Ltd.
DRY CLEANERS
USE 567

Pavilion
An imprint of HarperCollinsPublishers Ltd
1 London Bridge Street
London SE1 9GF

www.harpercollins.co.uk

HarperCollinsPublishers
1st Floor, Watermarque Building
Ringsend Road Dublin 4
Ireland

10 9 8 7 6 5 4 3 2 1

First published in Great Britain by Pavilion, an imprint of HarperCollinsPublishers Ltd 2022



Richard Offen asserts the moral right to be identified as the author of this work.
A catalogue record for this book is available from the British Library.

ISBN 978-1-911682-73-8

This book is produced from independently certified FSC™ paper
to ensure responsible forest management.

MIX
Paper from responsible sources
FSC™ C007454

For more information visit:
www.harpercollins.co.uk/green

Printed and bound in China by RR Donnelley APS



**PREVIOUS PAGE:** Ernie Polis's pin-sharp depiction of ordinary Perth street scenes will provide a lasting record of the late 20th-century city.

# A Perth Camera

**Richard Offen**

PAVILION

# Ernie Polis

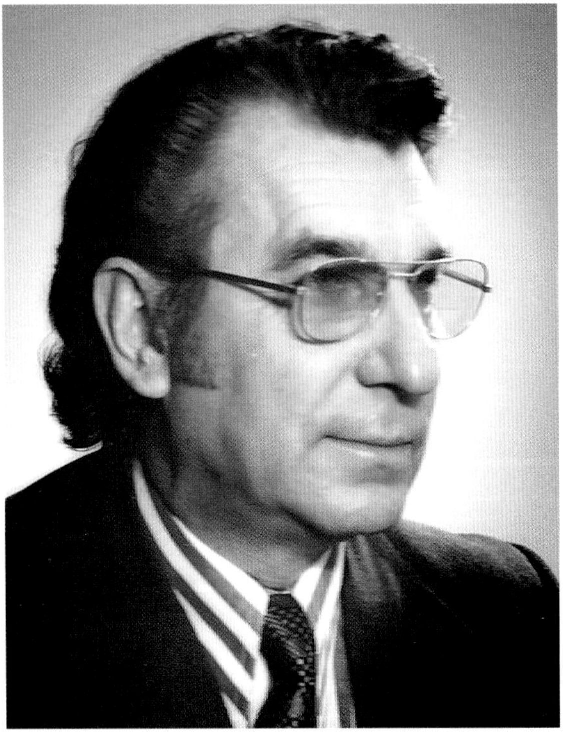

**Ernest Polis** was born in October, 1921 at Virbi, Latvia, the only child to Fricis and Olga Polis. At the age of 10 he bought his first camera and during his high school years studied photography and learnt to develop film and print photographs. After high school he studied architecture, but the Soviet occupation of Latvia in 1940 brought this to a premature end.

After the War, Ernie found himself in Wurzburg, Bavaria, where he was reunited with his childhood sweetheart, Austra, and they married in 1947. Unable to return to their beloved Latvia due to Soviet occupation the couple decided to leave war-torn Europe and migrate to Australia.

Arriving at Fremantle in September 1949, Ernie and Austra were eventually transferred by train to Lake Biddy, just north of Newdegate. Living in tents, Ernest was obliged to work for the Western Australian Government Railways (WAGR) as a fettler.

Whilst living at Lake Biddy, Ernie made friends with Tom Marsden, a local bank manager, who quickly discovered Ernie's talents as an artist, draftsman and photographer. Tom managed to convince Government officials that Ernie's skills could be better employed elsewhere. As a result, after a year at Lake Biddy, Ernie and Austra moved to Perth, where Ernie was taken on by the State Planning Department as a draftsman. Ernie's photographic skills were soon put to use, and he began taking photographs for government publications.

In 1965 Ernie gained a position with the City of Perth as Chief Draftsman in the Planning Department and was later appointed as the Council's official photographer. This gave him accreditation as a press photographer, which he discovered would gain him access to many events and functions without a ticket.

Photography was his passion and he managed to purchase high quality cameras and accessories, building a large dark room with state-of-the-art equipment. In the early 1970s he entered the world of colour film processing, much of which was self-taught.

In his spare time, Ernie continued to perfect his photographic skills, joining various camera clubs in order to do so. This led, in 1957, to him winning the Kodak Trophy for the best amateur photo taken in Western Australia. He continued to win the award for the next nine years until 1965, when he was made a judge, putting an end to his winning streak!

Following success in numerous state, national and international competitions, Ernie's abilities were given further recognition when he was admitted as an Associate of the Royal Photographic Society of Great Britain in 1969.

Ernie never left home without a camera and the shutter was constantly clicking away wherever he went: social events, picnics, weddings, or just a walk through Perth City all became subjects of his photographs.

Ernie's early interest in architecture probably helped him to realise the historic value of photographic records and he often commented, "what is here today is gone tomorrow and people forget." This resulted in commissions from historians and authors, with his photographs being published in a wide range of books and publications across Australia.

Ernie and Austra had two children, son Ernest Jnr born in 1951, and daughter Ina born in 1966. Both grew up with the never-ending experience of staring into the lens of a camera, the enduring memories of which now survive and are cherished by the Polis family.

Ernest died in 1993 aged 72 and the world of photography lost one of its masters.

**BELOW:** The Royal Hotel, Wellington Street from the corner of Horseshoe Bridge in the 1950s and still with us today.

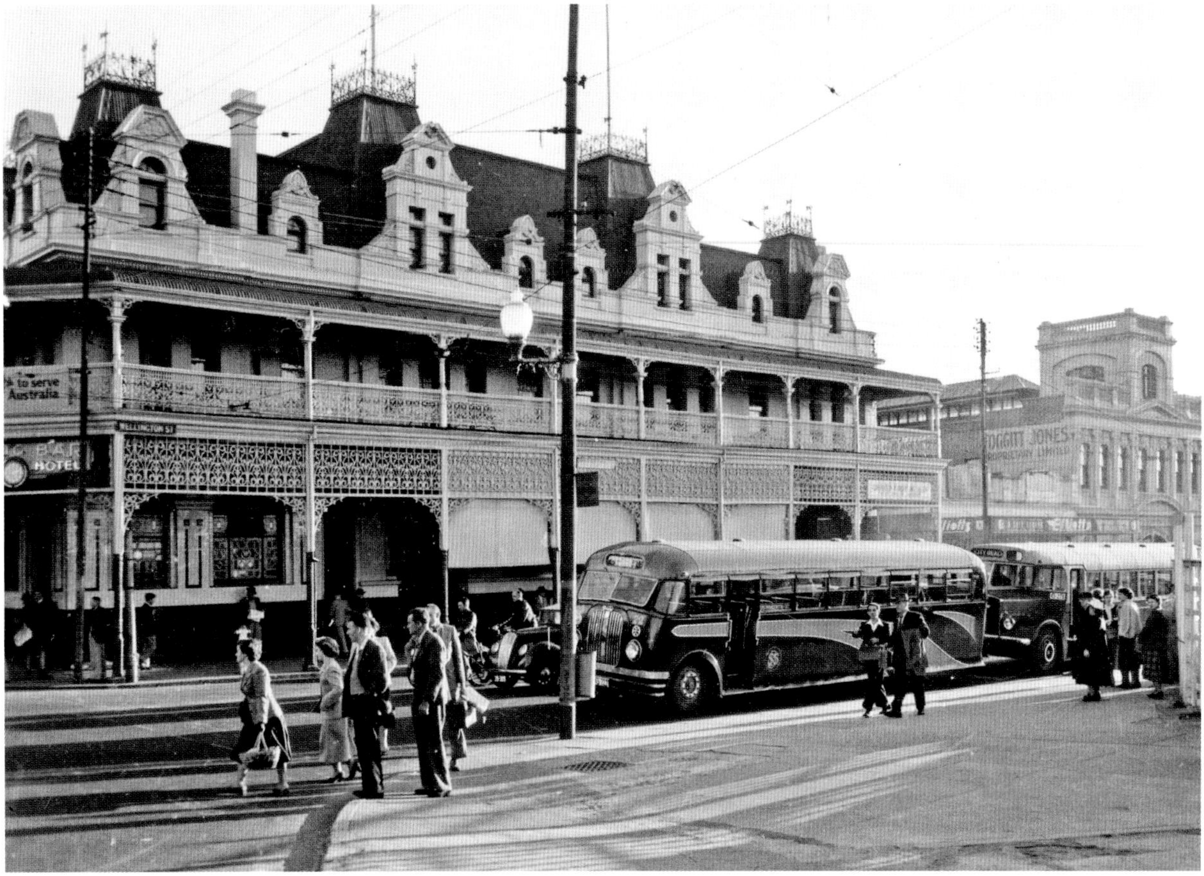

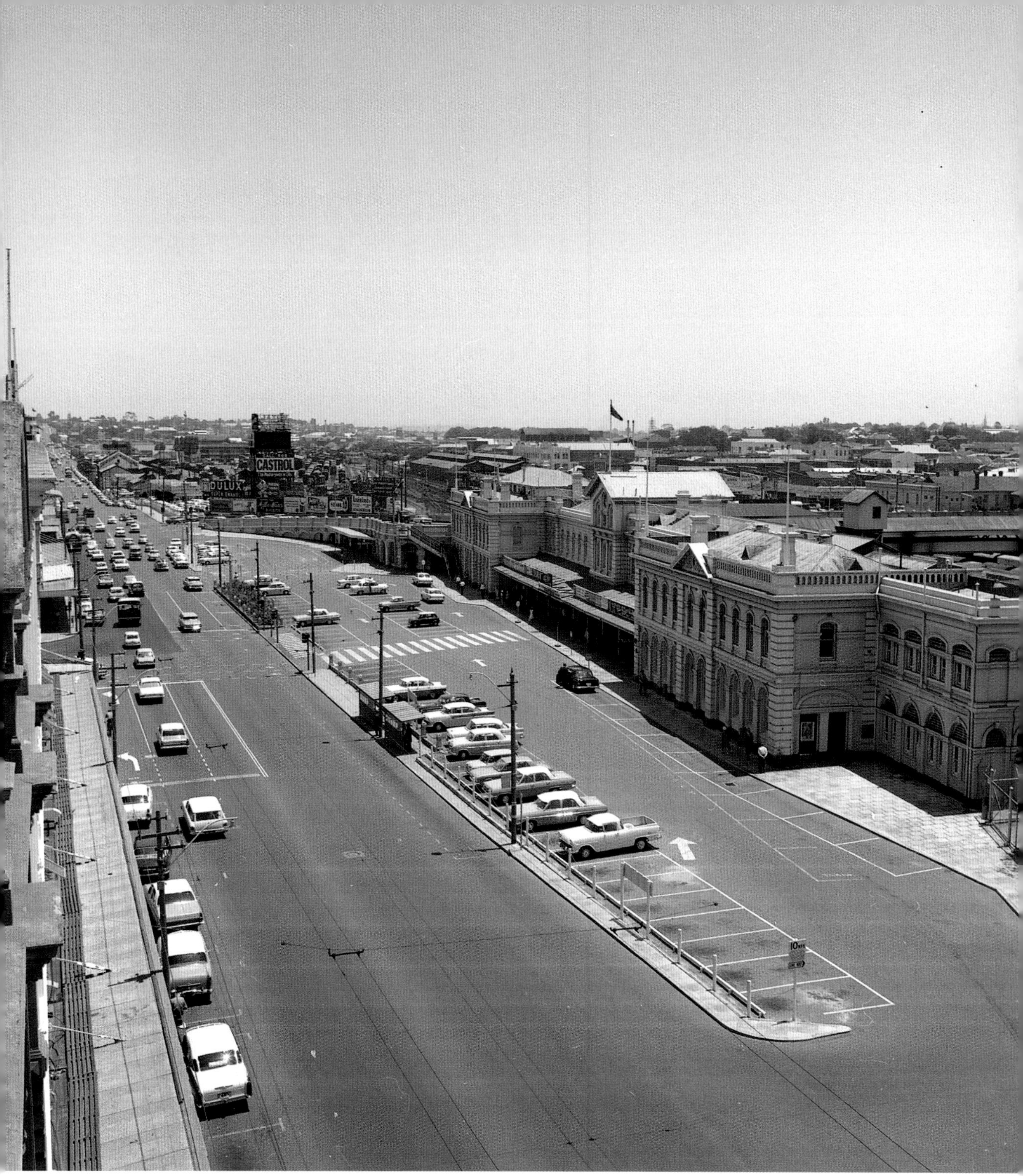


**ABOVE:** A view of Perth Railway Station in the late 1950s, with a low-rise cityscape.

# Introduction

## Perth: The new city

During the period immediately following World War II the Perth metropolitan area experienced a housing shortage, with an estimated 250-300,000 homes needed to accommodate a rapidly growing population. This shortfall was exacerbated by a lack of raw materials and skilled labour to make the Australian dream of home ownership a reality.

At about the same time, the Federal Government created an Assisted Passage Migration Scheme as part of their 'Populate or Perish' policy. Adult migrants, principally from Britain, were charged only £10 for their fare, with children travelling free. Those who took up the scheme became known as 'Ten Pound Poms'.

Around a million Britons took up the scheme during the 1950s and 60s, of whom three-quarters made Australia their permanent new home. As a result of this influx, the population of Perth changed in size and character during the 1950s as immigration brought new cultures and traditions to the city.

By 1952 it became clear that a carefully formulated strategy was required to create a systematic and well-planned way to accelerate city expansion to accommodate the growing population.

To achieve this, the State Government invited renowned town planner, Professor Gordon Stephenson, to draw up plans for the future development of the metropolitan region. Together with local planner Alastair Hepburn, Stephenson put together a blueprint that was to shape city planning for the rest of the 20th century.

The Stephenson-Hepburn plan accepted that the age of the automobile had arrived and envisaged a system of freeways and major highways enabling commuters to cross the city easily from far-flung suburbs. The rush to 'modernise' Perth began.

A major phase of development, spurred on by further mineral booms of the 1960s, 70s and 80s saw skyscrapers built and the city skyline radically change, at the cost of much of its built history and heritage. For many this was an inevitable trade-off, a casualty of progress.

Into this post-World War II Perth entered a young and talented photographer, Ernie Polis. Working for the City Council, Ernie got to know about buildings that were being knocked down, modernised or reconfigured and was determined to capture them on celluloid for posterity. In doing so, he did not just photograph the large and architecturally spectacular buildings of Perth; he also captured the humble domestic and commercial structures that would have been long forgotten had it not been for Ernie's camera.

This book contains a selection from the hundreds of photographs of Perth and the surrounding area taken by Ernie over a thirty-year period. While the bricks of Perth's past may be buried beneath today's buildings and freeways, here they stand fully assembled as a permanent record, as viewed through the steady lens of Ernie Polis.

1

# Lost from the Landscape

Like all cities, Perth has undergone significant growth and change during its history. The most significant changes began during the first gold rush of the 1890s and continued throughout the 20th century. Ernie Polis recorded many of the losses in the city, with a variety of buildings photographed on the eve of demolition.

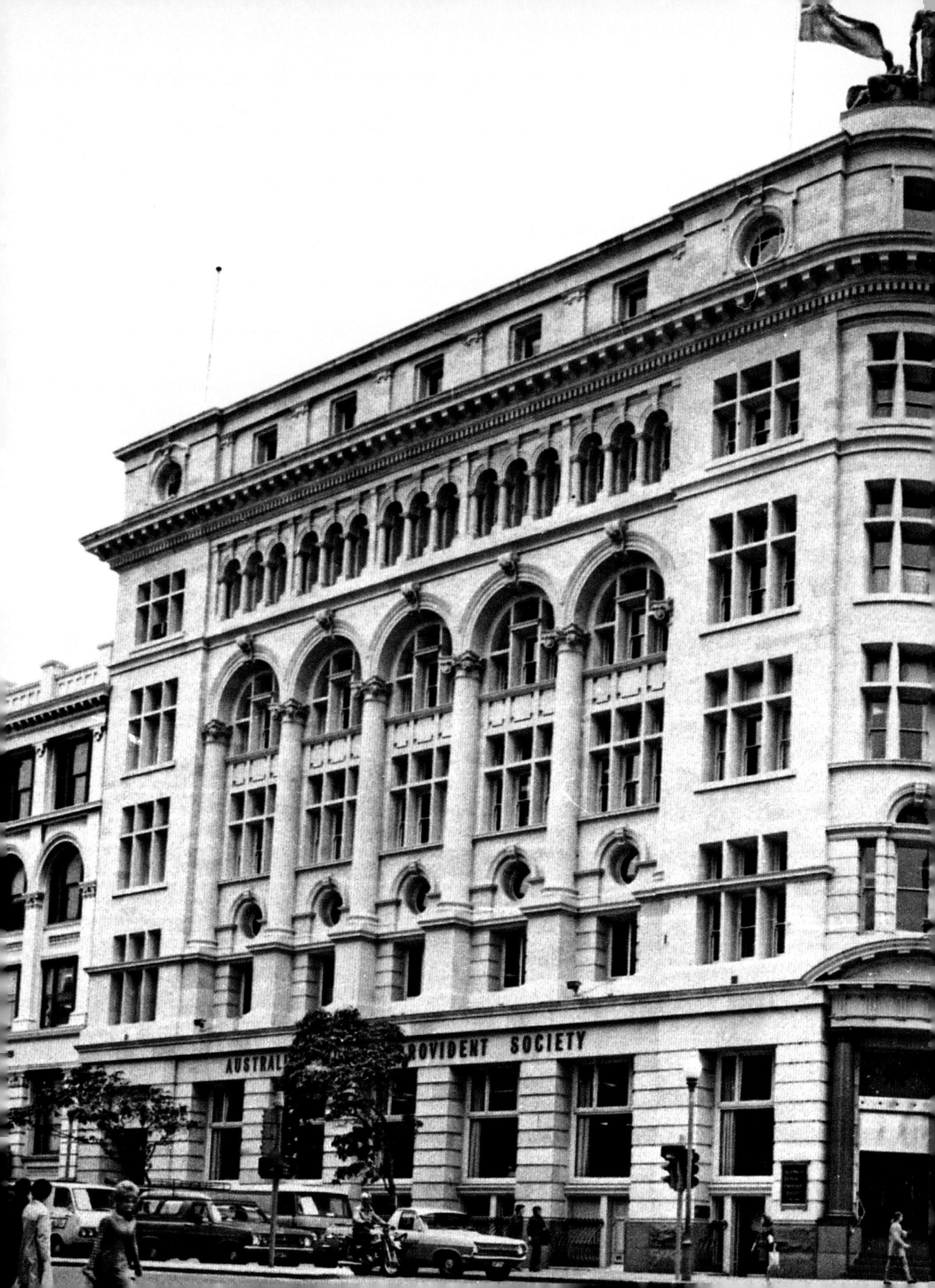
AUSTRAL
ROVIDENT SOCIETY

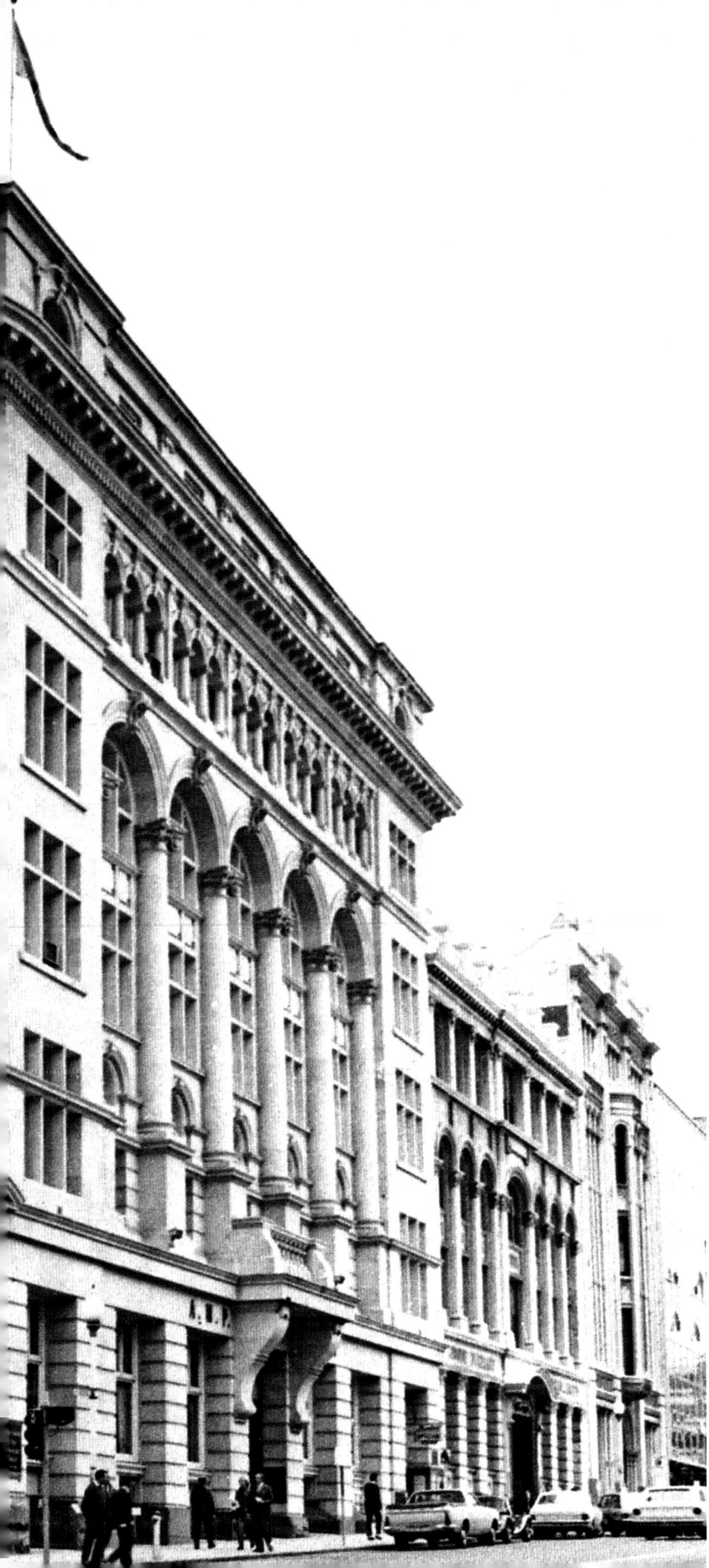

## **AMP Building** 1970

The AMP Building, on the north-west corner of the junction between St Georges Terrace and William Street is probably one of the greatest architectural losses to Perth during the last quarter of the 20th century.

Built for the Australian Mutual Provident Society, the foundation stone was laid by the Governor of Western Australia, Sir Edward Stone, in a ceremony on 8 November, 1912. This six-storey, plus basement, building was designed in what the local newspapers described as 'a dignified adaptation of the Romanesque style' and clad in white Donnybrook stone, with an interior decorated with jarrah. The top of the new building featured an iconic bronze statue of a central figure, symbolising 'protection', flanked by a man, woman and child.

Following the demolition of the building in 1972, the statue was purchased by millionaire collector Lew Whiteman. After Whiteman's death it was sold to a private buyer and can now be seen on an island in Herdsman Lake.

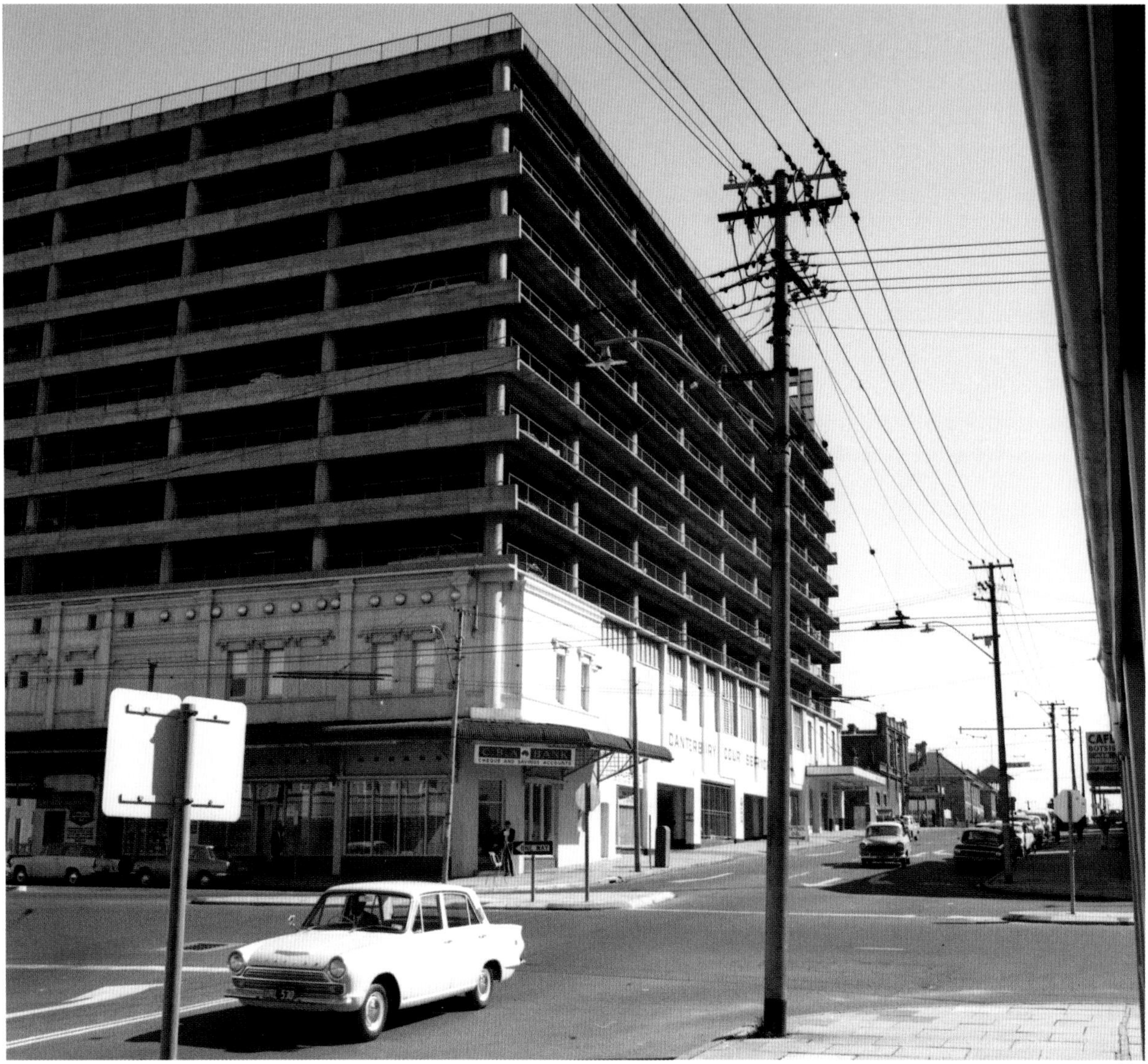

## Canterbury Court c.1970

Ernie's image of Canterbury Court does not, perhaps, show it at its architectural best, but it is probably how most Perth residents remember it. The Stirling Street site became an entertainment venue in 1911 when it was transformed from a wood yard into the Shaftesbury Picture Gardens, among the first outdoor cinemas in Perth. The cinema's programme usually changed twice a week and consisted of a feature film, plus vaudeville acts and live music. After World War I, film screenings ceased and the theatre became 'Perth's home of vaudeville'.

In 1949 the theatre was converted into Western Australia's first ice rink (a novelty in warm-weathered Perth) and five years later it became the Canterbury Court Ballroom. A multi-storey car park was added to the top of the building in 1969 and dancing continued, until the entire building, which had probably undergone more name changes than any other entertainment venue in Perth's history, was visited by a wrecking ball in 1990.

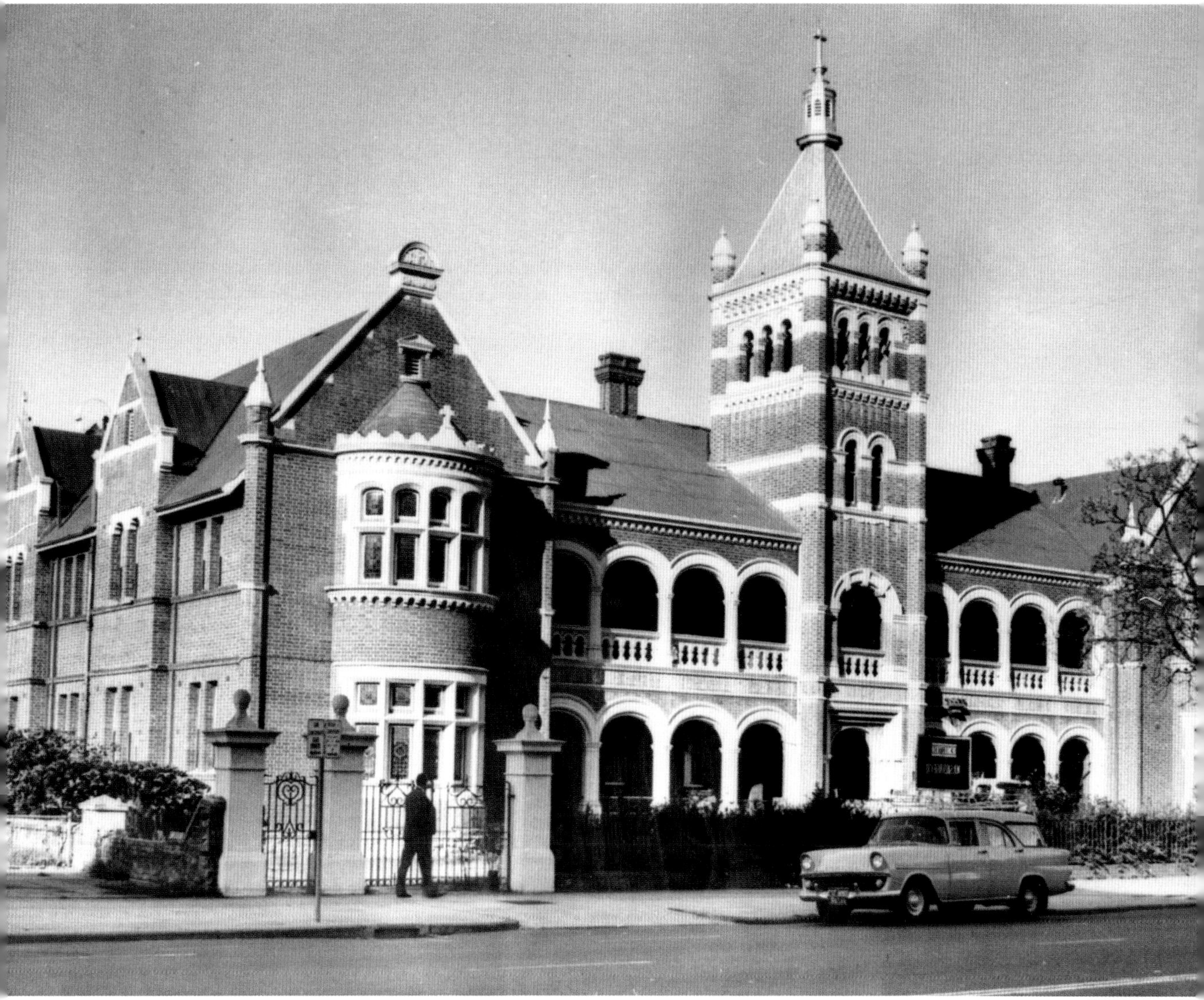

## **Christian Brothers School** c.1965

On arrival in Perth in 1893, the Christian Brothers purchased a 3-acre block on the corner of St Georges Terrace and Victoria Avenue on which a house and other buildings already stood. This house was used as the Brothers' residence and another 'wretched brick structure' was converted into a school which opened in February 1894 with 13 students.

By the beginning of 1895 the old building was found to be too small. To address the problem, plans were made for a new school building, which was eventually built in three stages. To fund the new building, one of the brothers went round the goldfields asking for donations and raised £2,000 in the process.

In 1938 boarders and some day-students were moved to the new Aquinas College at Salter Point, but the Perth campus continued as a day school until 1961 when Perth City Council acquired the site and demolished the building in 1965 to make way for the Duxton Hotel.

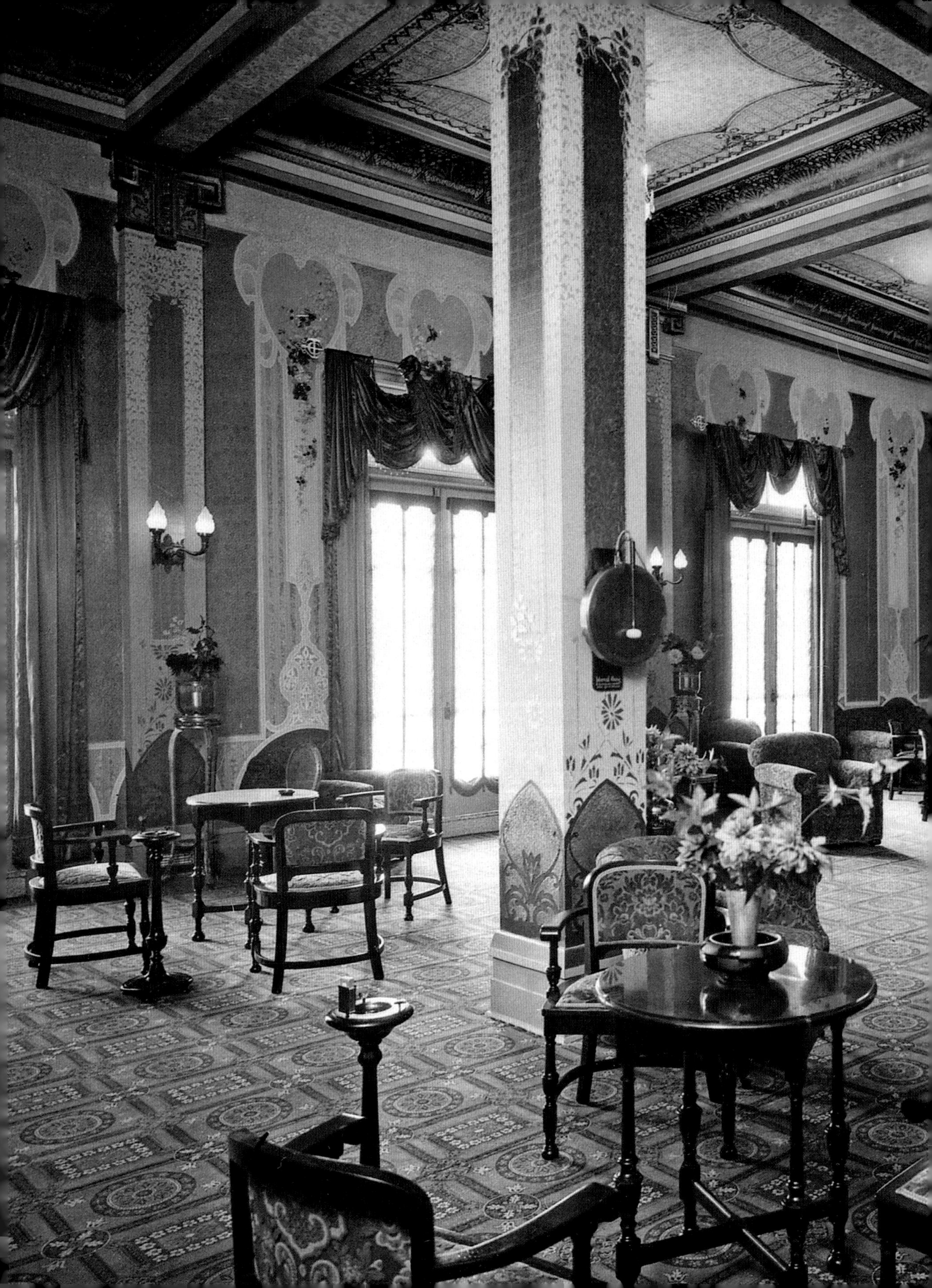

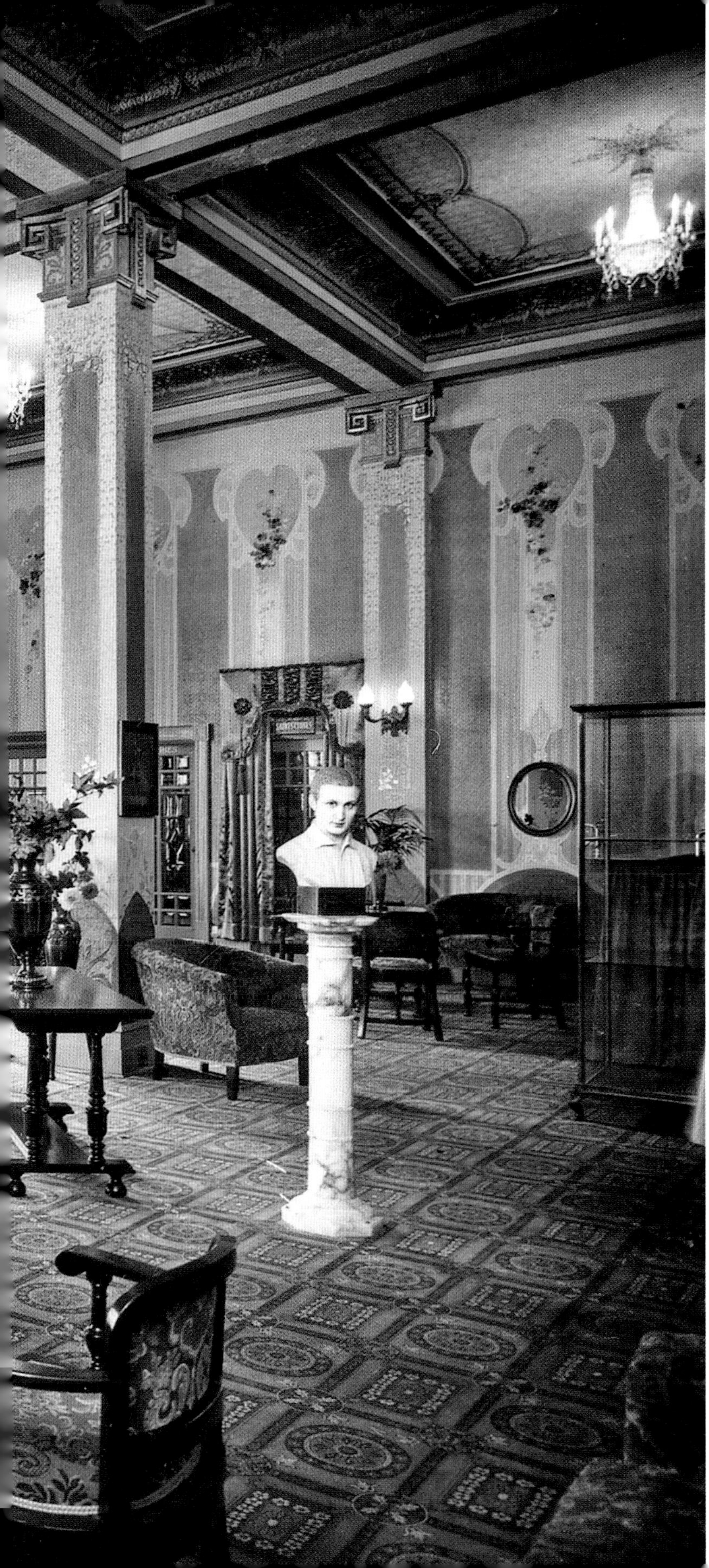

## Capitol Theatre 1968

**LEFT:** The Capitol Theatre was designed by George Temple Poole and Christian Mouritzen in the Art Nouveau style. It opened in May 1929 and was the first cinema in Australia with an RCA 'Photophone' – one of the earliest 'talkies' projectors. Other features included a huge illuminated sign on the roof and a bust of the late Rudolph Valentino, said to have permanently red lips from the kisses of his Perth fans.

While the majority of Ernie Polis's images featured external architecture, he seems to have enjoyed shooting interiors, treating them as if destined for a magazine or promotional brochure. This shot, in particular, shows the quality of his interior work.

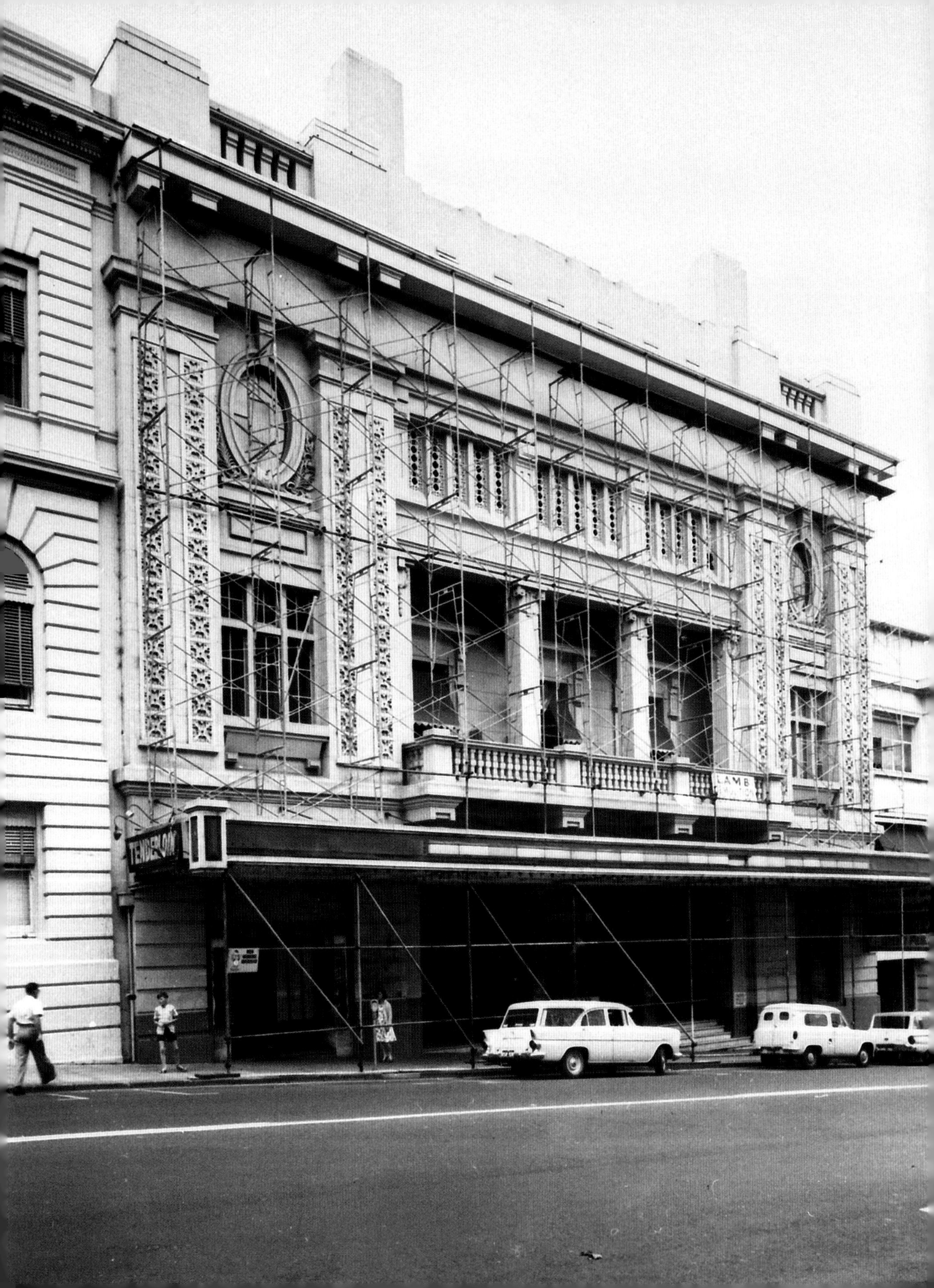
TENDERLOIN
LAMB

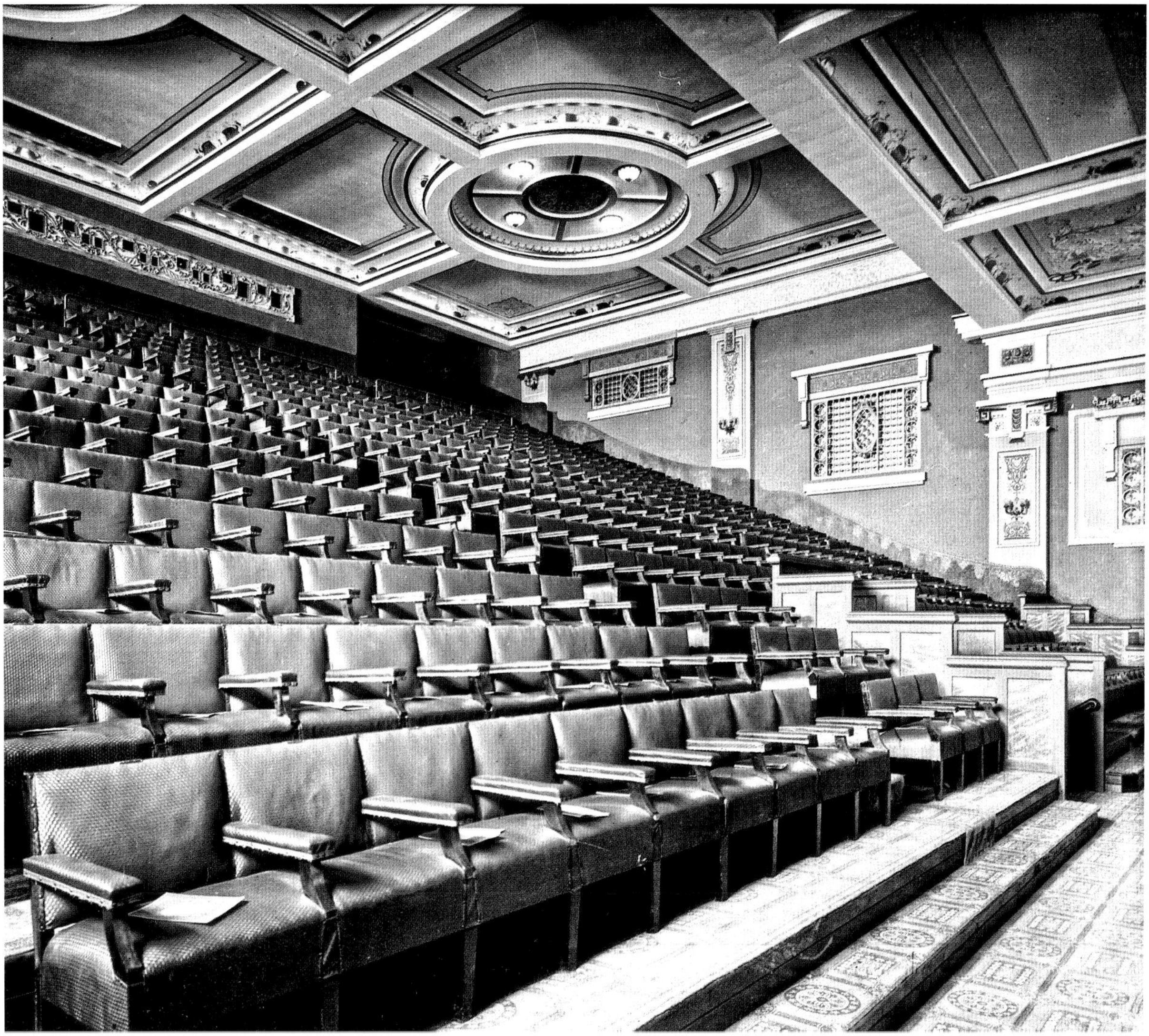

## Capitol Theatre 1968

Despite the extremely plush interior, the Capitol was not a great success as a cinema, being too large to be viably supported by the modest population of Perth. Add to this a reputation for poor acoustics and strong competition from other nearby cinemas the building rapidly became a white elephant.

Despite the appalling acoustics, in 1930 the theatre became the main concert venue in Perth and a popular place for large meetings and formal civic functions. Sadly, the building was demolished in 1968 and the photo at left was captured by Ernie at the start of the demolition process.

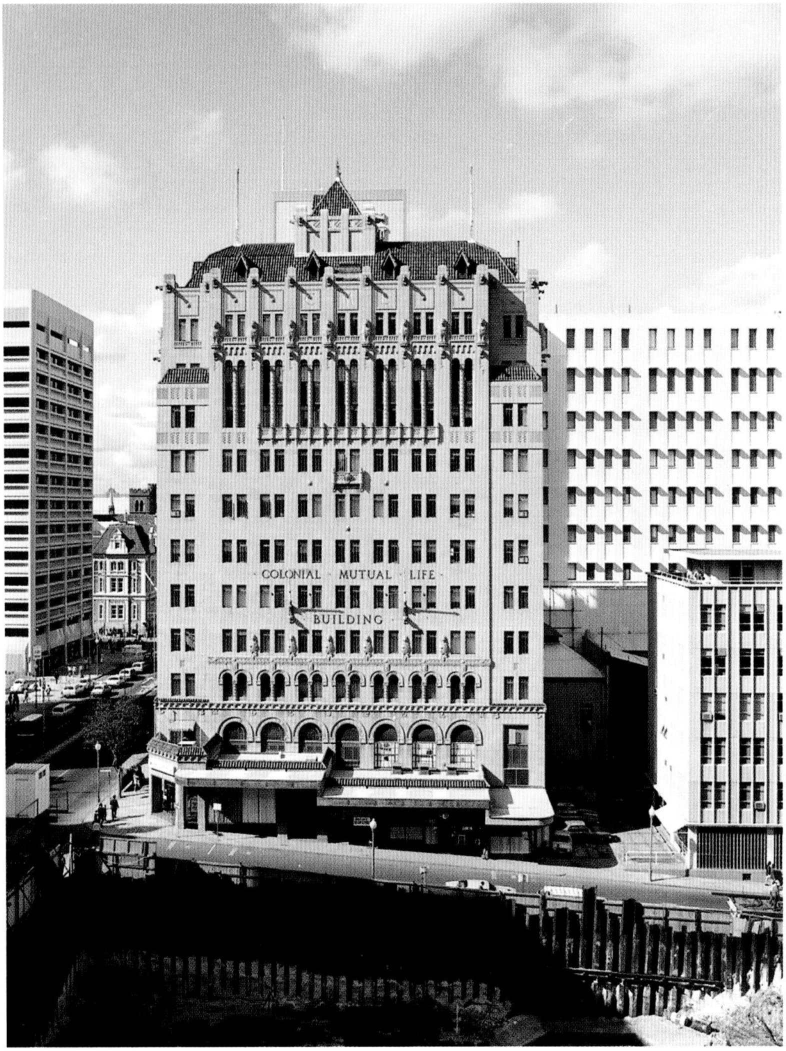


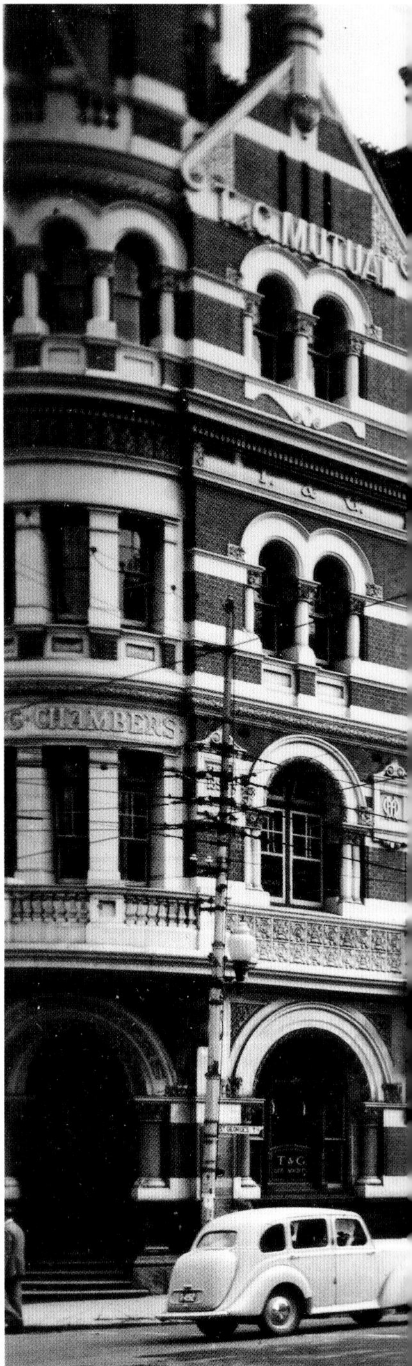


## **CMLA Building** 1960 and 1974

**ABOVE:** In September 1935, work commenced for the Colonial Mutual Life Assurance Company on what would become the tallest office block in Perth. Once built to ground level, a foundation stone was laid by the Governor, Sir James Mitchell, in May, 1936.

During the building works, the Daily News carried a story about the two 'billy boys' (tea boys), who, it was estimated, had carried some 3,000 gallons of tea around the site over a six-month period.

The Art Deco building had some delightful architectural features including carved figures said to be images of the CMLA Directors at the time the building was erected. The completed 11-storey building was the height of modernity and retained its title of 'tallest building' until 1962. Eighteen years later the 1930s giant had been felled.

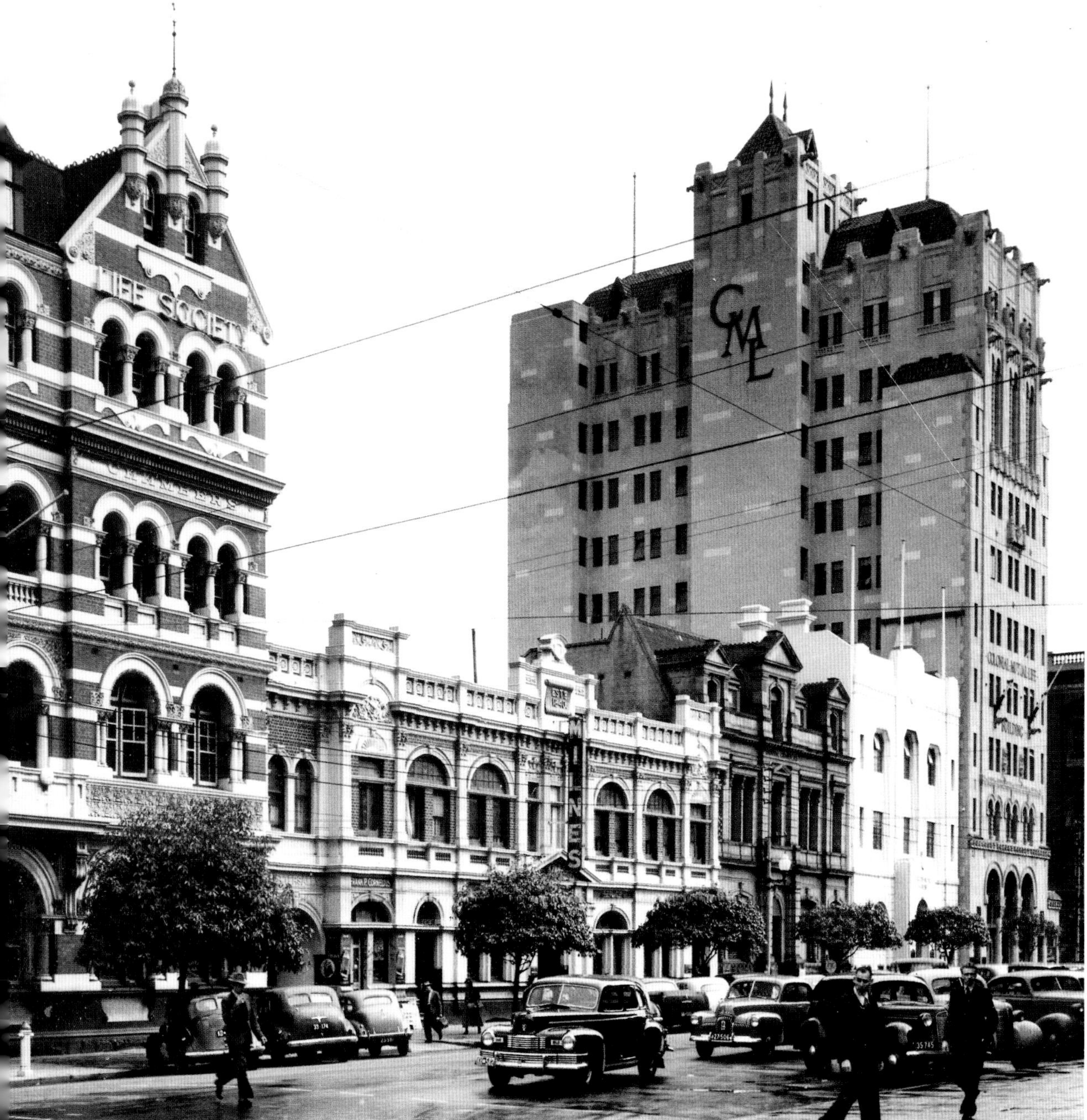


**ABOVE:** This photo was taken not long before Moir chambers (on the left) was demolished in 1960. Twenty years later the CMLA Building (right) followed it to a landfill site. Ernie's image gives us an idea of what modern Perth could have looked like if just a few more of these iconic buildings had been retained.

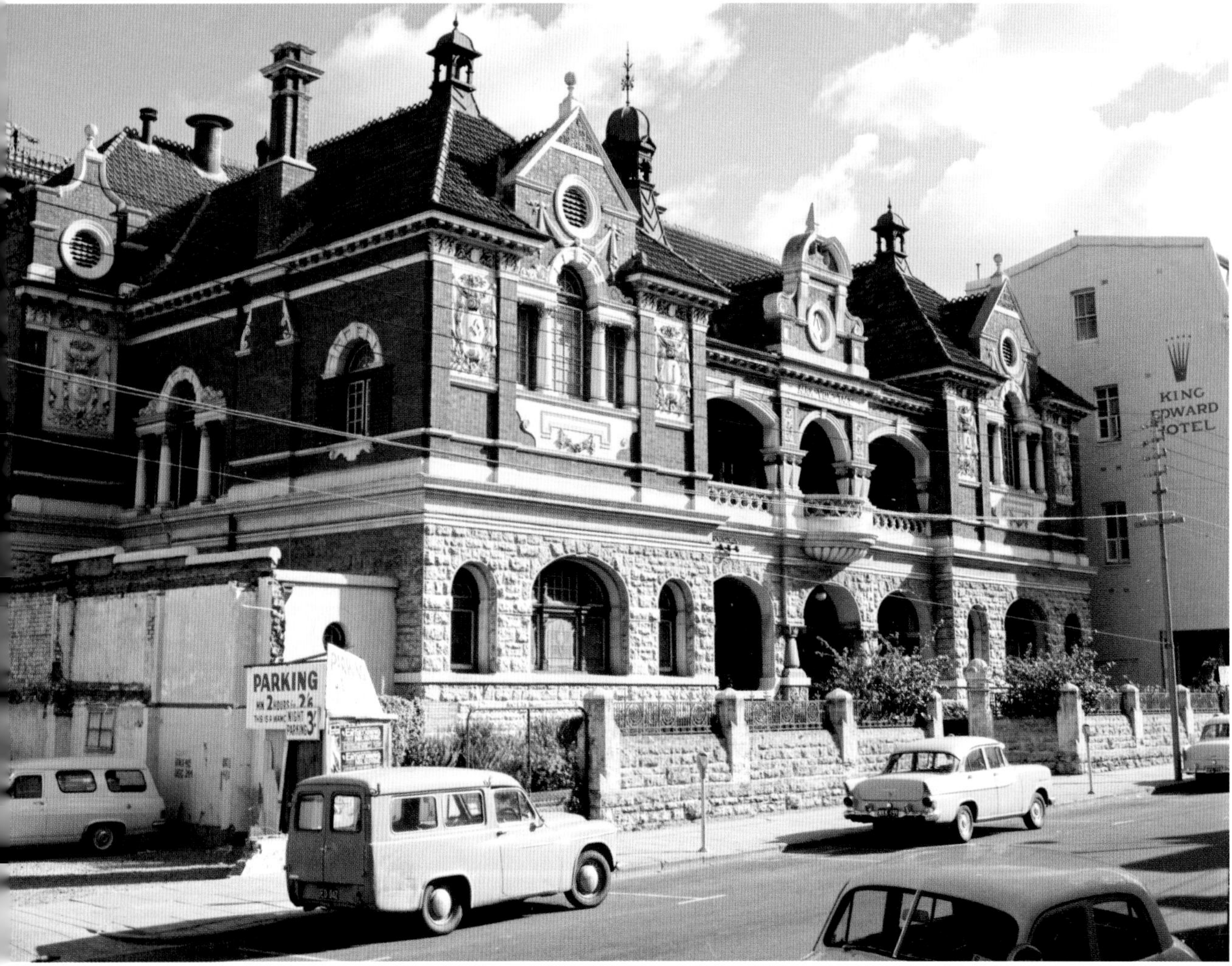


## Masonic Lodge, Hay Street c.1965

The first Masonic lodge in Western Australia was inaugurated at a meeting in the old Government House in 1841. For many years the Lodge met in the old King's Head/Leeder's Hotel on the corner of William Street and St Georges Terrace, but in 1867 moved into a custom-built Lodge near the Town Hall, on what is now Hay Street.

The growth of Freemasonry in Western Australia during the first Gold Rush warranted a much larger building and so the institution commissioned one of their members, architect J. J. Talbot Hobbs, to design a new and 'imposing' building a little further east along Hay Street, which opened in 1897.

The organisation vacated the building in 1967, moving to premises in Terrace Road and the old Masonic Hall was demolished in 1971, as another victim of the 'modernise our city' trend.

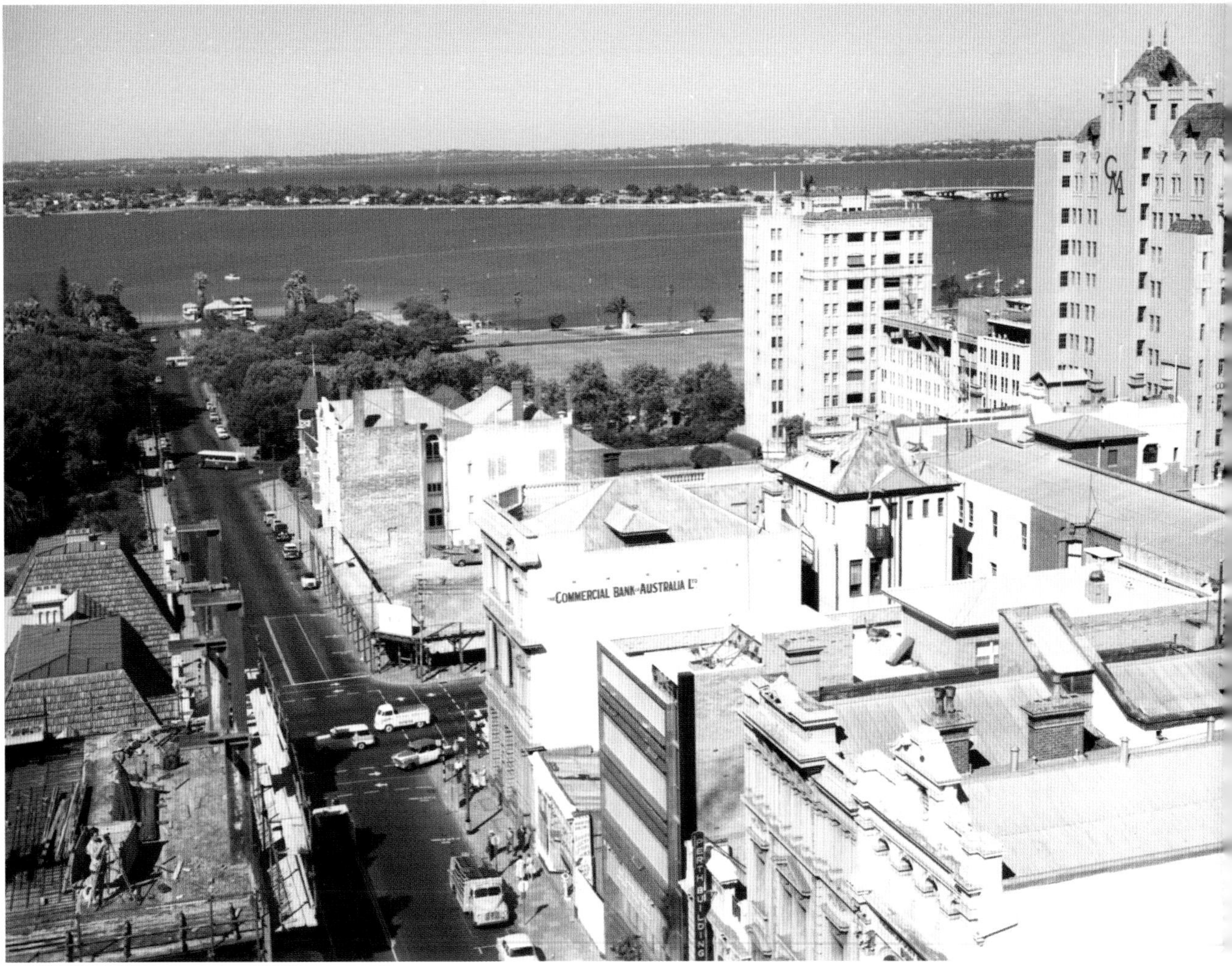


## Moir Chambers 1960

Built for Herbert Moir who made a large fortune in the first Western Australian Gold Rush, Moir Chambers was another fine building designed by J. J. Talbot Hobbs. Opening in 1897, the building was sold on to the Australasian Temperance & General Mutual Life Assurance Society in 1908, from whence it became known as the T&G Building.

Fifty-two years later, Ernie photographed the destruction of this building from Barrack Street. In the centre of the shot can be seen the old Commercial Bank of Australia building.

The photograph from the roof of the Town Hall not only shows the cleared site of the T&G Building, but also the Lawson Apartments and the old CMLA Building. At the time, the slate roof of the Central Government Offices was being replaced with clay tiles, which 50 years later had to be replaced because they were too heavy for the structure below.

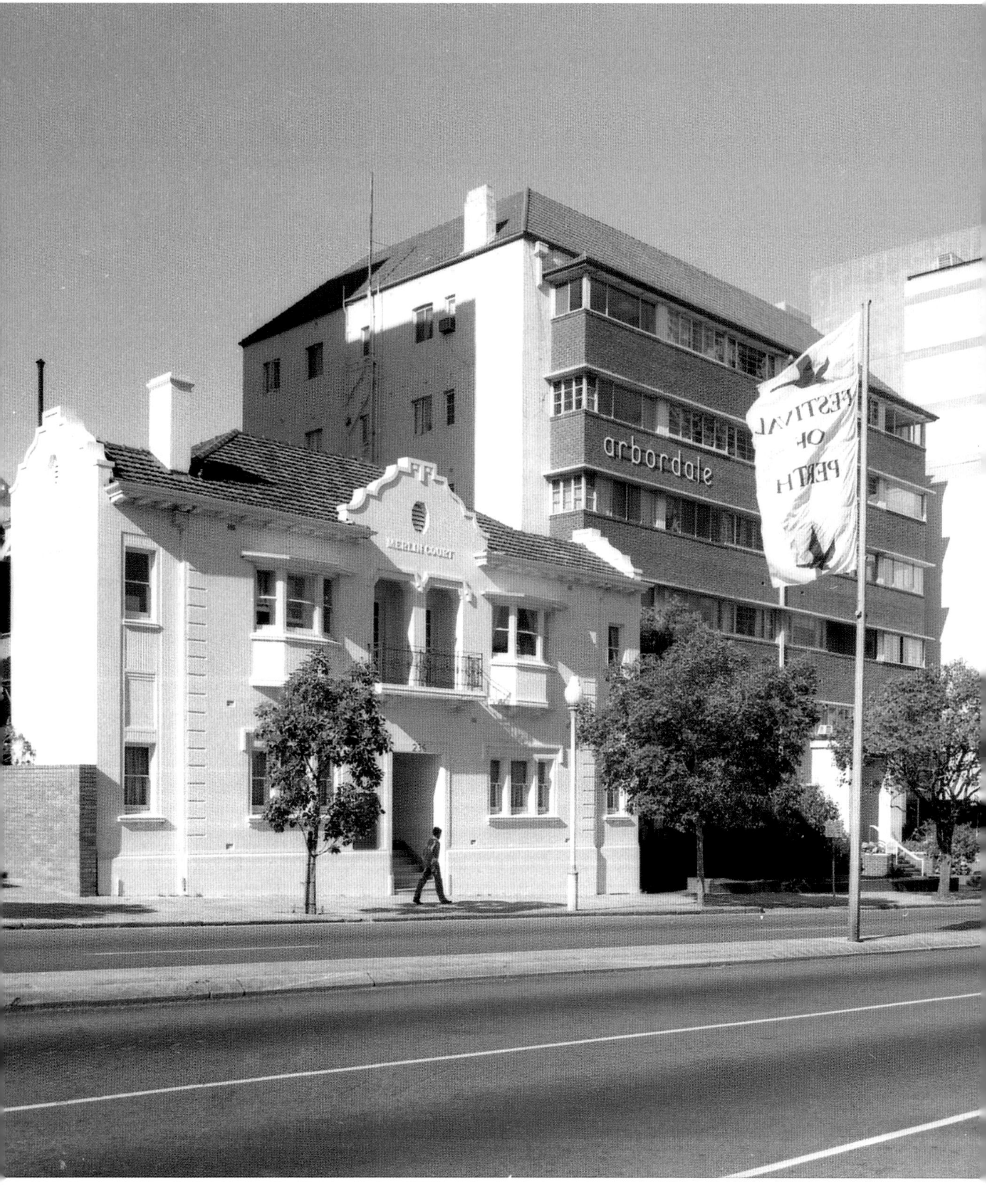
arbordale
MERLIN COURT
FESTIVAL OF PERTH

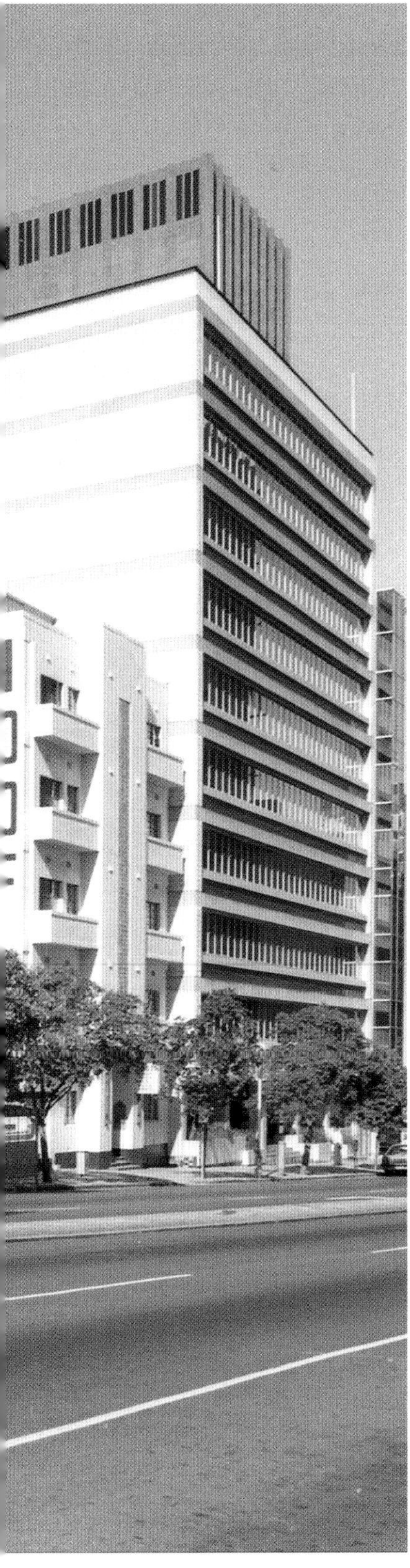

## Merlin Court, 236 St Georges Terrace 1982

Merlin Court, near the junction of Milligan Street and St Georges Terrace, was one of many developments in central Perth designed to aid Western Australia's economy recover from the Great Depression of the 1930s.

Incorporating the rear of a previous building, Merlin Court was designed in an Anglo-Dutch style by Perth architect Samuel Rosenthal. The complex consisted of seven flats, each consisting of a hall, lounge, bedroom, bathroom and kitchenette.

The neighbouring Arbordale Flats were designed by Harold Krantz. With thirty-six apartments, it was the largest block of residential flats in Perth at that time and boasted 'very modern' amenities such as rubbish chutes, an electric elevator and car garages.

The imposing office block next door was built in the early 1970s. Merlin Court and Arbordale Flats were demolished in the 1980s to make way for commercial premises, which in turn, along with the office block, disappeared in 2000 to be replaced by a twenty-five-floor building.

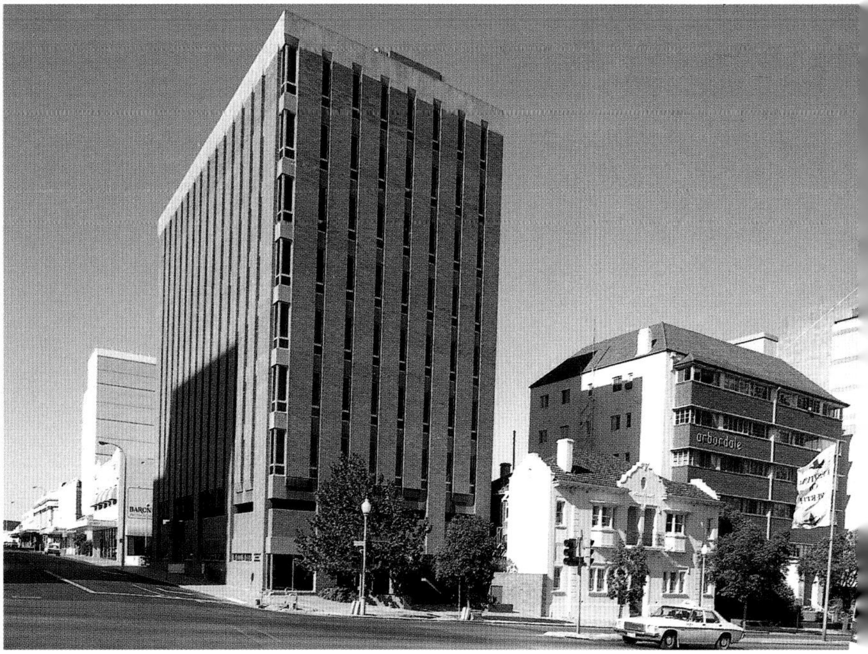

## Musgrove's 1974

Musgrove's music shop was founded in 1923 by Mandeville D'Oyley Musgrove with three others from the Perth music industry. It became one of Perth's major music warehouses, trading from a building in Murray Street that was named Lyric House after a radio set they marketed in the 1930s.

Although the company was very successful and is still in business, they were not so lucky with their Murray Street shop, which suffered two major fires. The first, in 1952, was found to have been started by a 14-year-old boy and caused serious damage.

In September, 1974, the shop was again engulfed by fire, which began on the ground floor, quickly spreading upwards causing organs and pianos to crash to the ground from the upper floors. The west wall of the building collapsed on to the neighbouring bank offices. This shot shows fireman hosing down after a ten-hour battle to try to save the building.

## Dunlop House c.1975

**FOLLOWING PAGE:** The inventors of the pneumatic tyre, the Dunlop Rubber Company, first opened for business in Perth at the turn of the 20th century, when their main products were bicycle tyres, rubber stops and tennis balls.

With the advent of the motor car in Western Australia, Dunlop rapidly expanded to supply the ever-growing market for vehicle tyres. As a result, they commissioned the construction of a new warehouse at 418 Murray Street and moved from their premises in Kings Street early in 1922.

By the 1970s, Dunlop had vacated the premises and it became a nightclub trading under various names including 'Beethovens' and 'Rumours' until the building was severely damaged by fire and subsequently demolished in July, 2001.

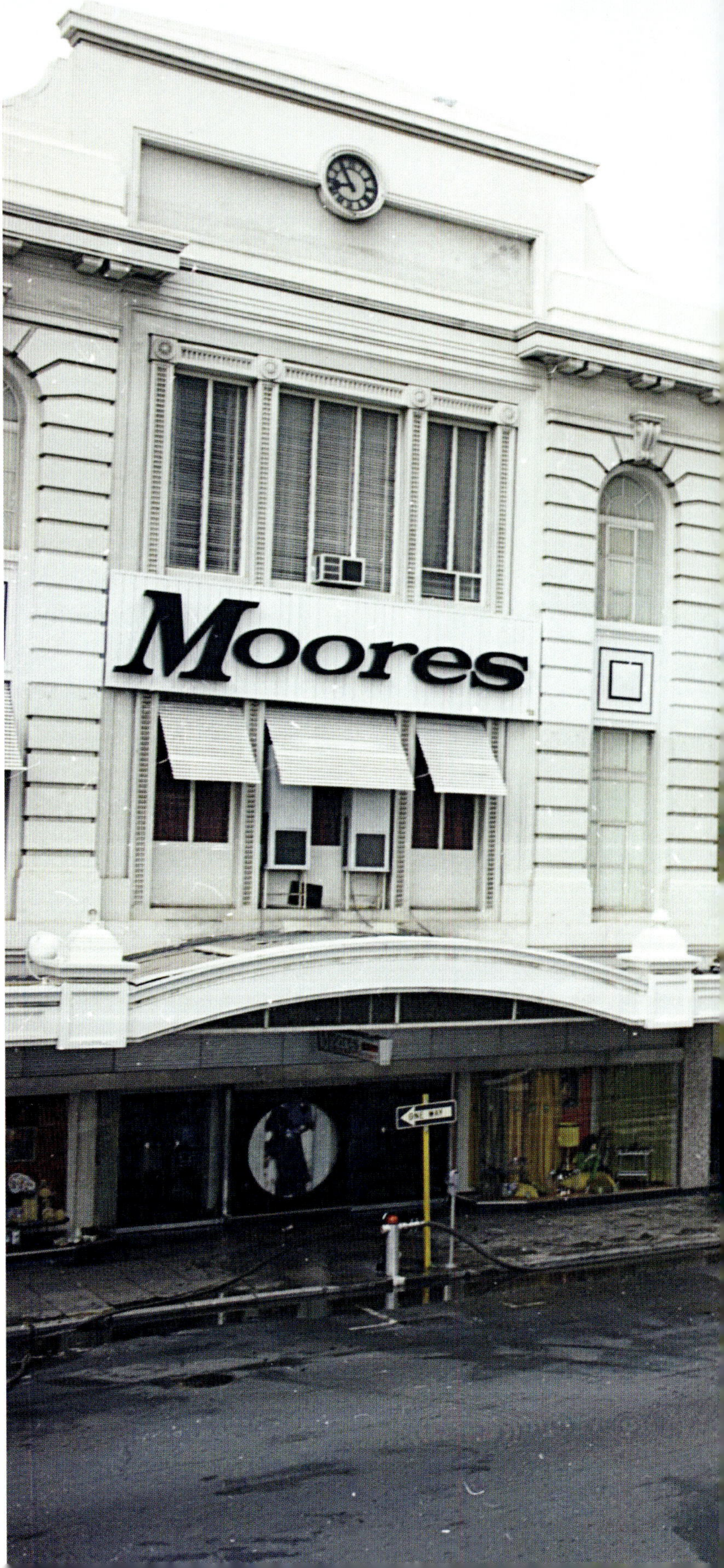

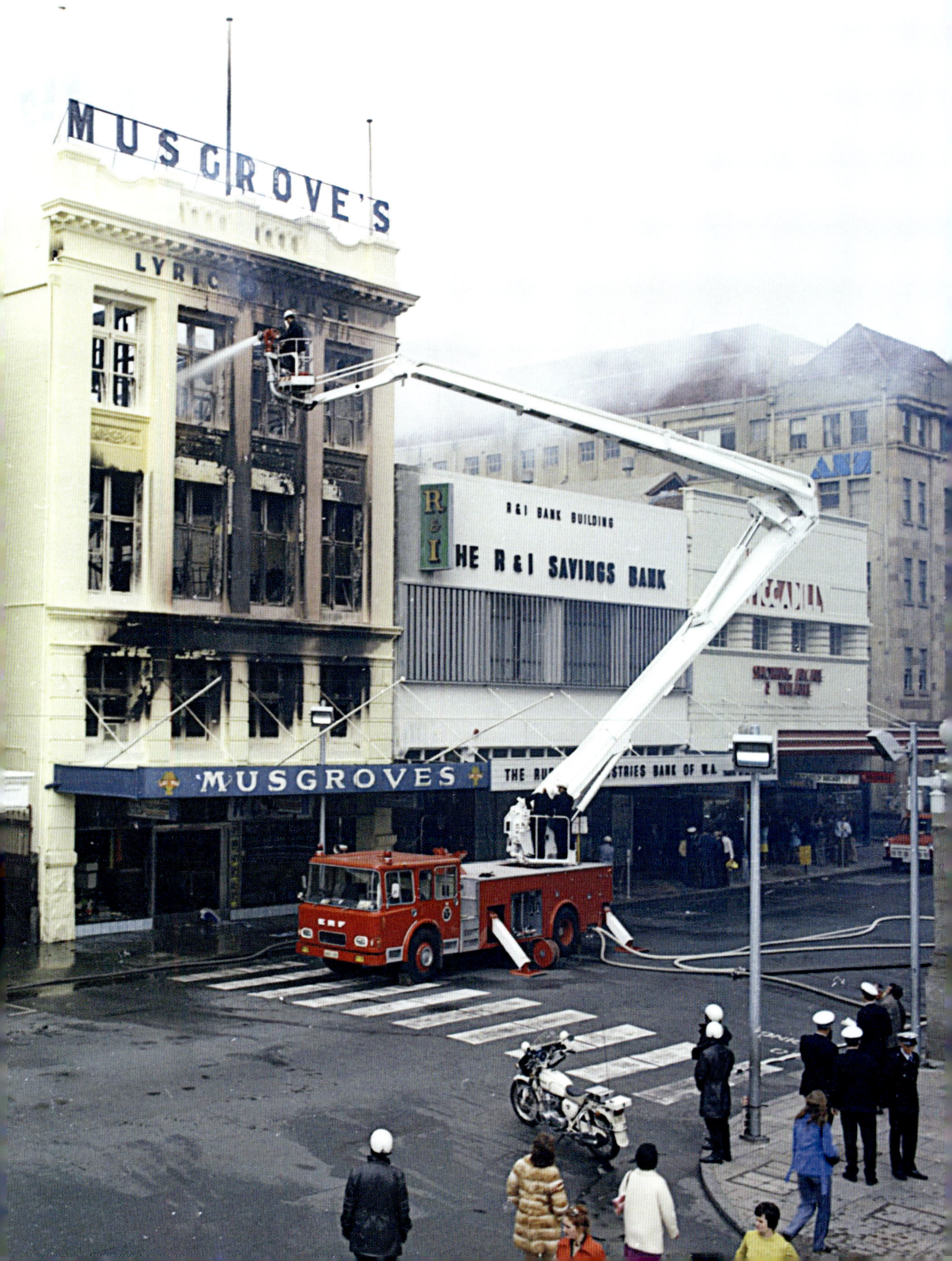
MUSGROVE'S
LYRIC
R&I BANK BUILDING
R&I
HE R & I SAVINGS BANK
ANZ
MUSGROVES

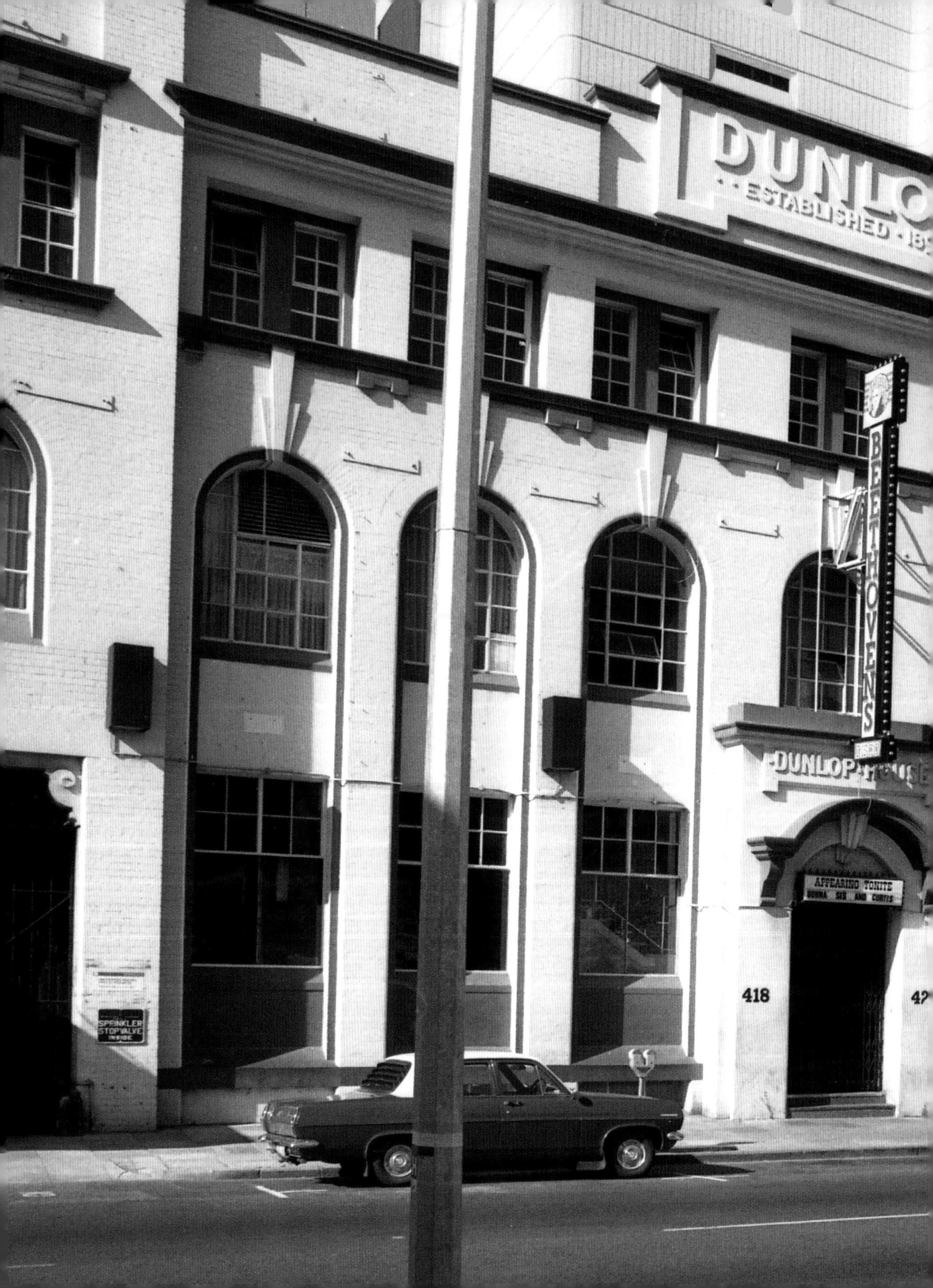
DUNLO
ESTABLISHED · 18
BEETHOVENS
DISCO
APPEARING TONITE
418
SPRINKLER
STOPVALVE
INSIDE

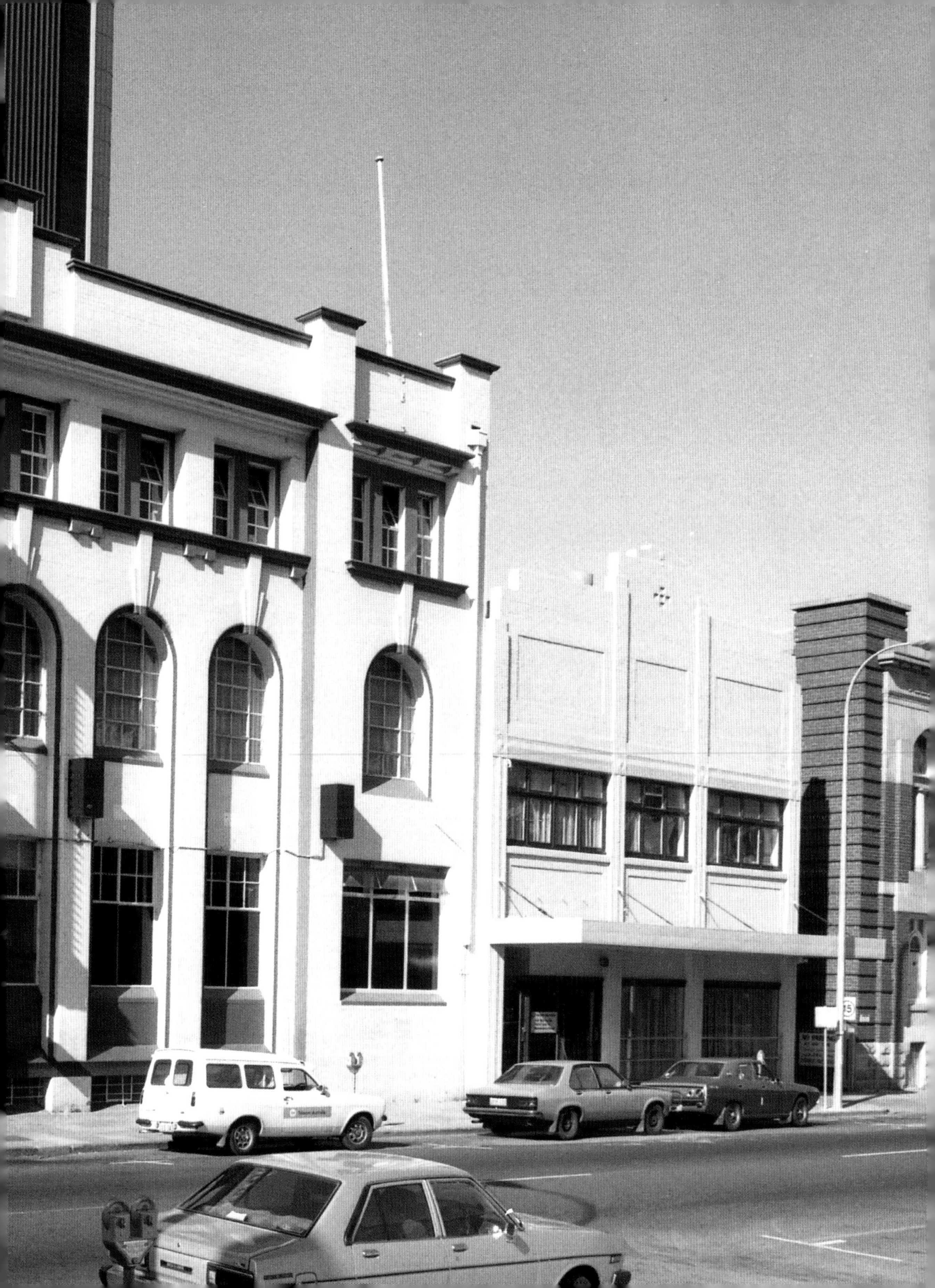

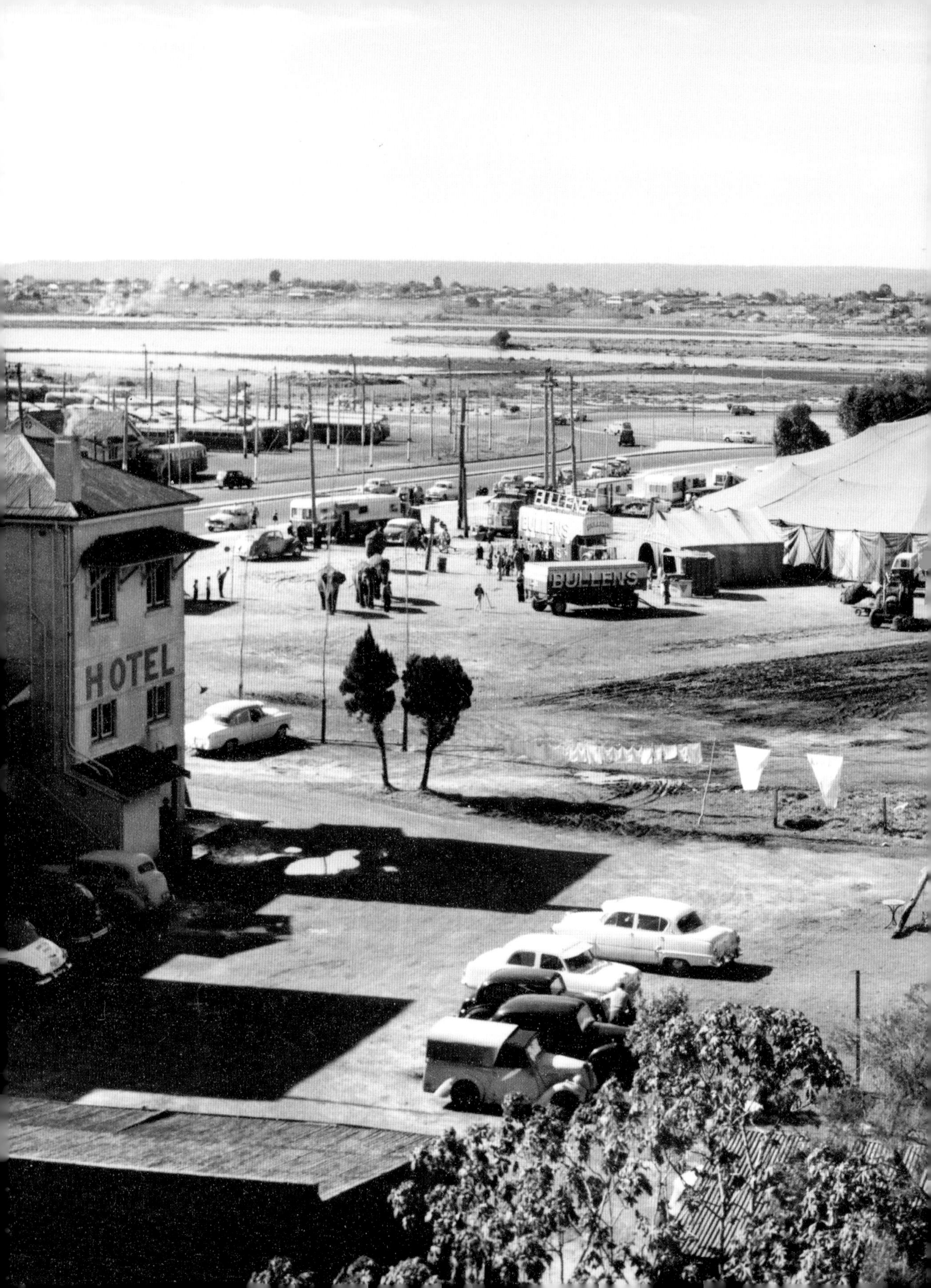
BULLENS
BULLENS
BULLENS
HOTEL

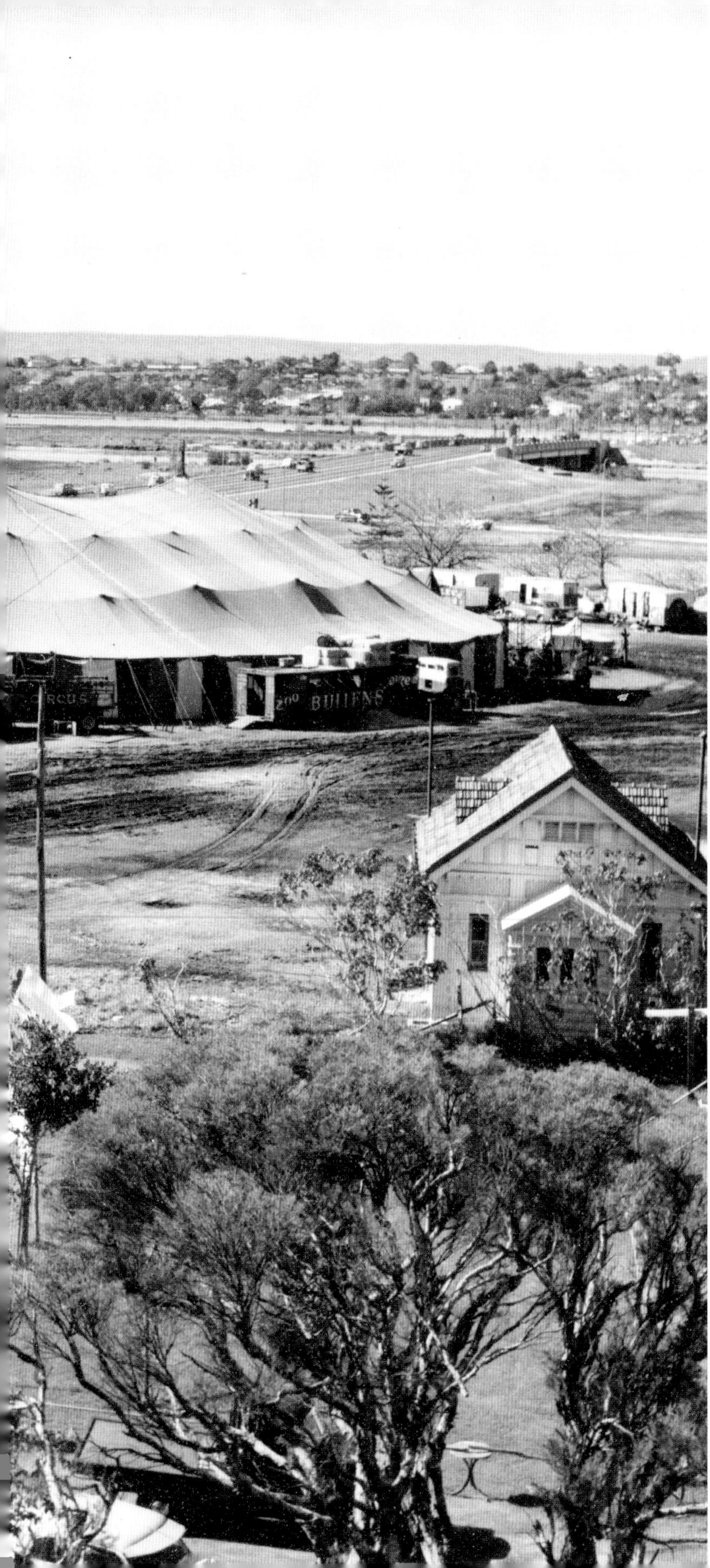

## 'The Drains' c.1962

In 1869, the city's 'Inspector of Nuisances' (public health officer), reported there had been much sickness in Perth, attributing it to bad drainage and problems with disposal of sewage because cesspits were either defective or non-existent.

In typical Perth style, after many written reports, incessant debate and much procrastination, the city finally began to build a sewerage system in 1906.

To improve the efficiency of the system, three pumping stations were built on Mill Street, Langley Park and the Causeway. Right through to the 1970s, pump attendants, known as 'pumpies', travelled a daily maintenance circuit of the pumping stations on bicycles.

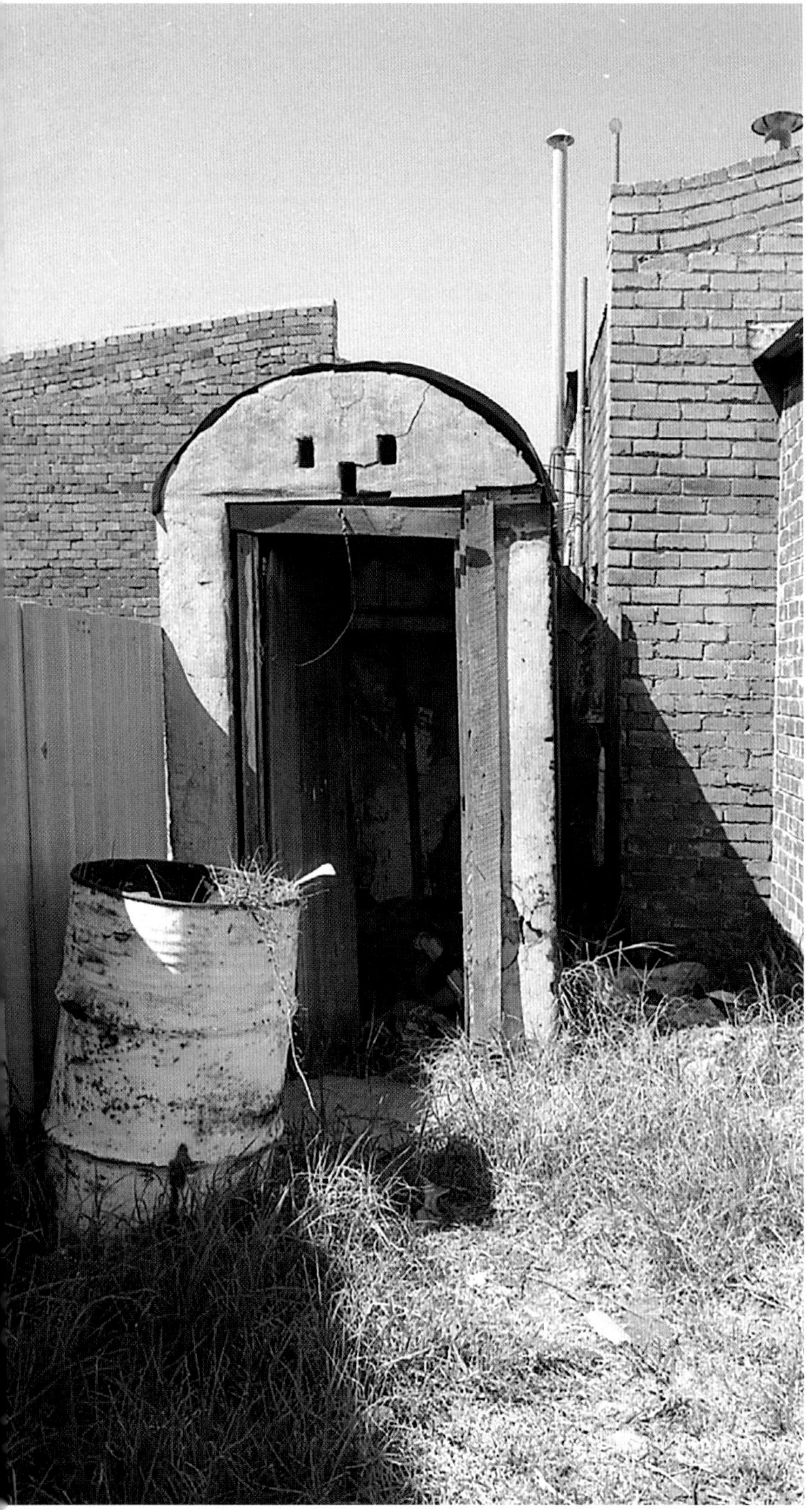

## Northbridge Dunnie
c.1962

**LEFT:** Even into the 1960s, when this photograph was taken, there were still some houses in Northbridge that retained their outside toilet or 'dunnie', although most had been connected to the sewerage system by then.

## Warwick House 1970

**RIGHT:** The corner of St Georges Terrace and Sherwood Court, where Allendale Square now stands, was a building named Warwick House.

Described by the Western Mail as, 'A notable addition to the architecture of St Georges Terrace', the five-storey Warwick House was designed by Frederick Upton and completed in the last months of 1914. The newspaper went on to say, 'The building is substantially built and fitted throughout with all modern conveniences, including lavatories' – journalists of that period seem to have been obsessed with every new building's lavatorial facilities!

One of the early tenants of the building was Stott's Business College. The College was founded in Melbourne in 1883 by Sydney Stott and was the first institution in Australia to provide specialised commercial training for those wishing to pursue a business career.

The building was demolished in 1973/74 for construction of Allendale Square.

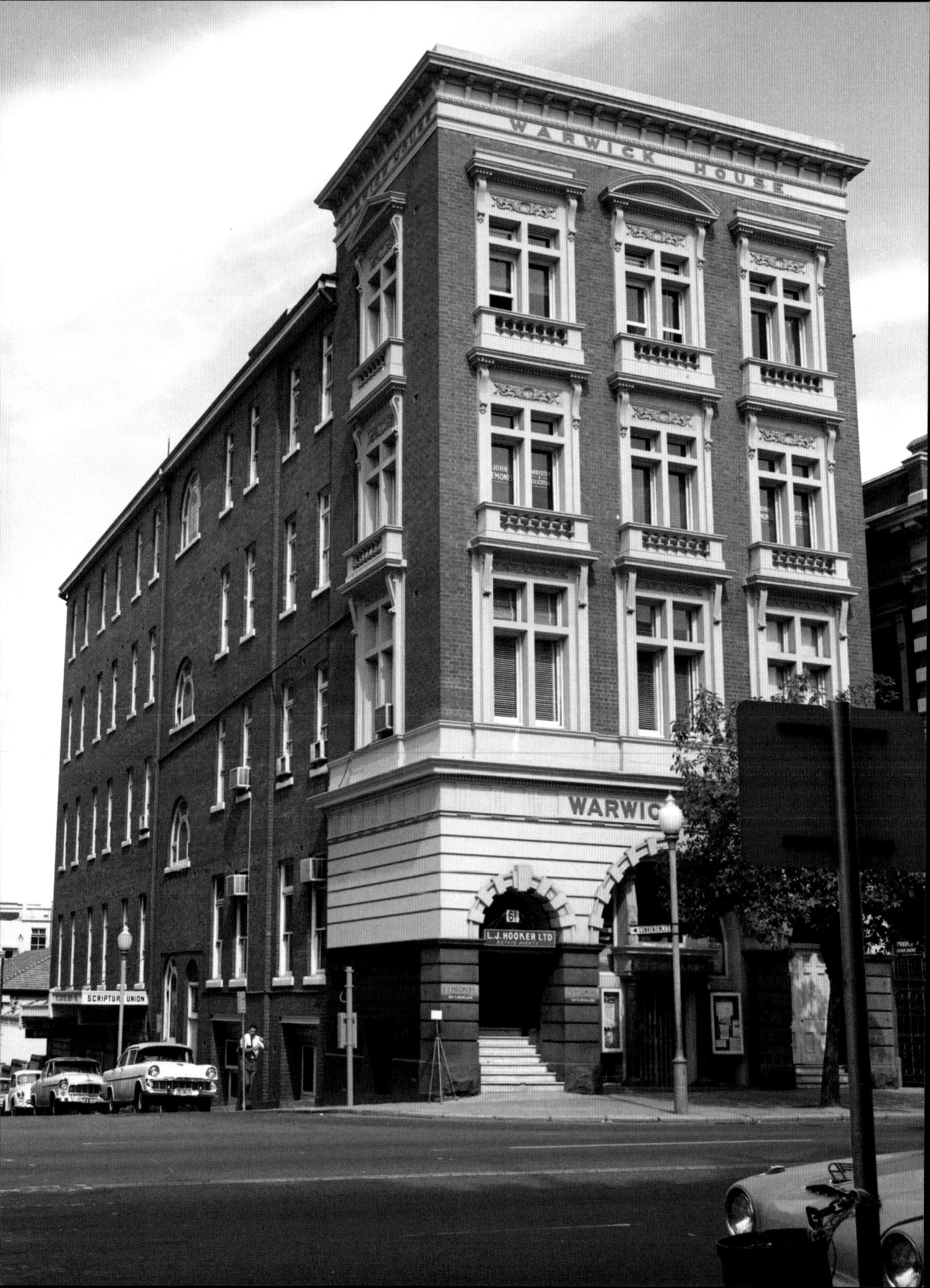
WARWICK HOUSE
WARWICK
61
L.J. HOOKER LTD
SCRIPTUR UNION

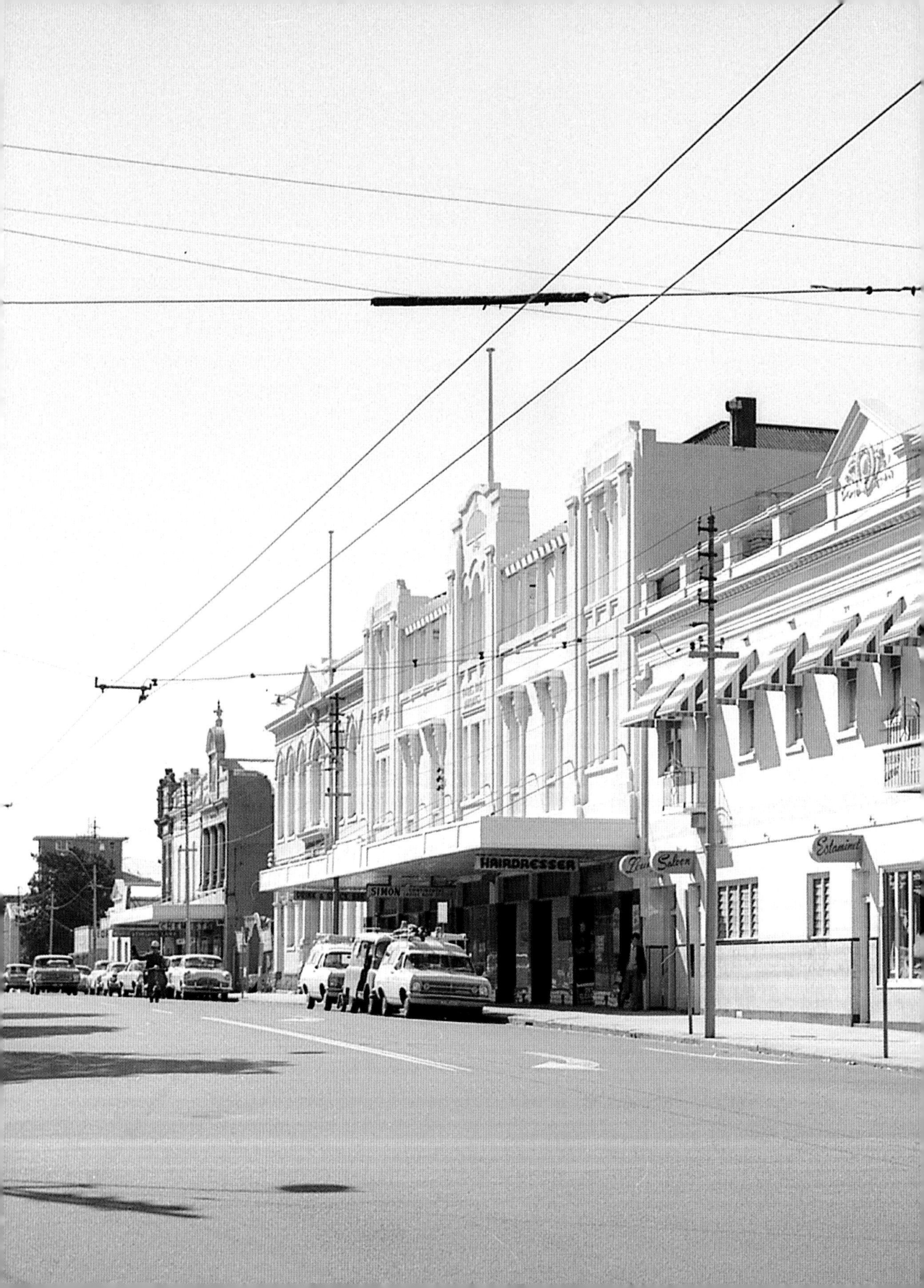
HAIRDRESSER
SIMON
Saloon
Estaminet

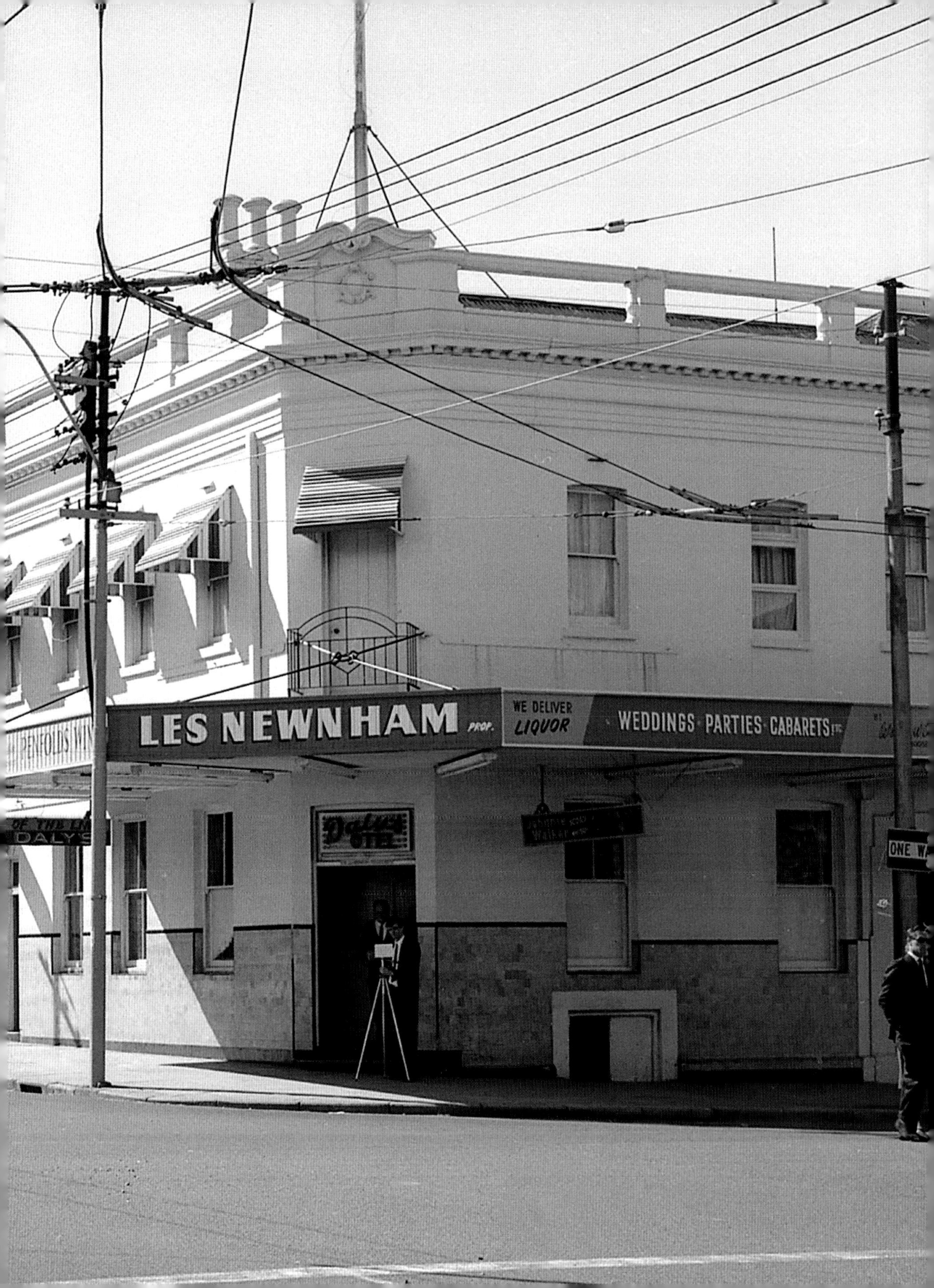

LES NEWNHAM PROP.
WE DELIVER LIQUOR
WEDDINGS · PARTIES · CABARETS ETC.
DALY'S
ONE WA

## Trade Hall Flats 1972

**PREVIOUS PAGE:** The first three buildings in this photograph have an interestingly linked history.

The furthest building is the Trades Hall, which was built in 1911 for the Western Australian Branch of the Australian Labour Federation. A year later the Federation formed the Perth Trades Hall Association (PTHA), with the power to acquire, lease and sell real estate.

Having purchased the block next door in 1934, the PTHA demolished what were said to be the oldest buildings on Beaufort Street (the newspapers of the time thought this a 'good thing'!) and constructed a three-storey building between the original Trades Hall and Court Hotel. It comprised seven ground-floor shops, a sixteen-room hostel on the first floor (later turned into flats), and two three-roomed flats above. This distinguished building, designed by Hobbs, Forbes and Partners, was demolished in 1973.

Nearest the camera is the Court Hotel which opened in November 1888. Close to the Trades Hall, this was the Unionist's much-frequented hostelry.

## Motor House 1982

**RIGHT:** Motor House, on the junction of Milligan and Wellington Street is described by real estate agents as being "like no other building in the Perth CBD", as it is situated on 'Milligan Island', which gives it three street frontages.

The land on which Motor House is situated was originally the location of St John's Anglican Church, which was demolished early in 1928 because of a dwindling congregation. Also on the site was a church hall, which was used as a paint spraying shop until it, too, was pulled down in 1935 to make way for the present building.

As the name would suggest, the new Art Deco building, completed in 1936, was the Courthorpe and Olifant service station and car showroom. It continued in the automotive trade until the early 1960s when it became a roller-skating rink. After a few years use as a car park, it was converted into offices soon after this photograph was taken in 1982.

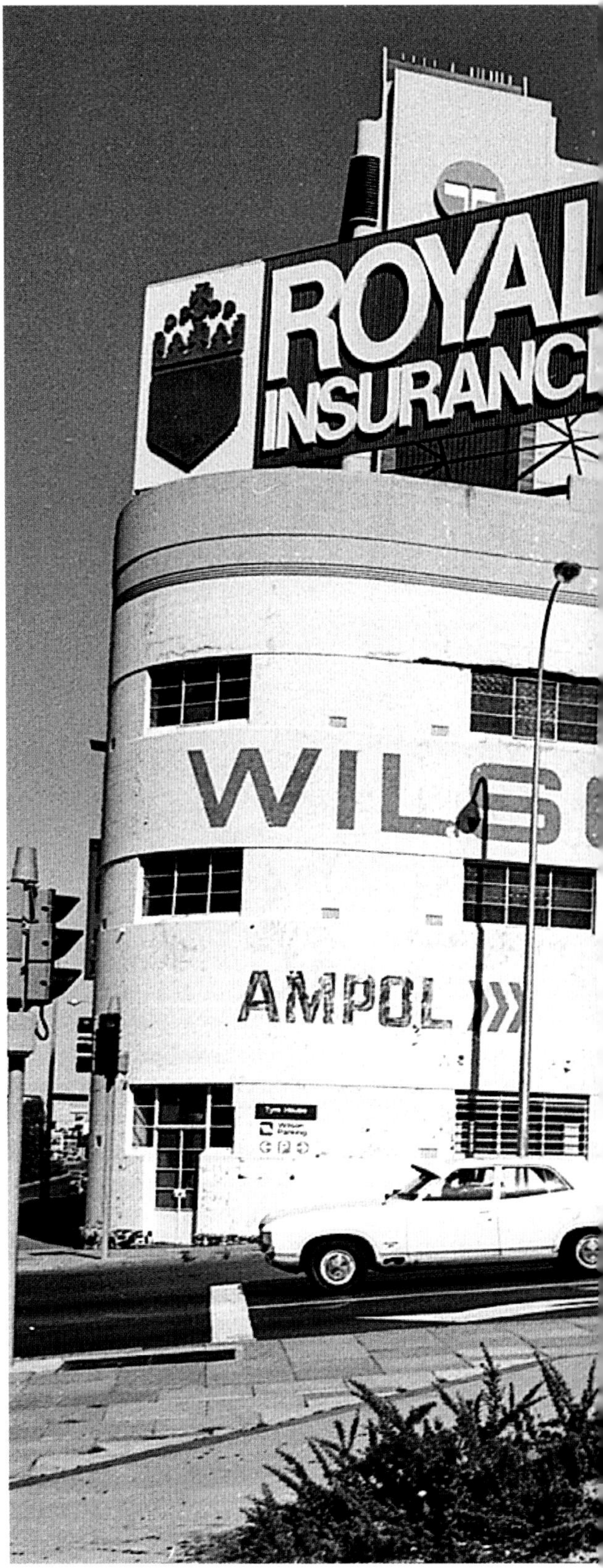

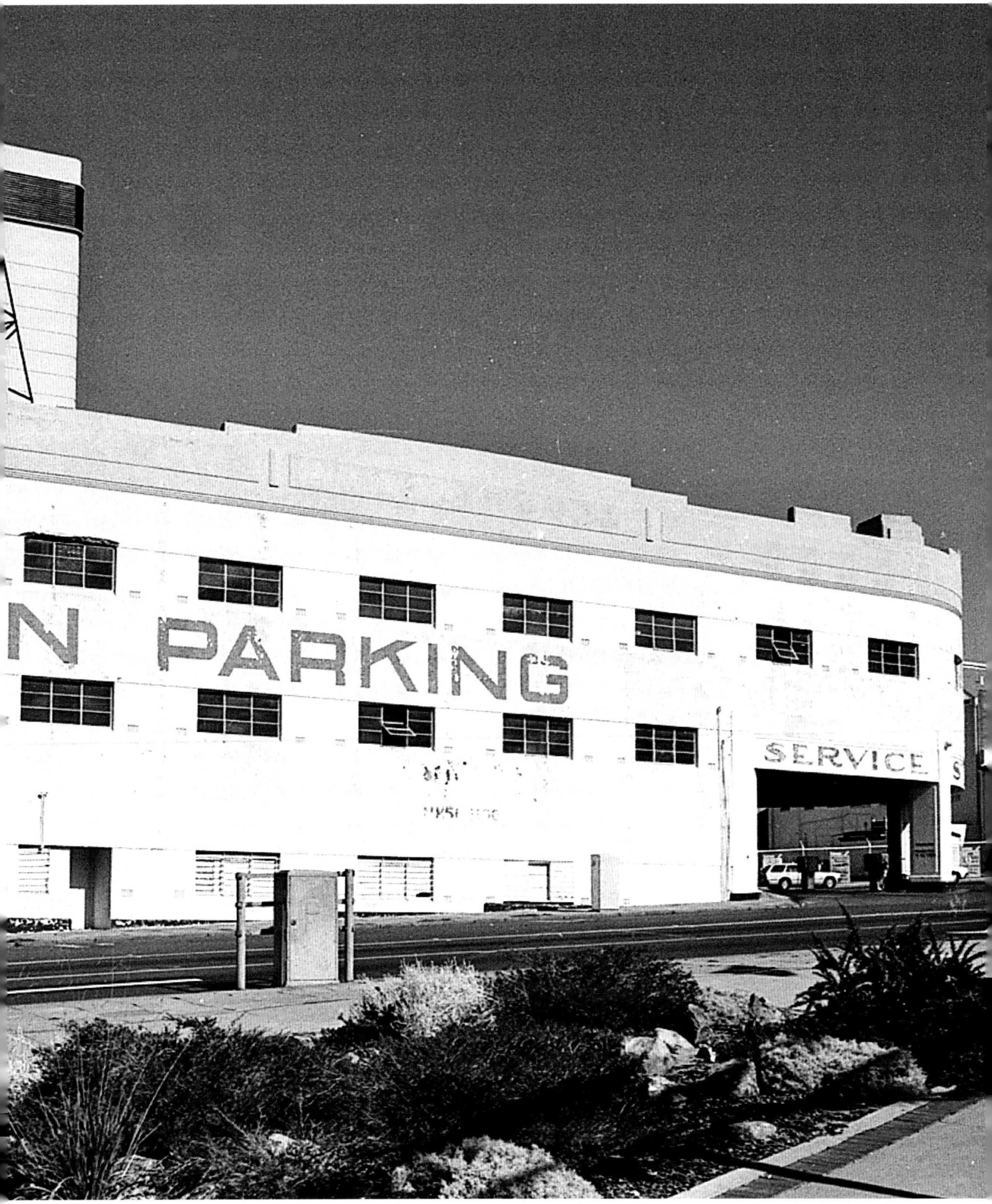
N PARKING
SERVICE

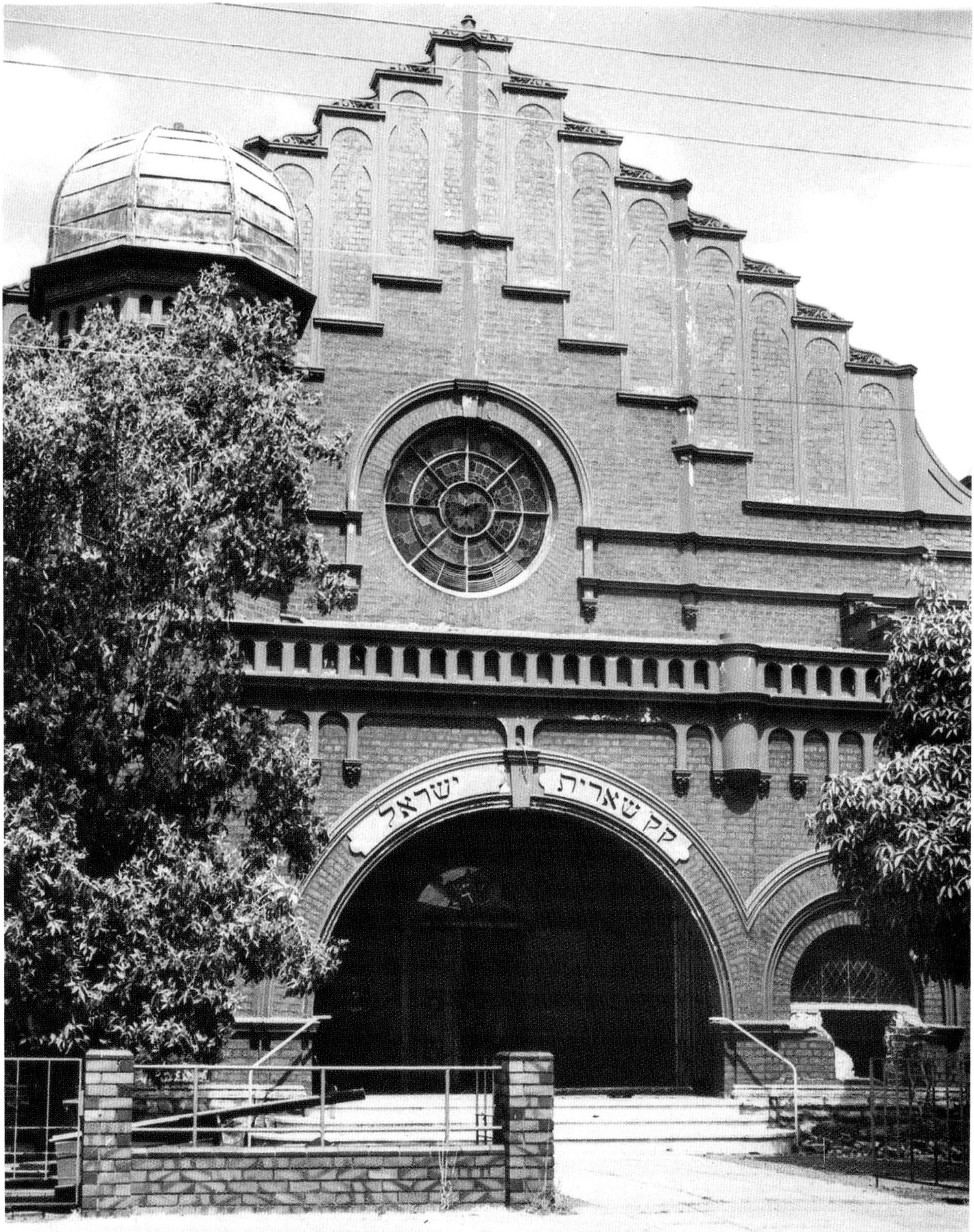
קק שארית ישראל

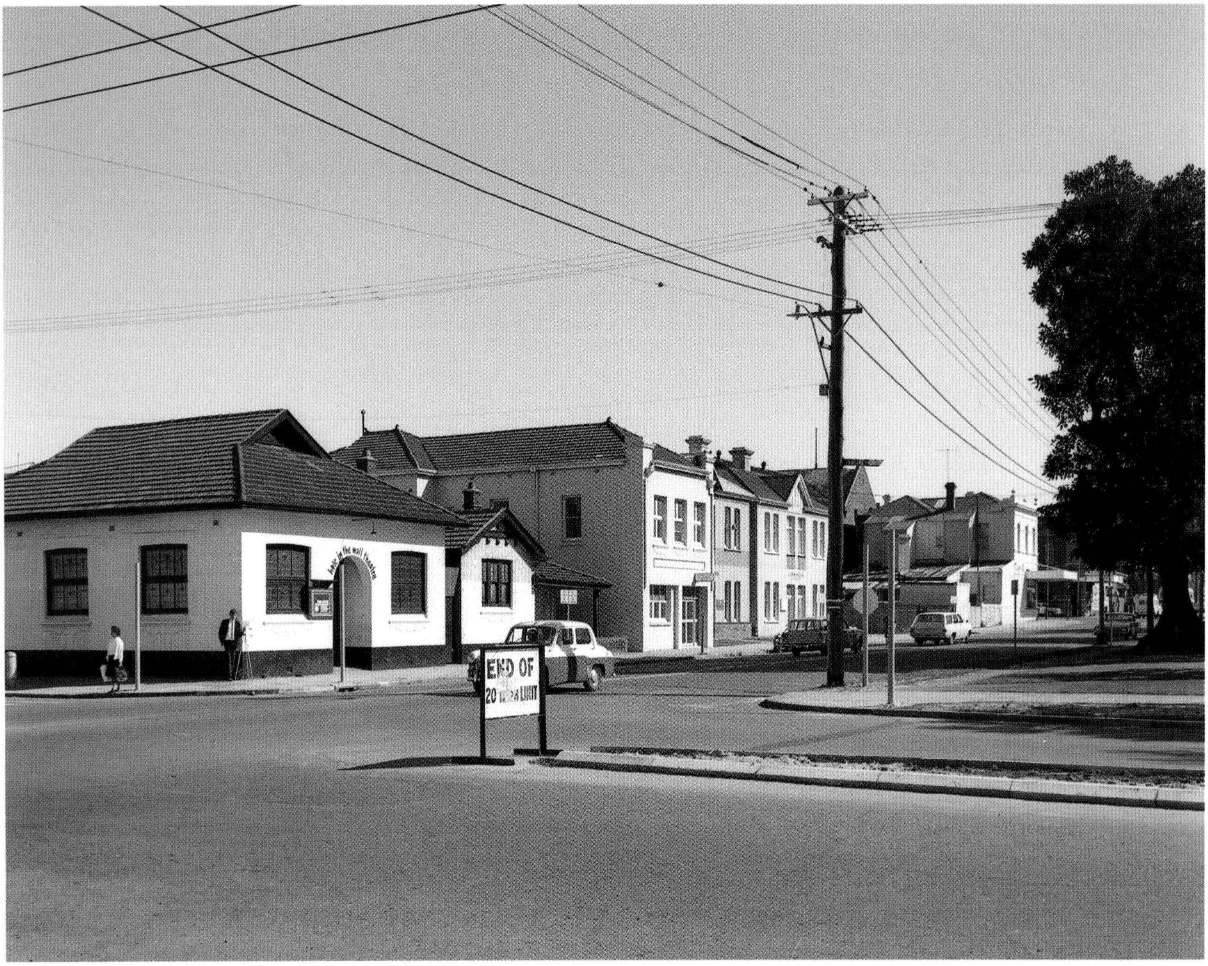


## Northbridge Synagogue c.1970

**LEFT:** Much of Perth's early Jewish community was centred in the area now known as Northbridge. The Jewish congregation opened a Synagogue in 1897 on Brisbane Street, the foundation stone of which was laid in October 1896.

The building was designed by William Wolf, who claimed to have gained his diploma as an architect in Heidelberg, Germany, which is dubious since there was no school of architecture in that city at the time. Whatever Wolf's qualifications were or were not, he was a very talented designer of buildings, as this, only his second commission after moving to Perth, shows.

The building was extended three times during its life to accommodate growing numbers. Eventually the congregation moved to Menora in the 1970s, closer to residential areas that had become home to many of the Jewish families, and the Brisbane Street Shul was demolished about ten years later.

## Hole in the Wall Theatre c.1972

**ABOVE:** Founded in 1965 by actor, director and theatre entrepreneur, Frank Baden-Powell, the Hole in the Wall Theatre Company was formed to enable a group of actors to perform alternative theatre. The company's first performances took place in the Braille Hall, on the corner of Newcastle and Stirling Streets, where they used stolen milk crates for seating and borrowed their stage lighting.

The Braille Hall has an interesting history and seems to date back to around 1917, when it was known as Mrs Keough's Recreation Hall – Mrs Keough being a well-known Perth caterer. Very popular for all sorts of functions, the hall was purchased by the WA Braille Society in 1950.

Once the theatre company had taken over, the building was renamed 'The Hole in the Wall Theatre'. The theatre company moved to Leederville in 1968, after which it became the 'Old Time Music Hall & Restaurant', and later, 'The Castle', before being demolished in the 1980s.

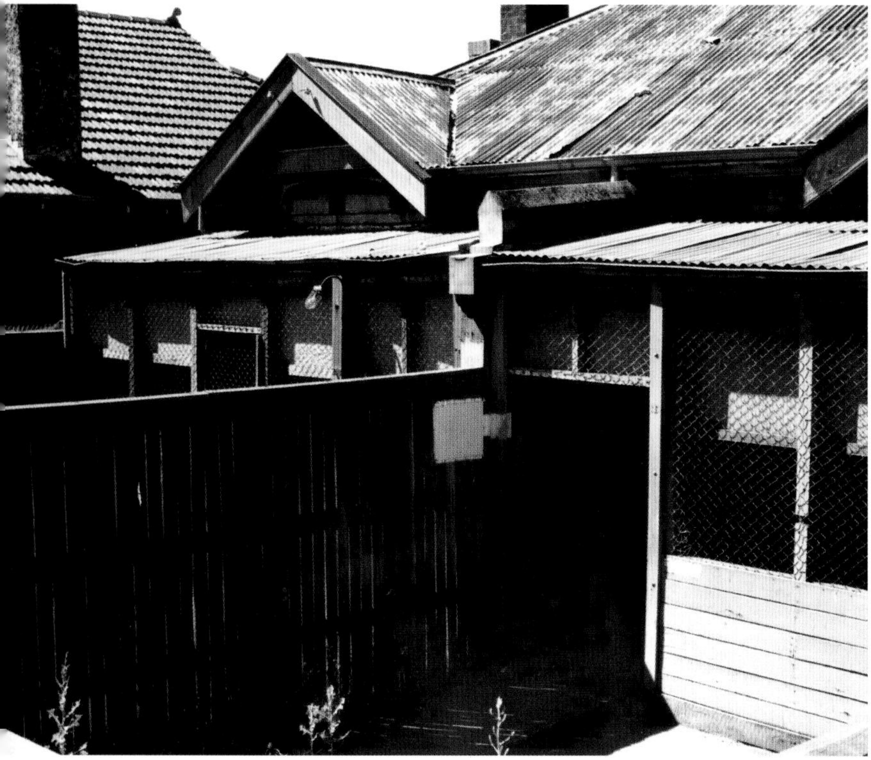

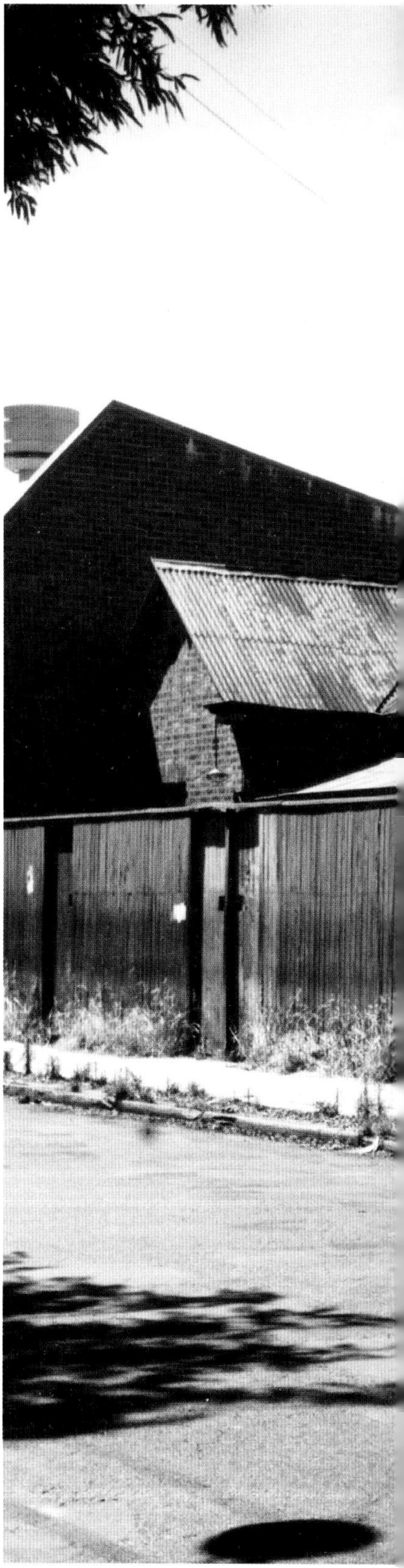

## **Roe Street** c.1965

**ABOVE:** Given the vast increase in population Western Australia experienced during the first gold boom, there is no doubt that 'service industries' (brothels) increased proportionately.

Whilst prostitution itself was not illegal in WA, the Police Act of 1892 prohibited activities such as street soliciting and operating brothels. Historically the police have used an unofficial containment policy to control the number and location of brothels. By the beginning of the 20th century, police records show that brothels were located throughout the centre of the city, particularly along Murray Street. However, at some point they began to migrate north, across the railway line into Roe and James Streets. In a police report of 1911, seventy-five houses around Roe, William, James and Aberdeen Streets were identified as brothels.

**RIGHT:** Perth City Council records show the Council came under considerable pressure in the early 1940s for Roe Street to be cleared of its brothels and this was claimed to have eventually been achieved in 1958. However, one Perth resident recalls being driven as a child down Roe Street one evening in the early 1960s. Seeing a queue of men outside one of the cottages she enquired of her mother, "what are those men doing?" "Queuing for fish and chips" was the reply!

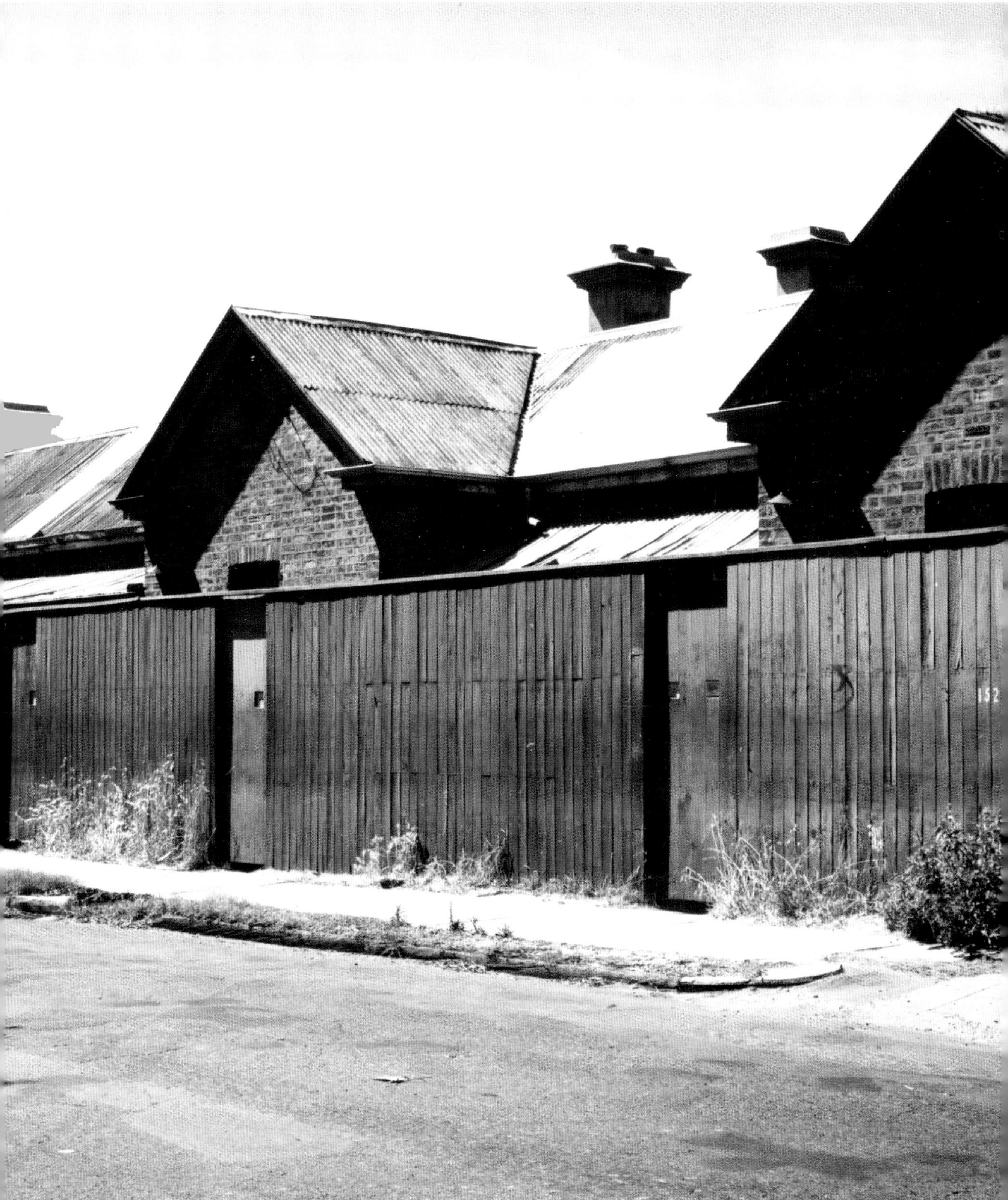
152

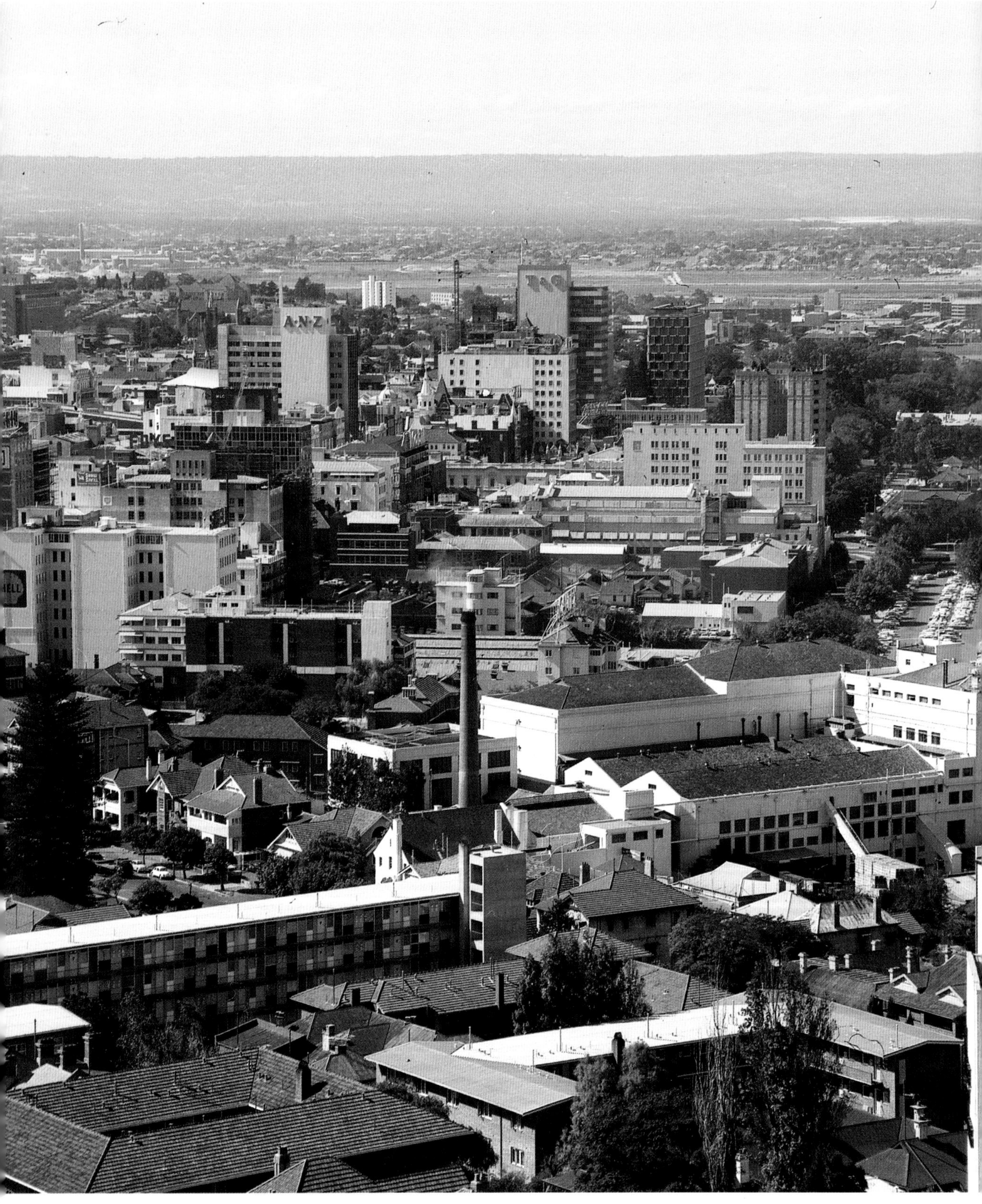
A·N·Z

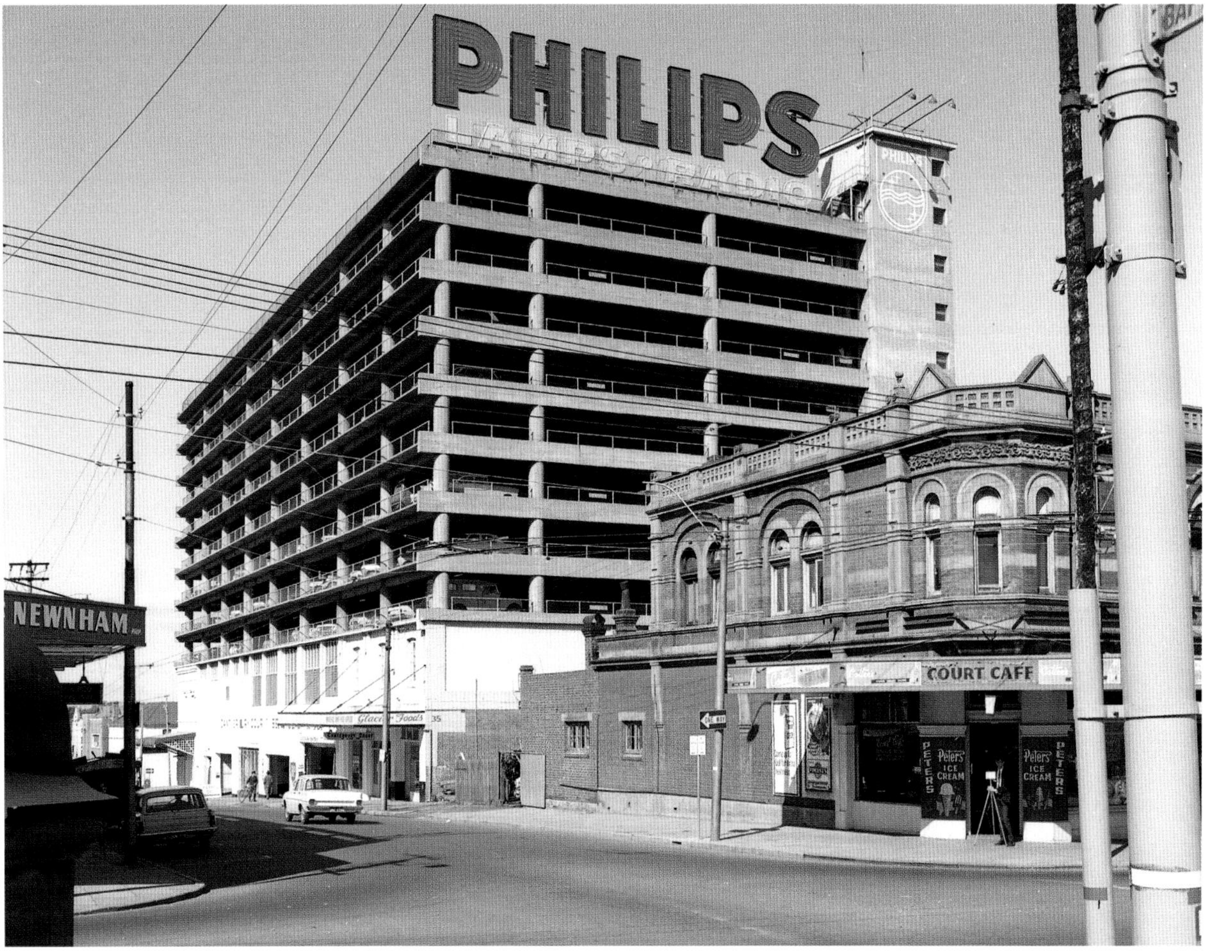


## Emu Brewery c.1968

**LEFT:** This photo is one of many aerial shots Ernie took of Perth in the 1960s. The Emu Brewery is the large factory building with an industrial chimney in the foreground.

The brewery was started in 1848 by James Stokes, who sold what he described as a 'nutritious body ale superior to any imported', costing £4 per hogshead. The brewery's most popular ale was sold under the 'Emu' trademark and the company was renamed as the 'Emu Co-operative Brewery Ltd' in 1908.

The brewery building seen in this photograph replaced the original in 1936. Built in the Art Deco style, it was topped off with a decorative bas-relief border created by local artist Edward Kohler, depicting the different stages in the brewing process.

Emu moved its operations to Canning Vale in the 1970s after which the old brewery remained empty for many years before being controversially demolished in 1991.

## Court Café c.1970

**ABOVE:** The building which became the Court Café first appeared in the Wise's Street Directory in 1899 as See Lung Laundry. Up until 1930 the premises was used by a number of different enterprises such as a tobacconist and newsagent.

From 1931, the street directory shows 48 Beaufort Street as the 'Court Café' with M.G. Peckow as proprietor. By the 1960s, the café had a local reputation for being an excellent place to meet and dine, particularly for those working in the area at lunchtime.

In 1990, along with its next-door neighbour, the Canterbury Court Ballroom with its multi-storey car park on the upper-levels, the cafe was demolished to make way for a Myer Megamart, occupying the entire block. This, in turn, was replaced by a car park complex a few years later.

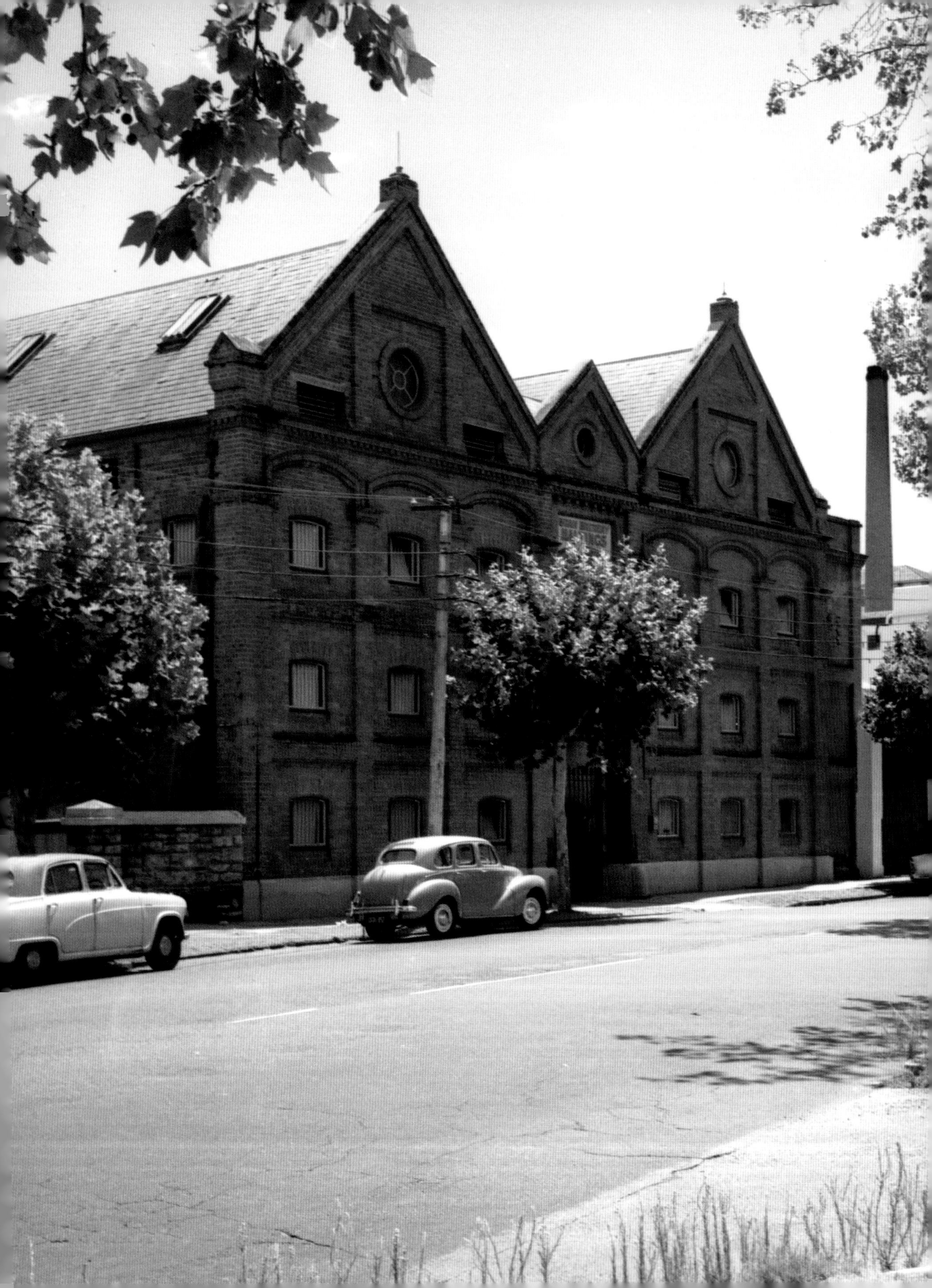

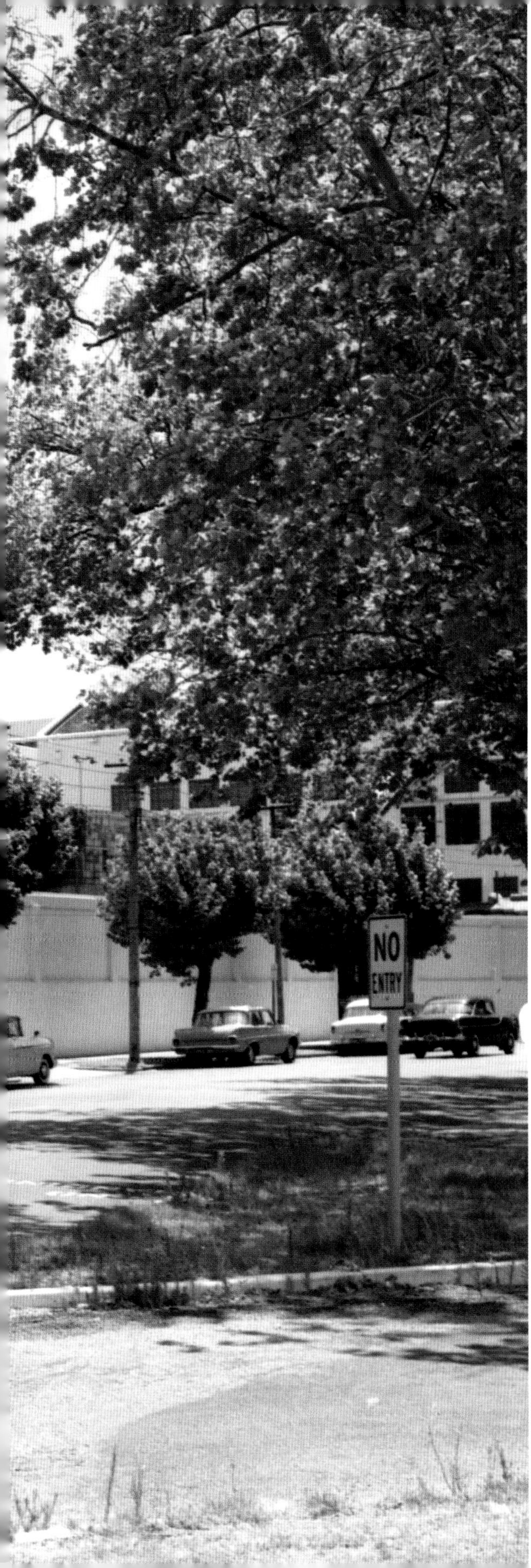


## Swan Brewery Malthouse And Bottling Plant 1967

Frank Sherwood established the famous Swan Brewery in 1857 and placed an advertisement in the Perth Gazette: 'The Public are respectfully informed that after the first day of November next, they may be supplied with superior Pale Ale.' In 1879 the brewery moved to the now familiar site at the foot of Mount Eliza, where it stands today.

Like most breweries of the time, Swan Brewery malted its own barley and in 1901 a larger malthouse was built to a design by the well-known Perth architect, J. J. Talbot Hobbs.

At the time of the building's demolition, there was some debate as to the style of architecture of the front facade. The debate on this point was inconclusive; however, the rear of the building was definitely industrial.

## West Perth Cottages

1963

**RIGHT:** During the first Gold Rush, the newly fashionable suburb of West Perth was characterised by grand homes facing major streets on the top of the Mount Eliza escarpment. These houses were designed to reflect their owners' prominent place in Western Australian society. Further down the hill to the north, small workers' cottages were also located, facing the backstreets of the vicinity and close to the various manufacturing businesses located in the area.

These semi-detached cottages, photographed in 1963, on the corner of Murray and Coolgardie Streets are typical of the housing stock being built in Perth suburbs around 1900. This row of cottages was demolished to make way for commercial buildings during the 1960s.

## West Perth Residence

1963

**FOLLOWING PAGE:** During the last 20 years of the 19th century development began to creep west towards Kings Park. This resulted in a slow transfer of wealthy and influential families from their original base around Government House to the delightful hilltop setting of West Perth, which was being laid out in the 1880s.

By the beginning of the 20th century, West Perth had become one of the more prestigious residential addresses in the area, with its convenient location and its proximity to Kings Park, making it a much-sought-after place to live. In 1906, the area between Hay Street and Kings Park was described as 'a very fashionable resort'.

This house, photographed in 1963, is typical of the residences built in West Perth during the first half of the 20th century. Sadly, it made way for a new development a few years after this picture was taken.

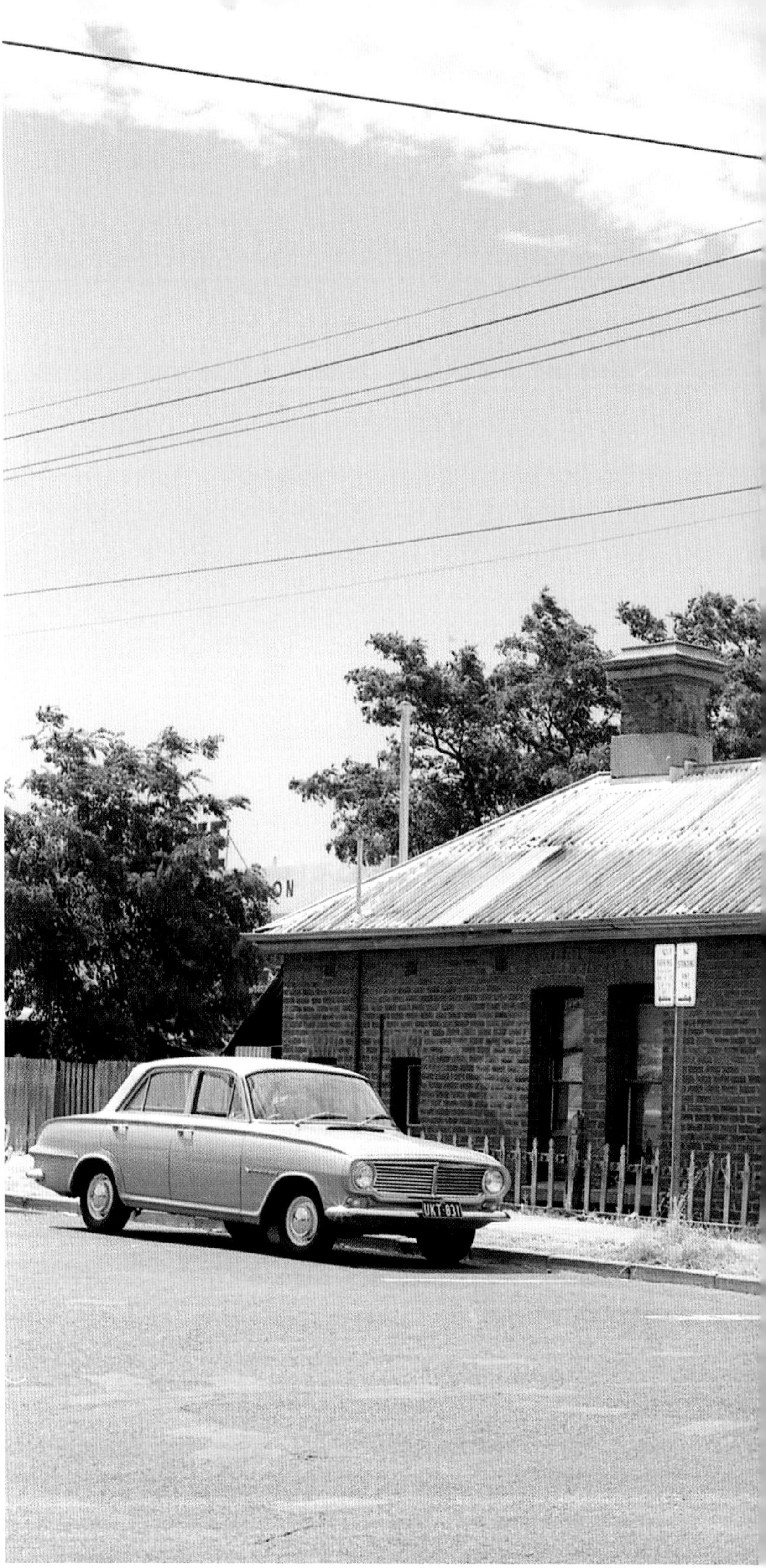

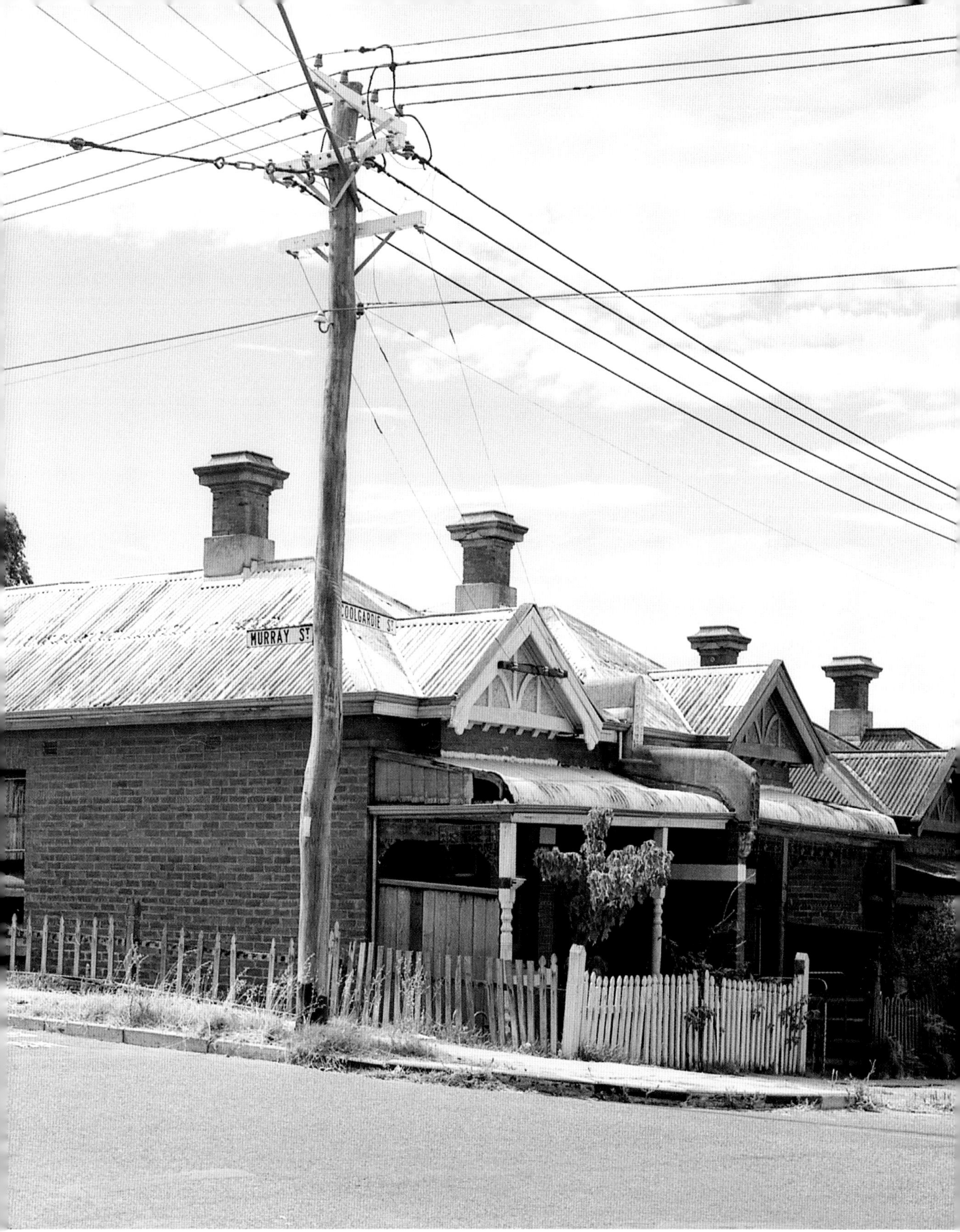
MURRAY St
COOLGARDIE St

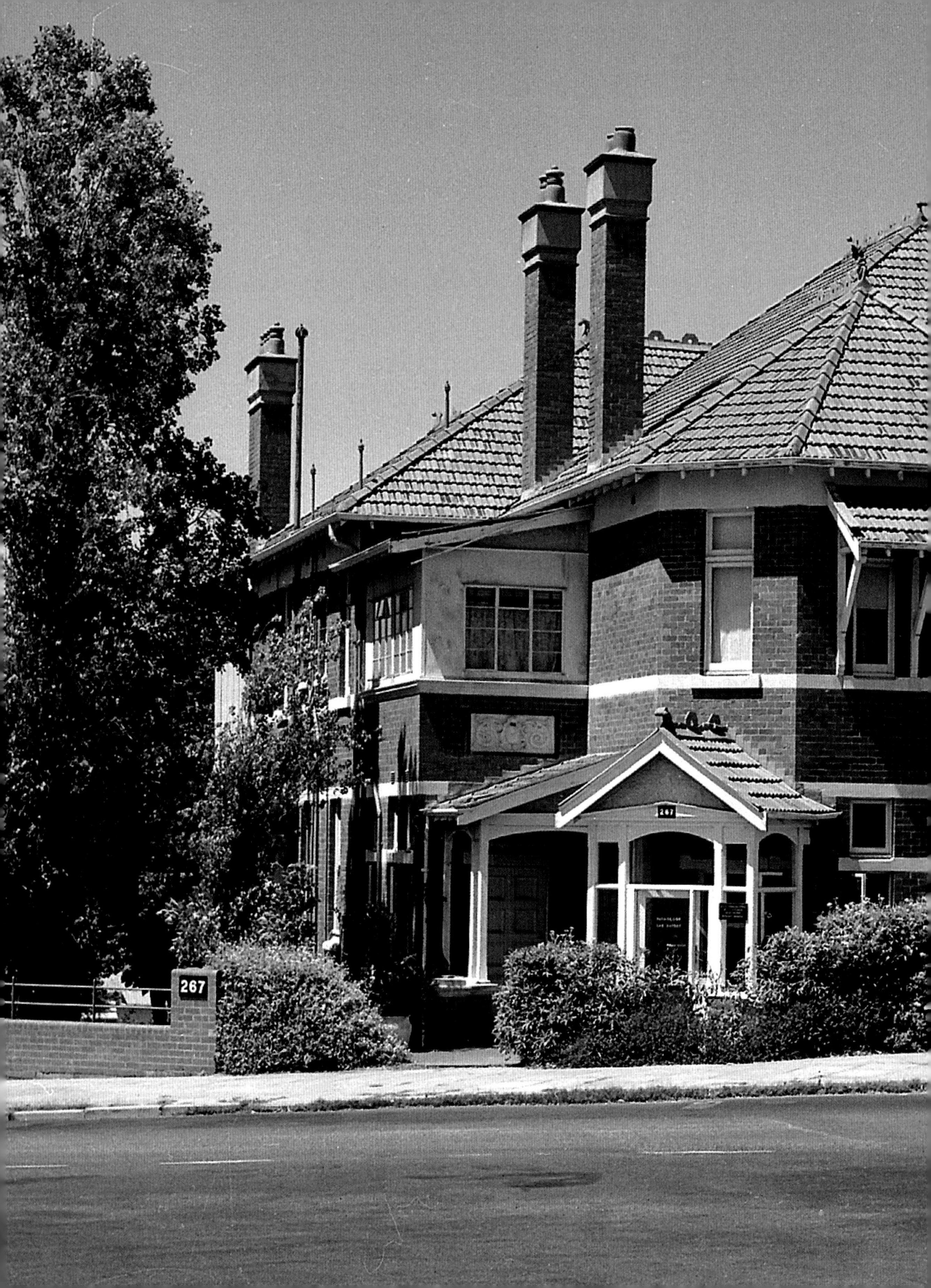
267
267

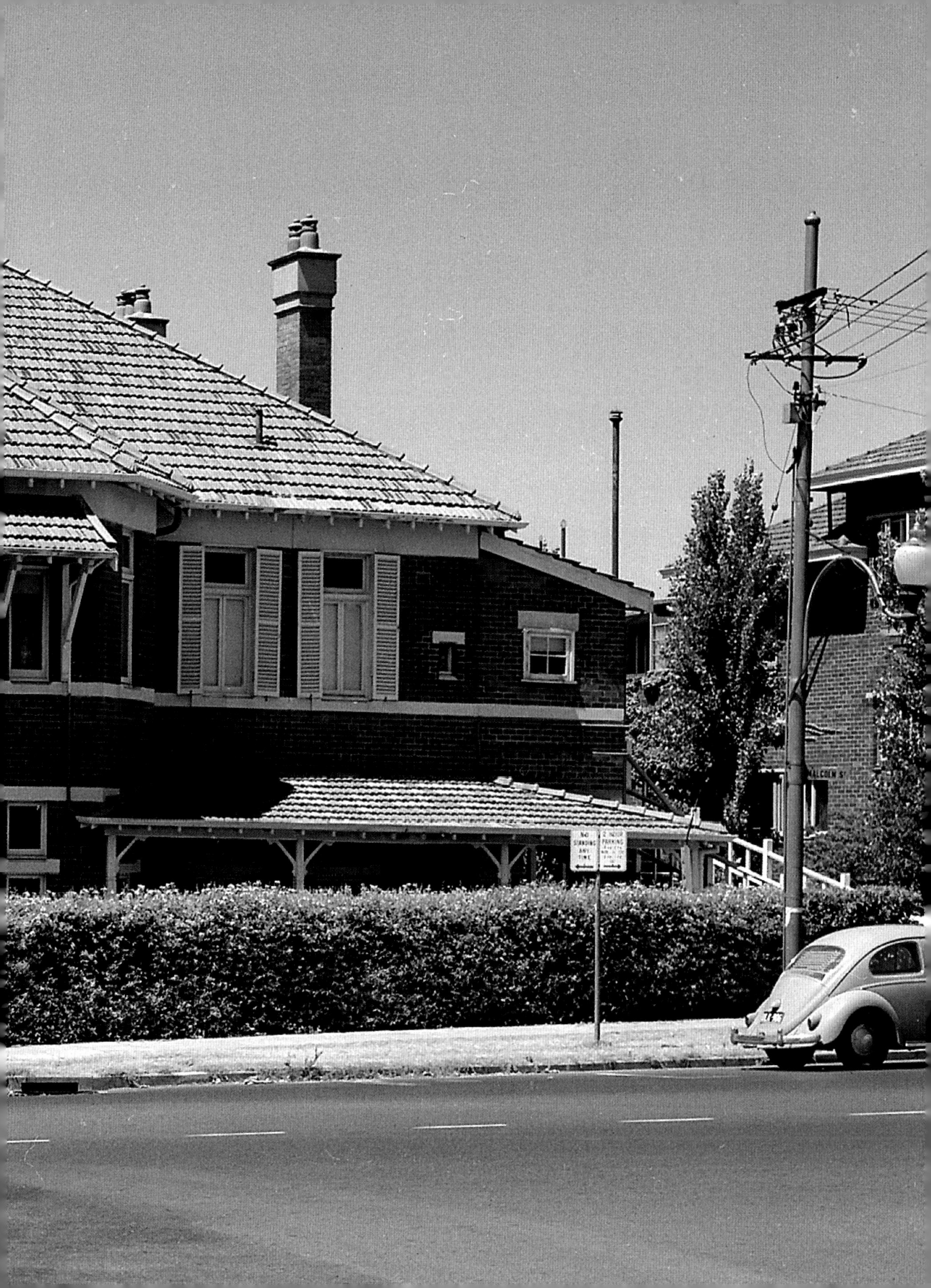
NO STANDING ANY TIME
2 HOUR PARKING
MALCOLM St

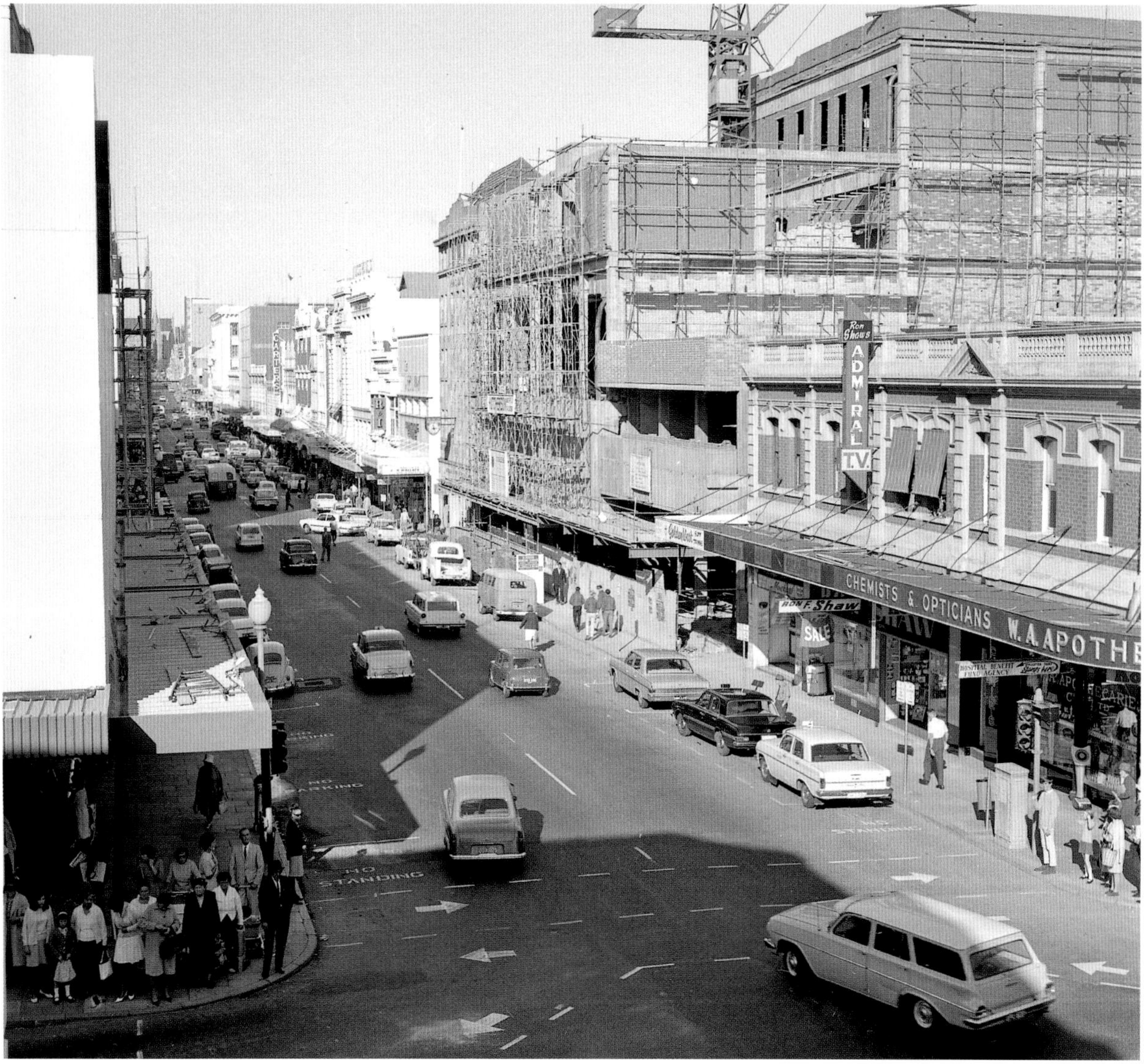


## Murray Street c.1963

Taken in the early 1960s, this photograph shows the demolition of the National Bank of Australasia on Murray Street, close to its junction with William Street.

Designed by Eales, Cohen & Fitzhardinge for the Bank, this rather bland Art Deco shopping arcade and office building was constructed in 1938.

Going down Murray Street, the Piccadilly Arcade and Musgrove's music shop are visible. In the foreground is WA Apothecaries Co Ltd, a pharmacy chain founded in Hay Street by Harry Armstrong in 1894. Of all these buildings, only the Piccadilly Arcade still exists.

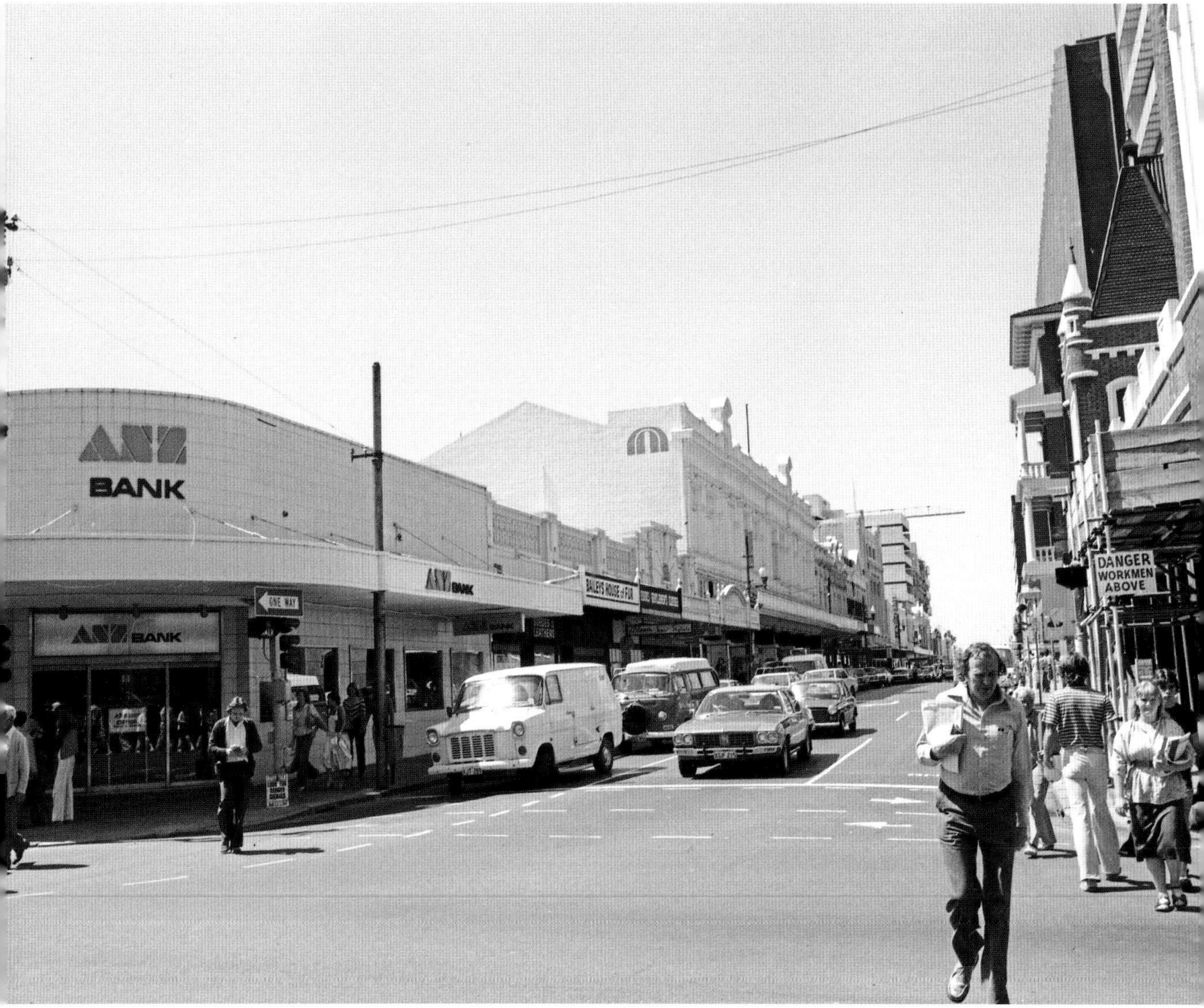


## ANZ Bank c.1972

Taken in about 1972, this photograph shows the Macay Building running along to the Cremorne Arcade, which thankfully still exists.

Constructed in 1926, the Macay Building had various tenants throughout its life, with the ANZ Bank being the last. The building made way for the four-screen, state-of-the-art Cinema City which opened in November 1980 with 'The Blues Brothers' playing in one of the auditoriums. Where high finance was once conducted, a well-known burger chain now plies its wares and Cinema City has made way for the Equus Apartments building, which from St Georges Terrace looks like an ocean-going liner coming in to dock.

The photograph, although undated, can be traced to 1972 by the scaffolding surround Perth Town Hall, which was undergoing major renovations at that time.

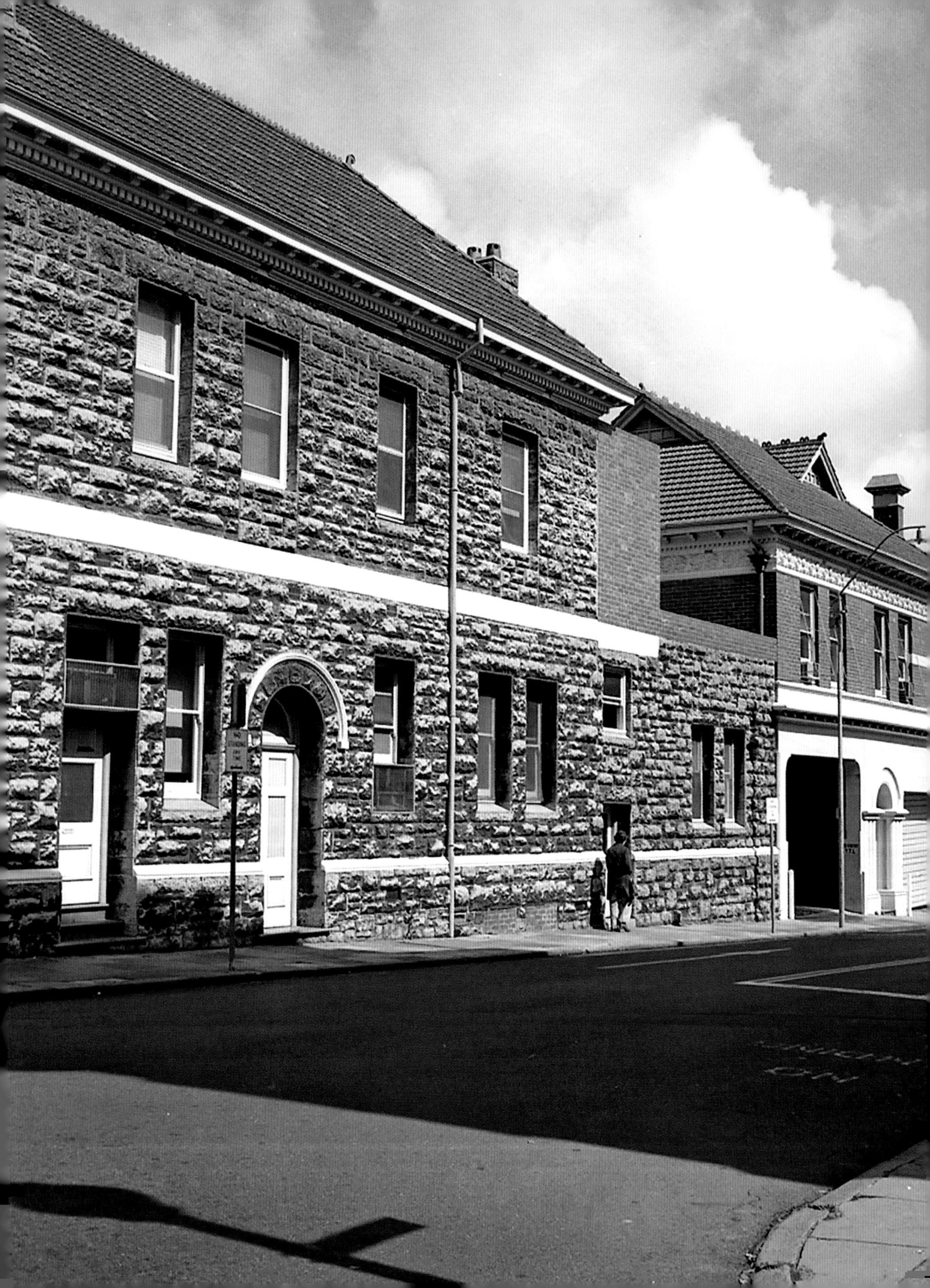

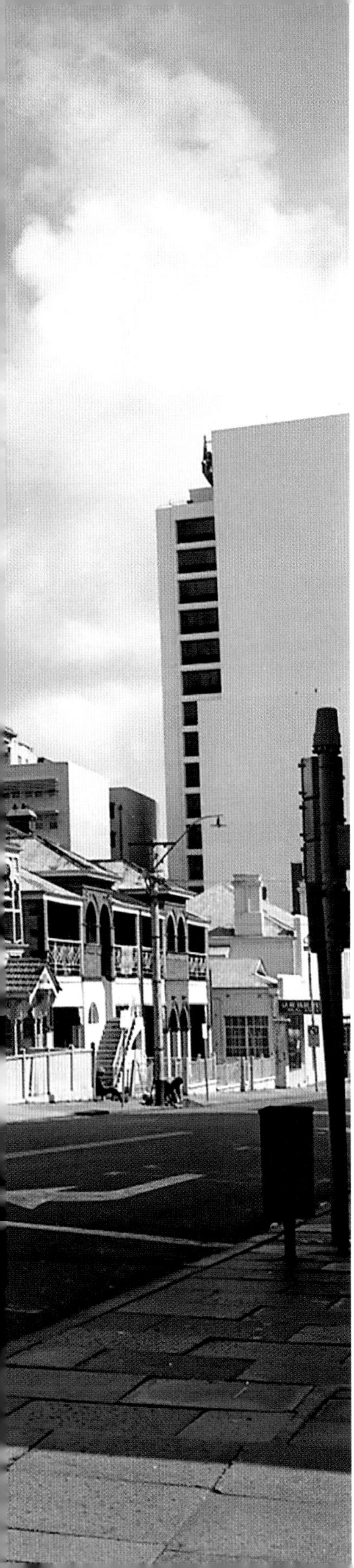

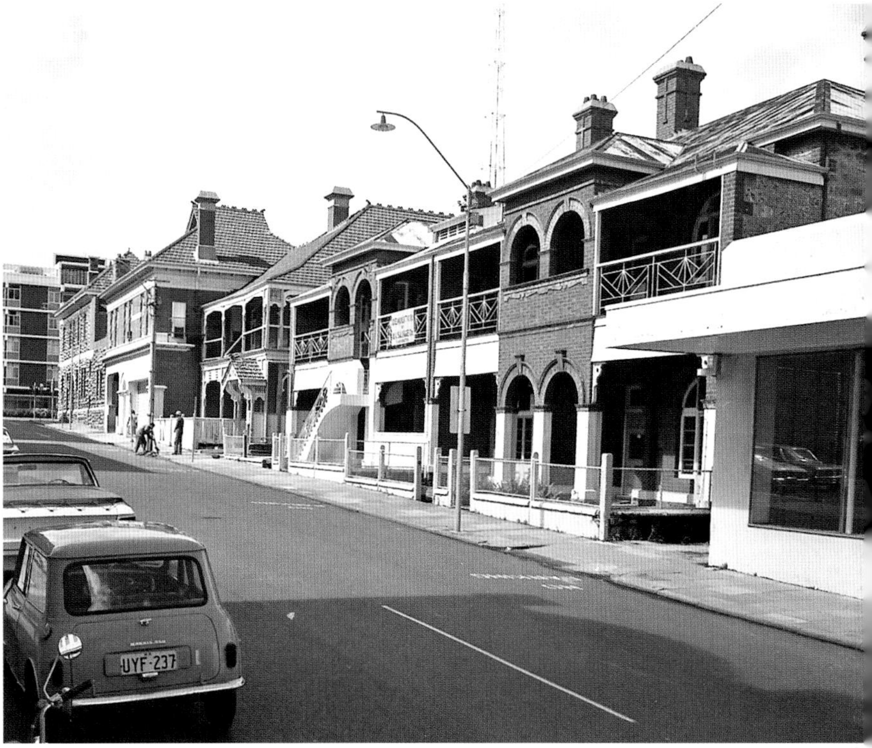


## **Irwin Street** c.1977

These two photographs of the eastern side of Irwin Street were taken just before demolition of the houses and fire station annex in about 1977.

According to Wise's Street Directories of the time, this row of cottages, built at the end of the 19th century, were all occupied by females, some of whom operated their premises as boarding houses, which was apparently a socially acceptable occupation for unmarried females of that era.

The large building in the foreground of the photo at left is the 1903 No. 1 Fire Station, the first custom built fire station in Perth. The brick building next to it was added in 1910 to provide better accommodation for the Brigade Superintendent and resident firemen.

The cottages and fire station annex were demolished to make way for the new Central Fire Station, which did not have a long life, being another victim of the wrecker's ball in 2015 to make way for a hotel complex.

# Hay Street 1956 and 1958

**RIGHT:** Until 1897, Hay Street west from Barrack Street was named Twiss Street, the eastern end being Howick Street. The name change came about when the City Council decided to rationalise the names and remove the anomaly of having two names for different portions of the same street.

Taken in 1956, possibly from the roof of Optical House, this photo shows people queuing to see Walt Disney's film 'Davy Crockett and the River Pirates' starring Fess Parker at the Plaza Cinema, which first opened its door in 1937.

Next door is the Savoy Hotel, which had the Betts and Betts shoe shop as a tenant on the ground floor. Alterations in 1961 enabled the shop to take over the entire ground floor and make the claim to be the largest shoe shop in Australia.

**BELOW:** Two years later and a little further west, on the opposite side of the street, can be seen the Perth branch of Sandover's Store, which opened in 1884 selling hardware and pharmaceutical goods. The store suffered a major fire in 1907, which at the time was the largest building fire ever seen in Perth. The business was taken over by Electronic Industries Limited a year after this photograph was taken.

Next door is Trinity Arcade, which was built for the Congregational Church and opened in 1927.

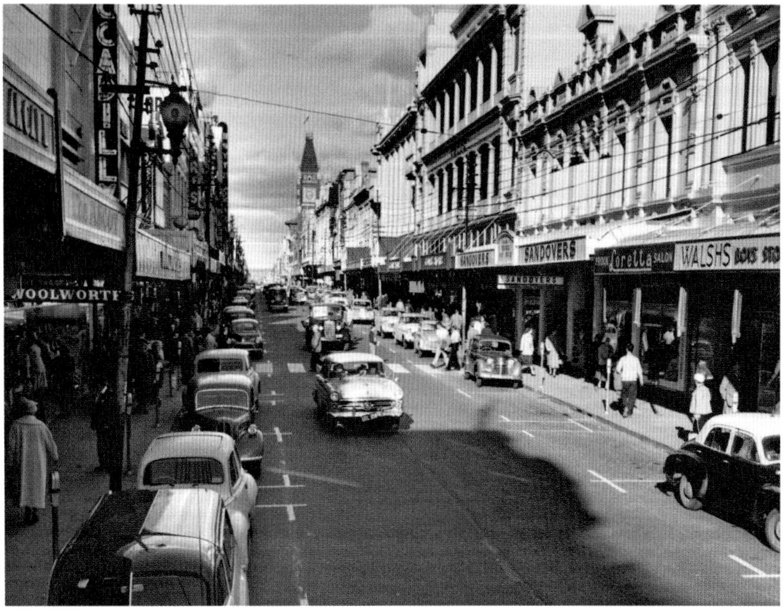


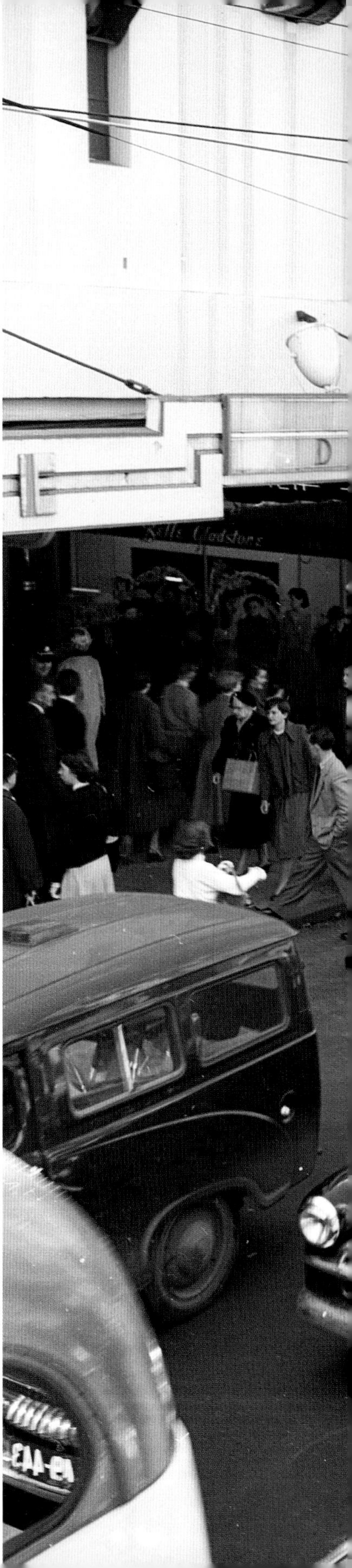

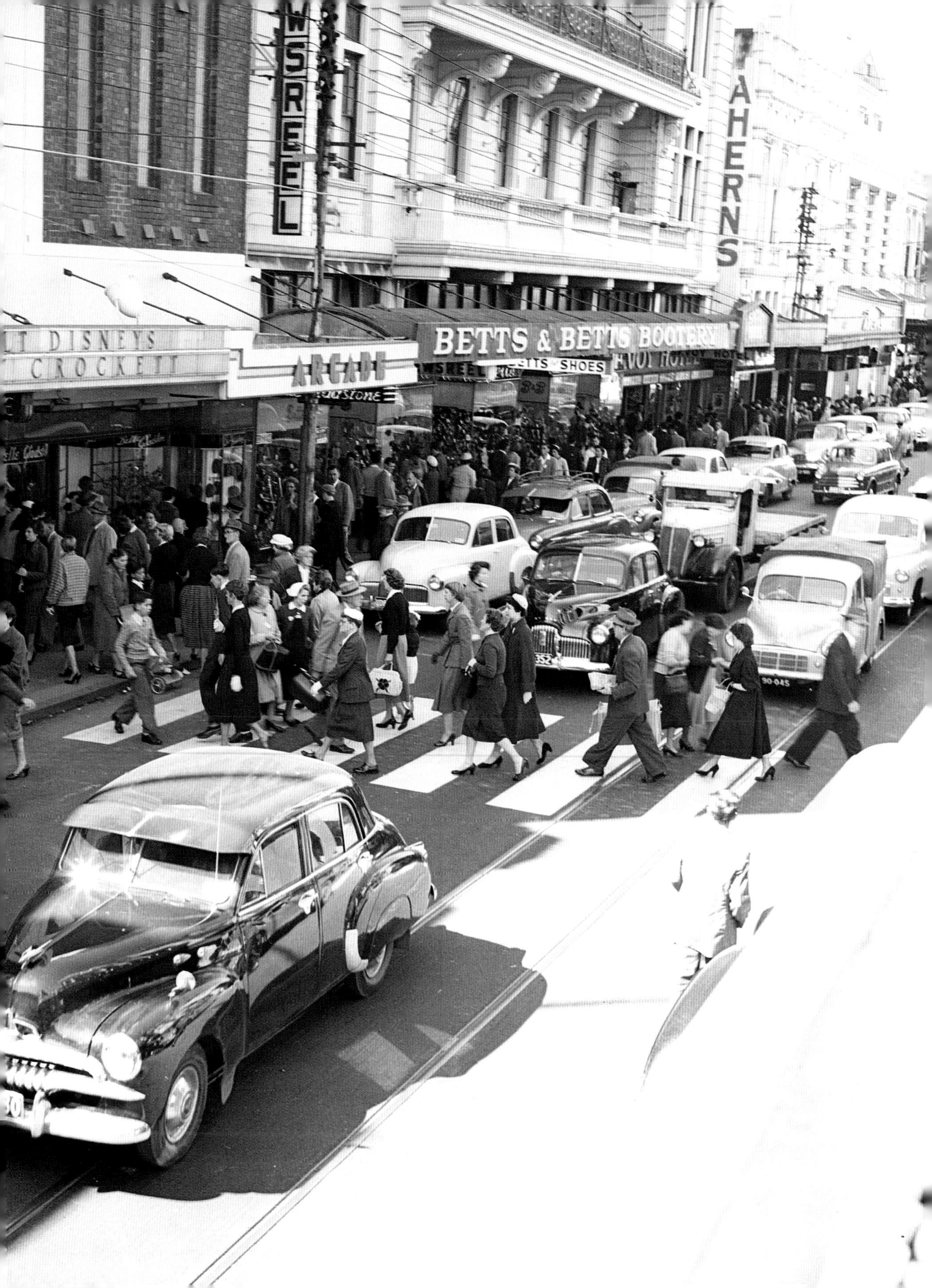
WSREEL
AHERNS
BETTS & BETTS BOOTERY
BETTS SHOES
DISNEYS
CROCKETT

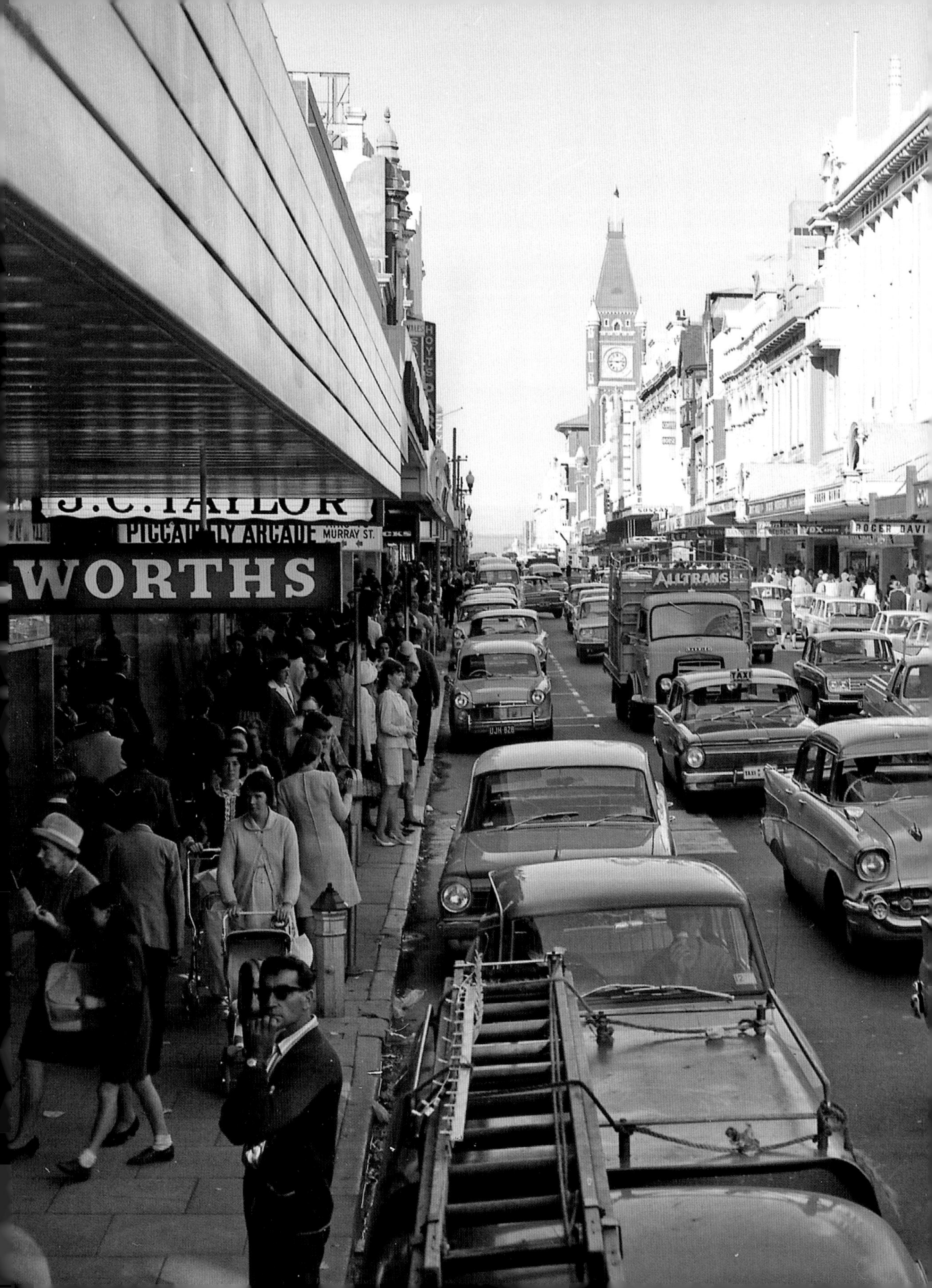
J.C. TAYLOR
PICCADILLY ARCADE
MURRAY ST.
WORTHS
ALLTRANS
TAXI
ROGER DAVI
UJH 828

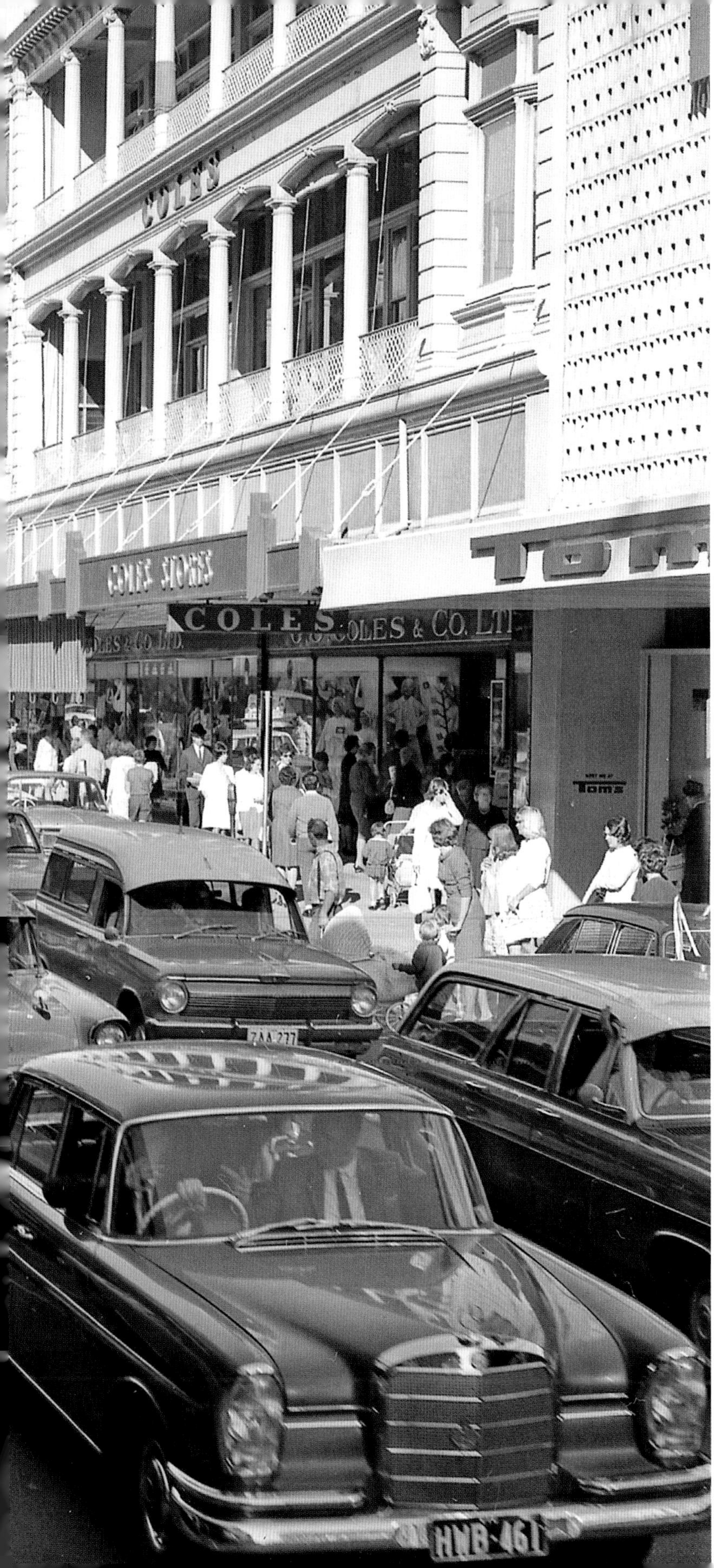


## Hay Street 1966

By the time this photo was taken in 1966, the Sandover store site had been redeveloped, the Hay Street frontage of the Trinity Arcade was a Cole's grocery store, and the traffic congestion had got much worse!

2

# Vintage Perth

Ernie's architectural and photographic training gave him a keen eye, not only for things of architectural interest, but also a keen sense of photographic composition. The following photographs show how he combined those two skills to depict the evolving Perth, warts and all, in an artistic and engaging manner.

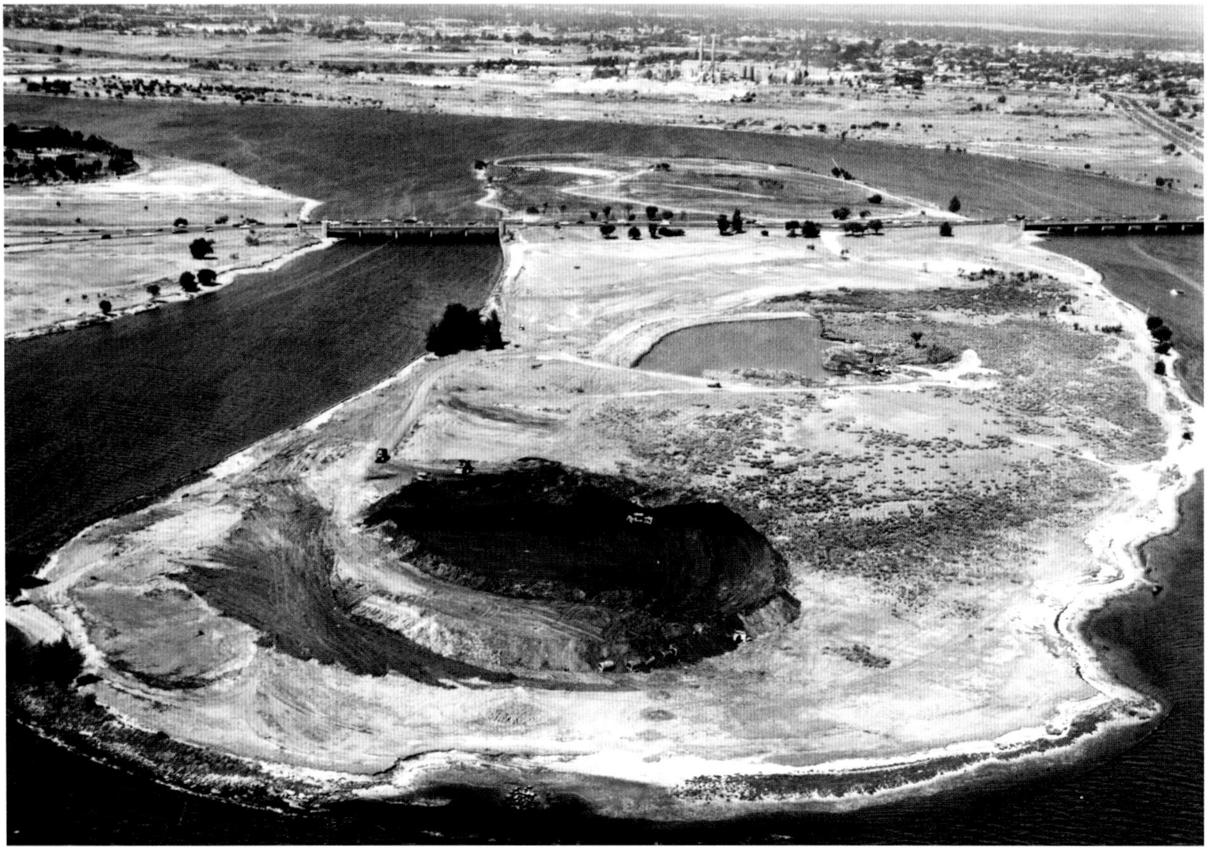

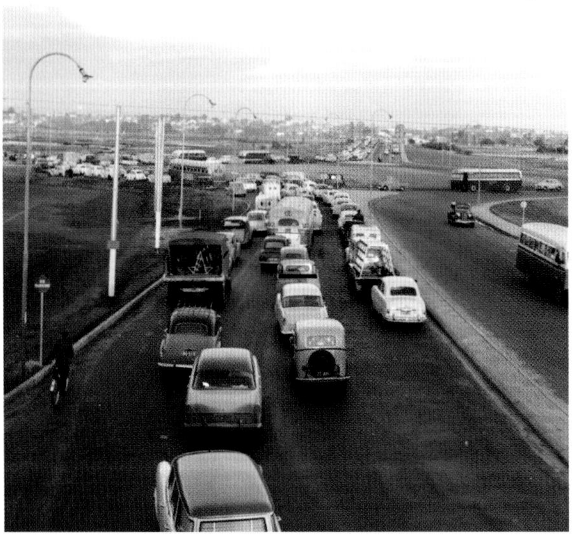

## The Causeway 1954 and 1959

**ABOVE:** The first Causeway Bridge across the mud flats around Heirisson Island was officially opened in May 1843, but by the 1860s the bridge was described as being in 'a moribund state', having been weakened by heavy use, frequent battering by vessels and being completely submerged during the floods of 1862. A replacement bridge was opened for traffic in August 1865.

Widened for a tramway in 1904 and again in 1932, by the late 1930s the bridge was only strong enough for a limited traffic-carrying capacity. War delayed the construction of a replacement bridge, but in 1949 a two-bridge, composite steel and concrete structure was built and opened for traffic in September 1952.

This aerial image shows the rawness of the new landscape around Heirisson Island and the river floodplain.

**LEFT:** Despite the improvements the Causeway remained a serious bottleneck for traffic trying to cross the river until the opening of the Narrows Bridge in 1959.

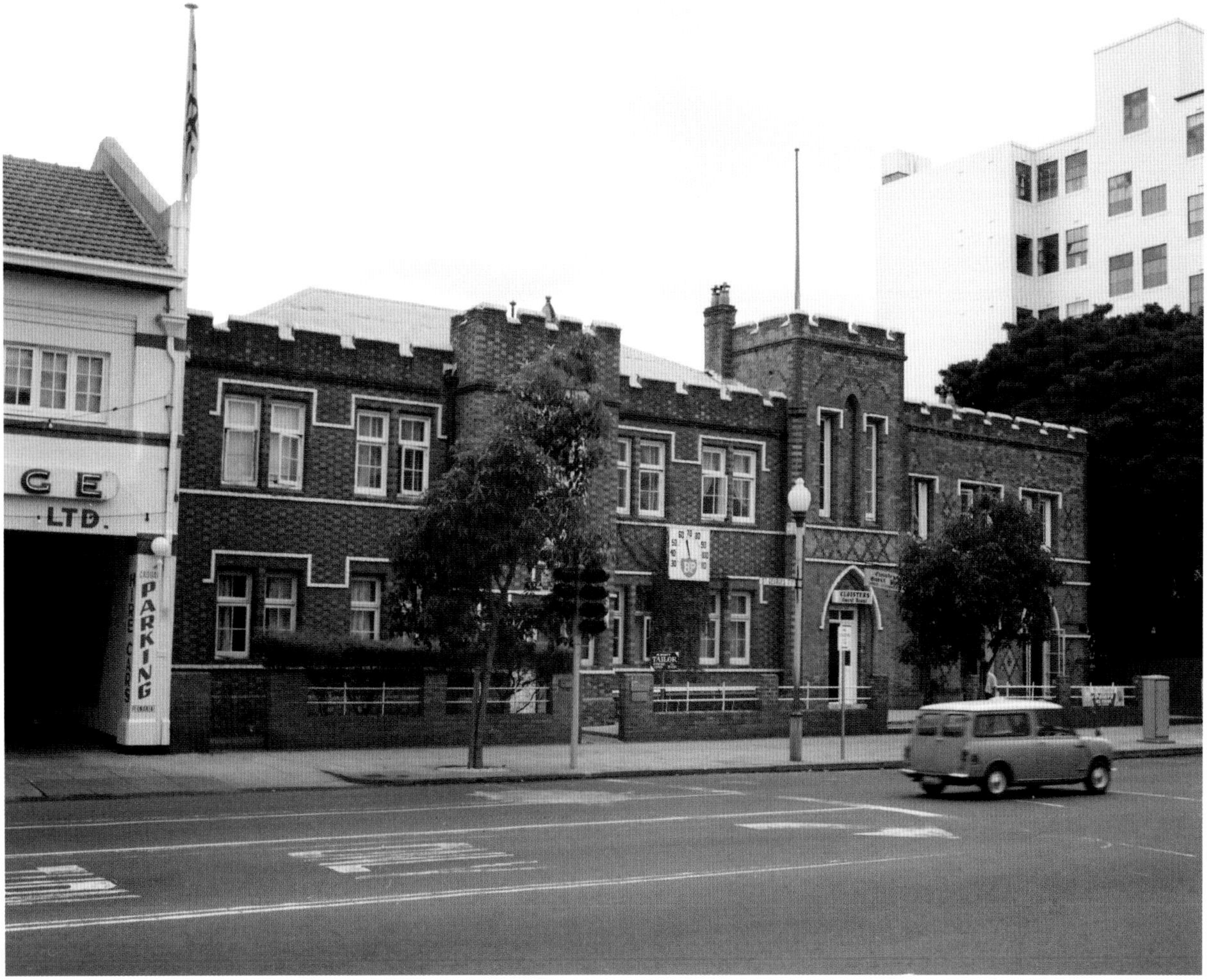


## The Cloisters c.1960s and 1971

**ABOVE:** The Cloisters has a close association with Bishop Hale, the first Anglican Bishop of Perth, who had it built to house the 'Perth Church of England Collegiate School'. The school opened in June, 1858 with an initial role of 23 pupils – 'a very good commencement' wrote the Inquirer newspaper.

The building continued to be used as a school until 1914, after which it had a number of different uses and narrowly escaped demolition following a fire in 1931.

**RIGHT:** This photograph was taken in 1971 during the building's restoration for use as a commercial outlet. By modern standards, this was an extremely invasive restoration of such an historic building, with little of the original remaining other than its walls.

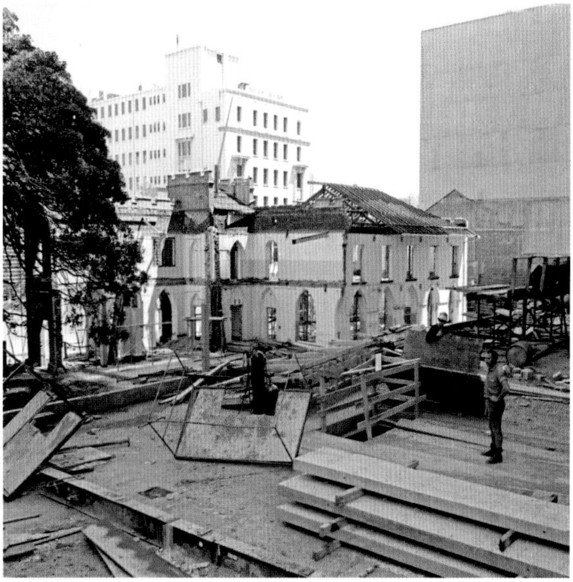

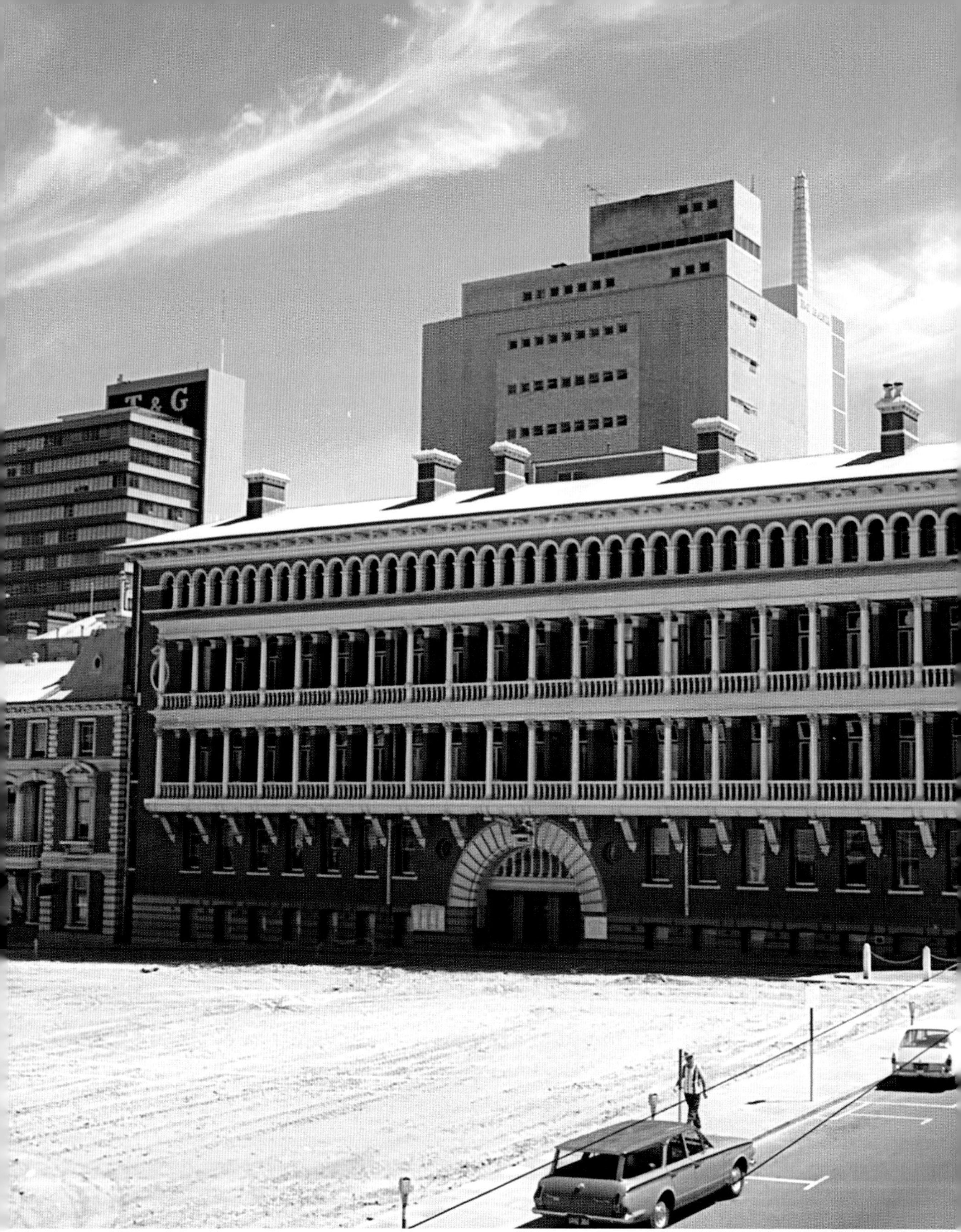
T & G

## Land Titles Office 1968 and 1969

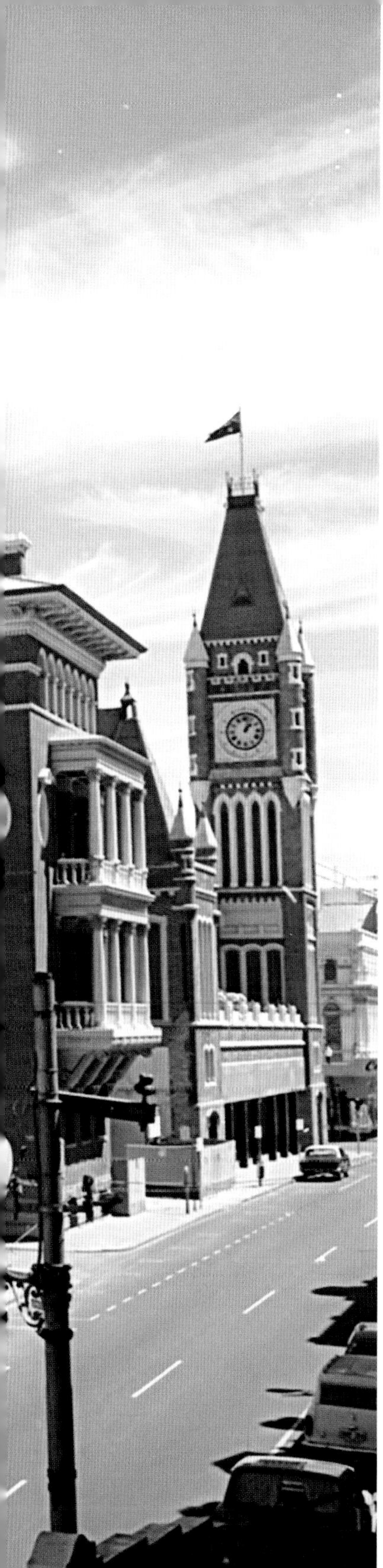

**LEFT:** This photograph, taken in 1969 just after the demolition of St Georges Chambers, offered Ernie a rare, uninterrupted view of the Land Titles Building. This view was briefly glimpsed 50 years later when the west end of the Law Chambers building was demolished to open up Cathedral Square and make way for the new City of Perth Library.

**BELOW:** Heralded by many architectural historians as one of the grandest classical style buildings in Australia, the Land Titles Building was designed by State Architect, George Temple-Poole and completed in 1897. This building forms one wing of the Central Government Offices, more recently referred to as the 'Old Treasury Building'. The building continued in government use until 1996 when it was vacated. After a long period of disuse, the building has spectacularly been given a new lease of life as a hotel and public plaza.

This image shows the proximity of the government buildings to the land allocated to the Anglican cathedral. The smaller building to the right is part of St Georges Chambers designed by J. J. Talbot Hobbs and constructed in 1897. It was occupied by the administrative offices of the Anglican Church, the Agricultural Bank and Land Titles Department.

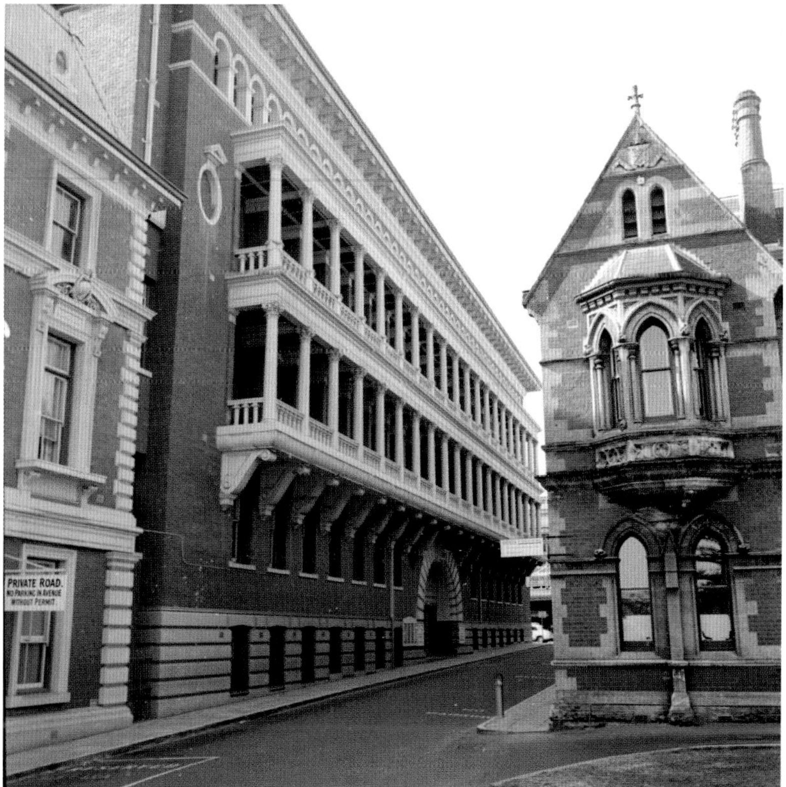

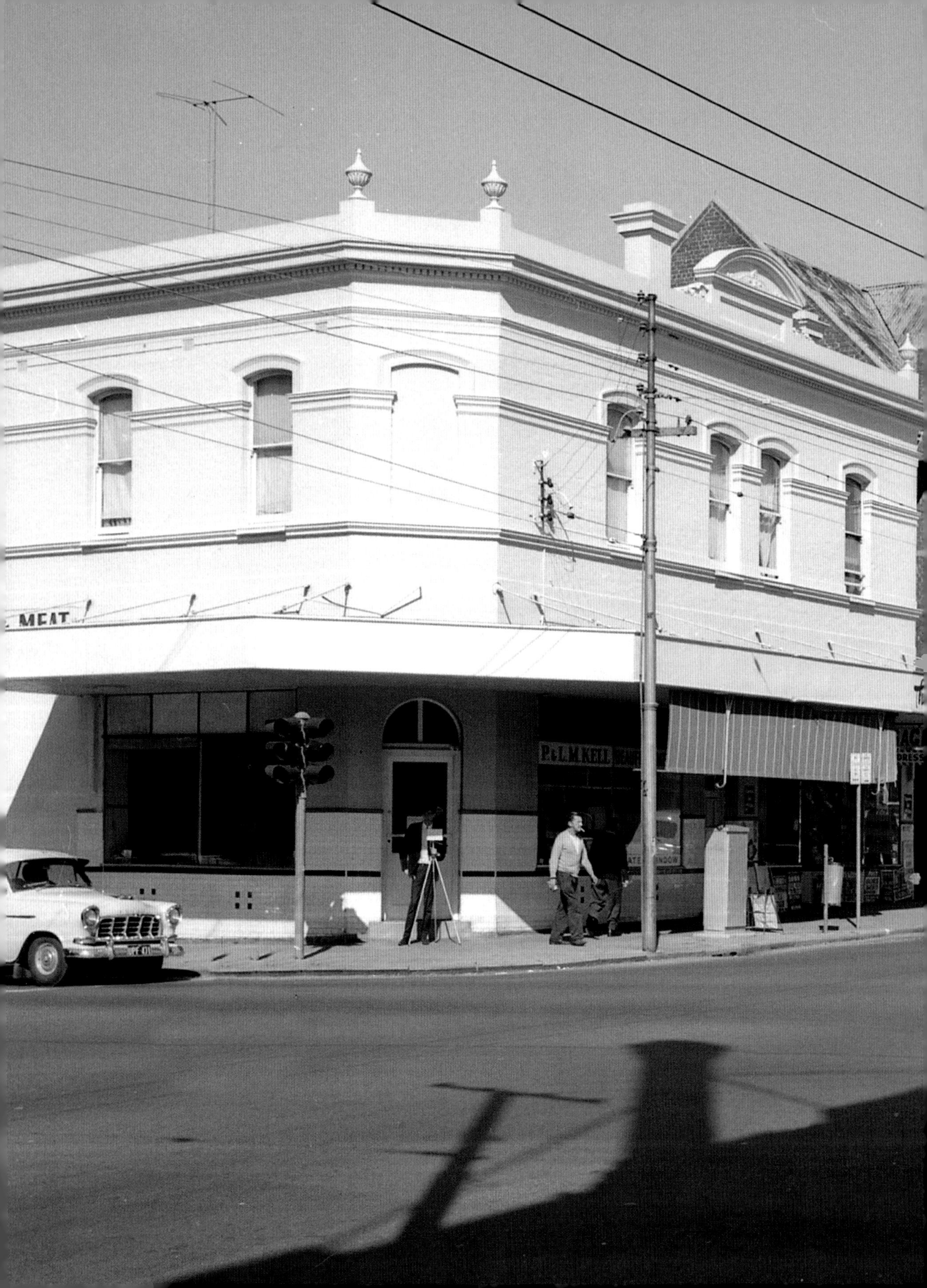
MEAT
P. & L. M. KELL

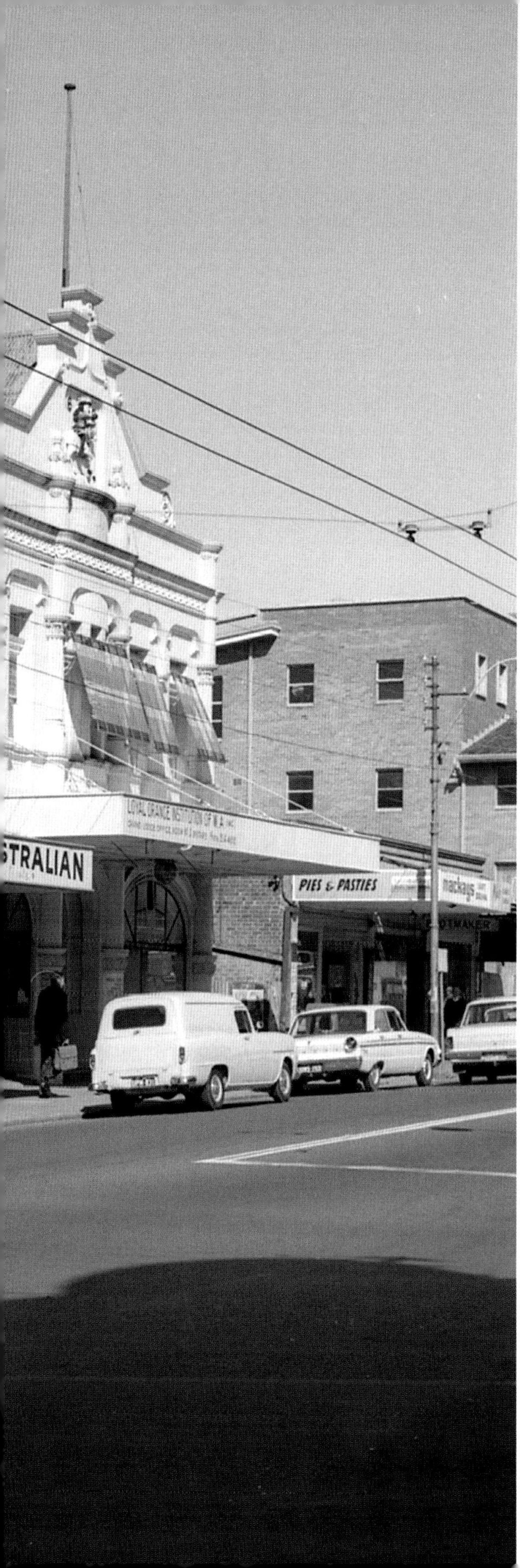


## Protestant Hall c.1970

**LEFT:** The date of 1690, written along with a relief of William of Orange on horseback, has often confused passers-by into think it was the date of the building – a time long before the British colonisation of Western Australia.

William of Orange (1650-1702) 'good King Billy' was a staunch Protestant, which made him the obvious emblem for the Protestant Alliance Friendly Society (PAFS), formed in Perth in 1892. The main function of the Society was to provide economic assistance to members before social welfare was introduced.

Originally, the Society met at various locations across Perth through the 1890s, before finally building its own meeting hall in Beaufort Street. The two-storey building with ground-floor shops, a main hall behind, and living quarters above was designed by Henry Trigg, and opened in February 1901.

The PAFS vacated Protestant Hall in 1981 when social changes rendered the purpose of a Friendly Society obsolete. Today, the Protestant Hall provides office space for commercial concerns.

## Concert Hall 1973

The need for a dedicated concert venue in Perth became critical when the Capitol Theatre was demolished in 1968. Thankfully, with State Government support and a land swap, the City Council stepped up to the mark. Perth Concert Hall was designed by architects Jefferey Howlett and Don Bailey, (who had been responsible for the nearby Council House) and was built on land that was originally part of the Government Domain.

The building's design included the use of computer modelling to ensure the acoustic properties of the hall were the best they could be – the first time such modelling had been used anywhere in Australia.

Designed to seat a total of 2,000 people, the hall was officially opened on Australia Day, 1973. The occasion also marked the 21st anniversary of the Festival of Perth and the day of celebrations was rounded off with a midnight-to-dawn ball attended by around 1,700 people.

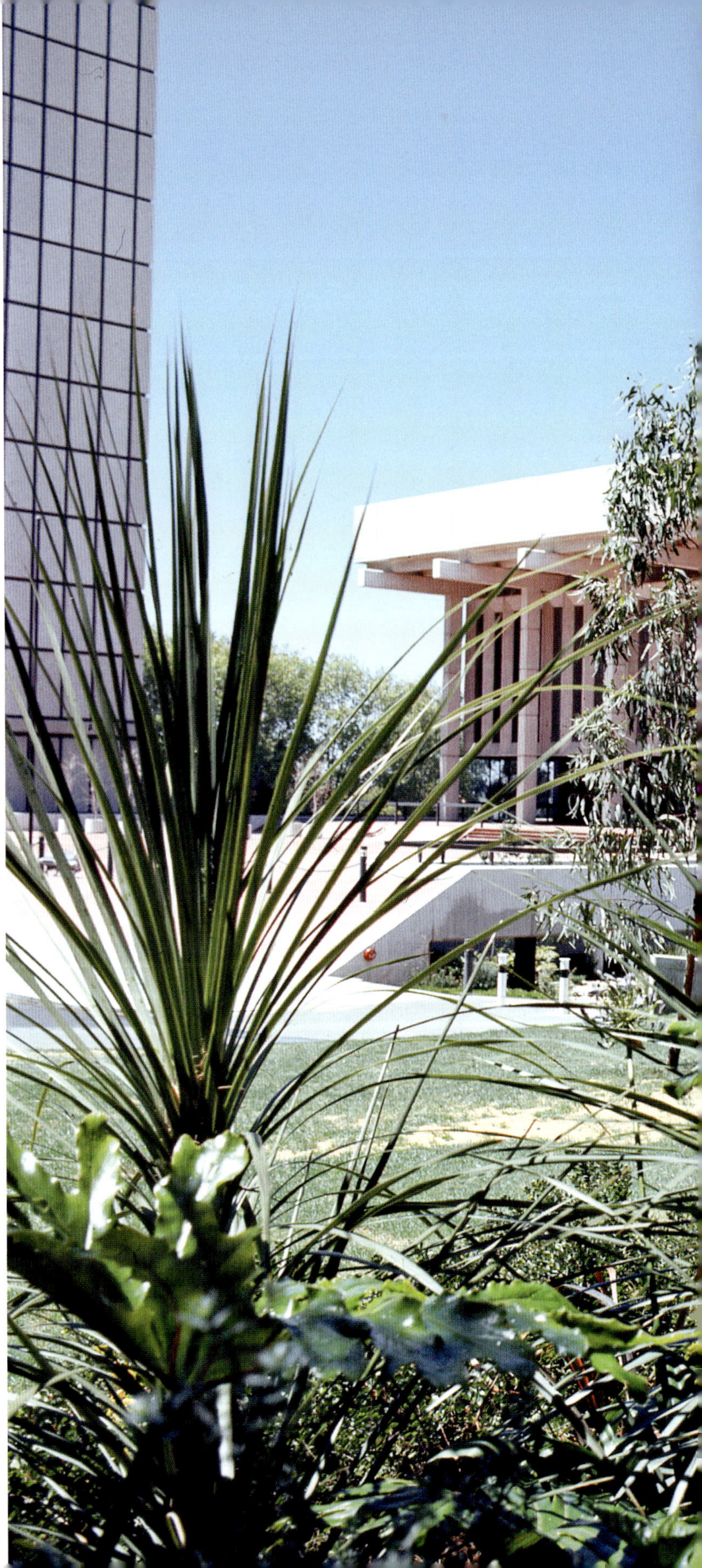

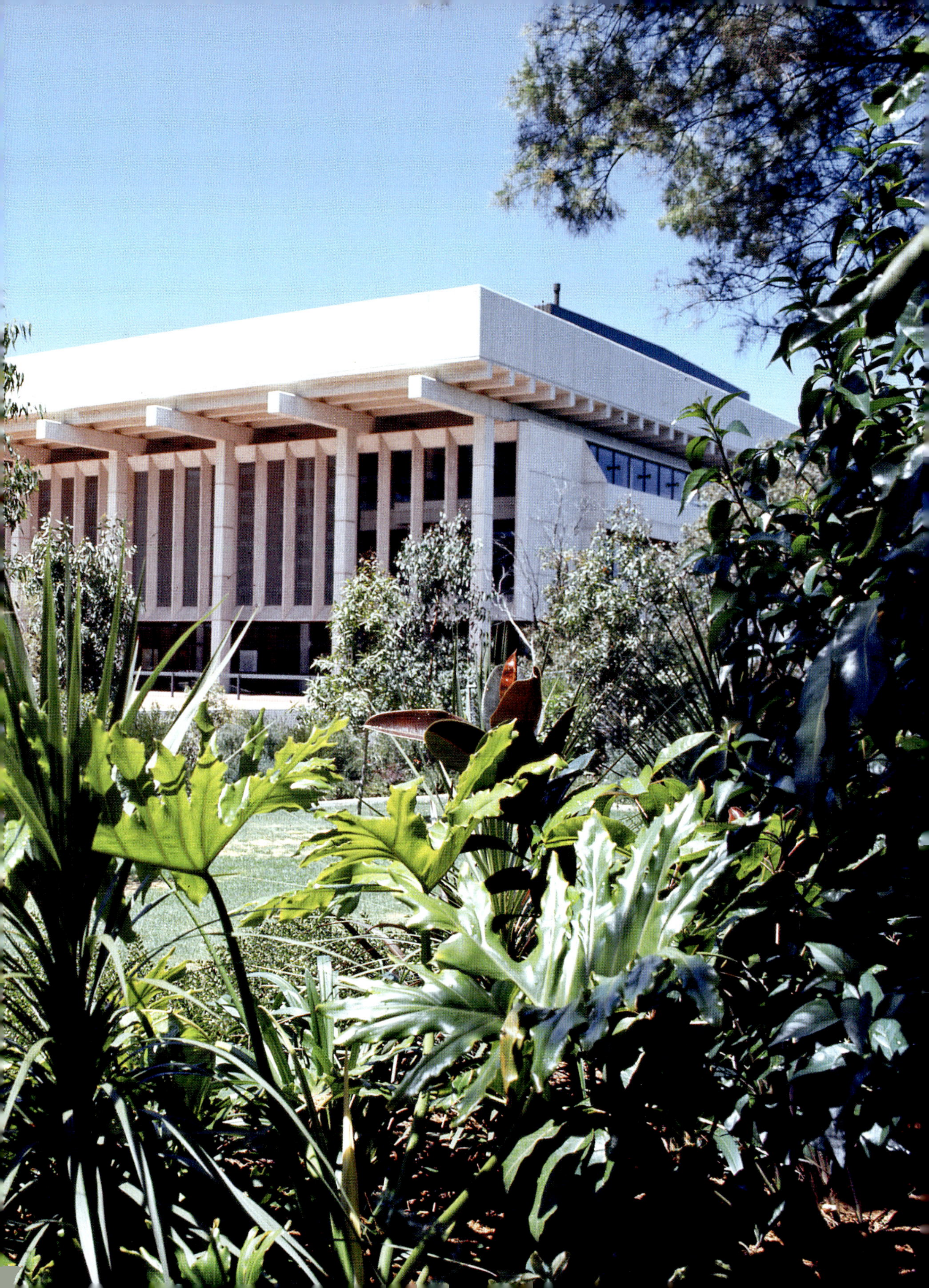

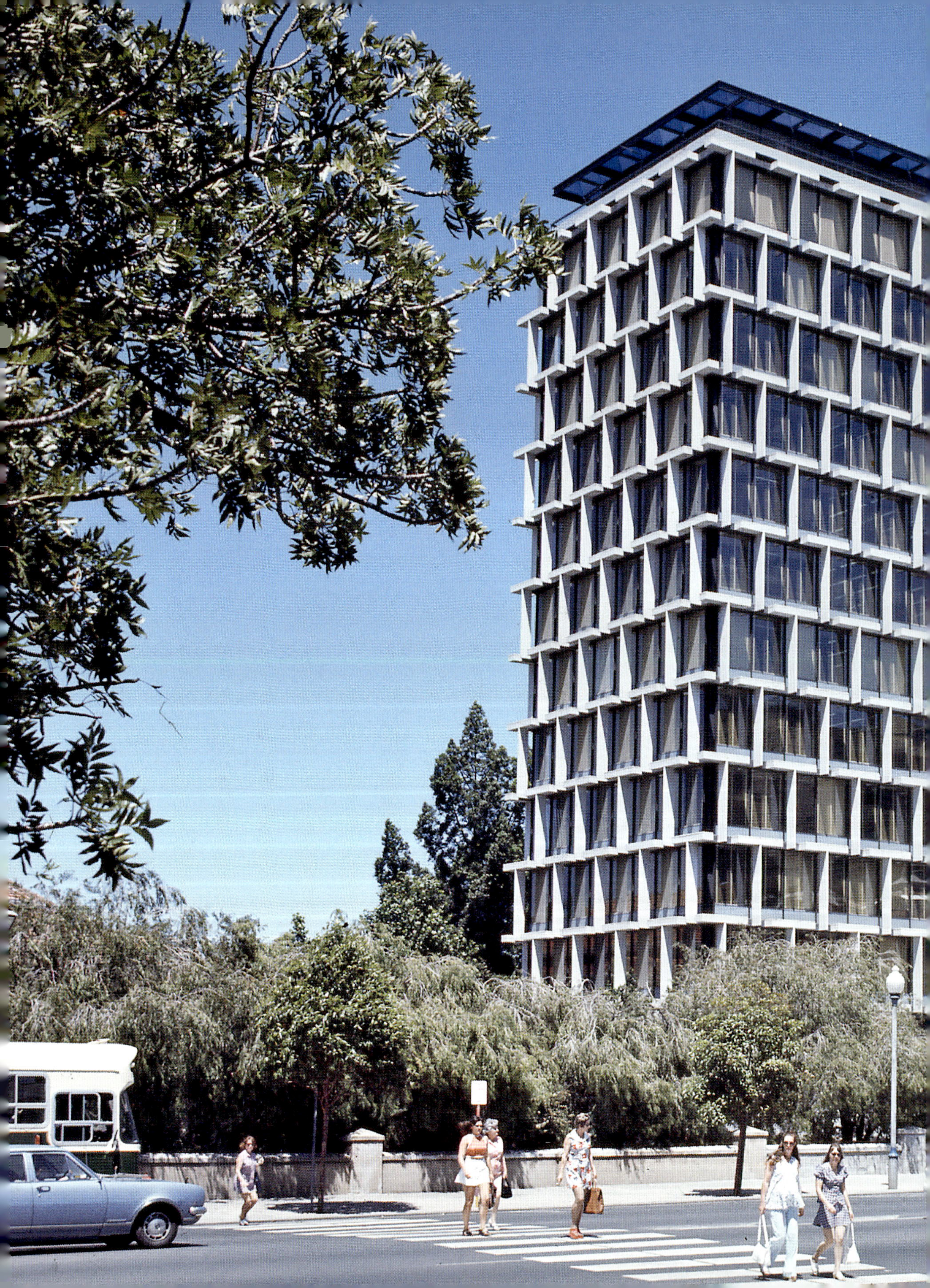

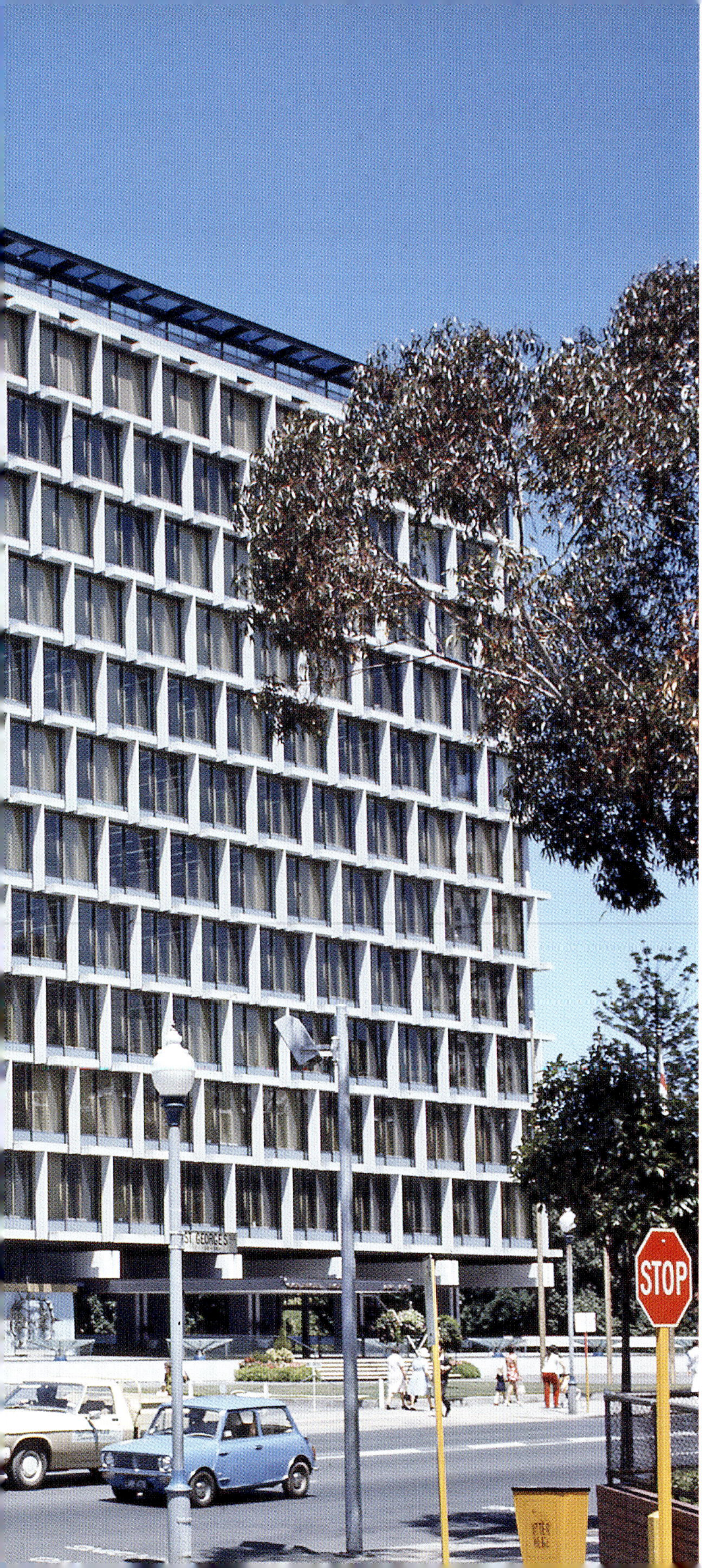


## Council House 1971

In 1961, the old Government Offices building was demolished to make way for Council House. The design for this new building came from a national competition, which was won by Melbourne architects, Jeffrey Howlett and Don Bailey. The resulting building is recognised throughout Australia as one of the finest examples of 1960s 'minimalist modern' office buildings in the country.

The uninterrupted floor-to-ceiling glazing provides occupants with spectacular views of the city and the river, while the building has a unique transparency, particularly at night, prompting one journalist to write that 'it has the effect of a glittering diamond in the city when night falls'.

Council House was officially opened by Her Majesty Queen Elizabeth II, in March 1963.

In the late 1960s, the T-shaped sunshades became the subject of comical references to the then Lord Mayor Sir Thomas Wardle, who ran a chain of cut-price grocery stores known locally as 'Tom the Cheap's' stores.

A few years after the opening of Council House, the Council's previous office accommodation, the Strelitz Building in Murray Street, was demolished to make way for Carillon City.

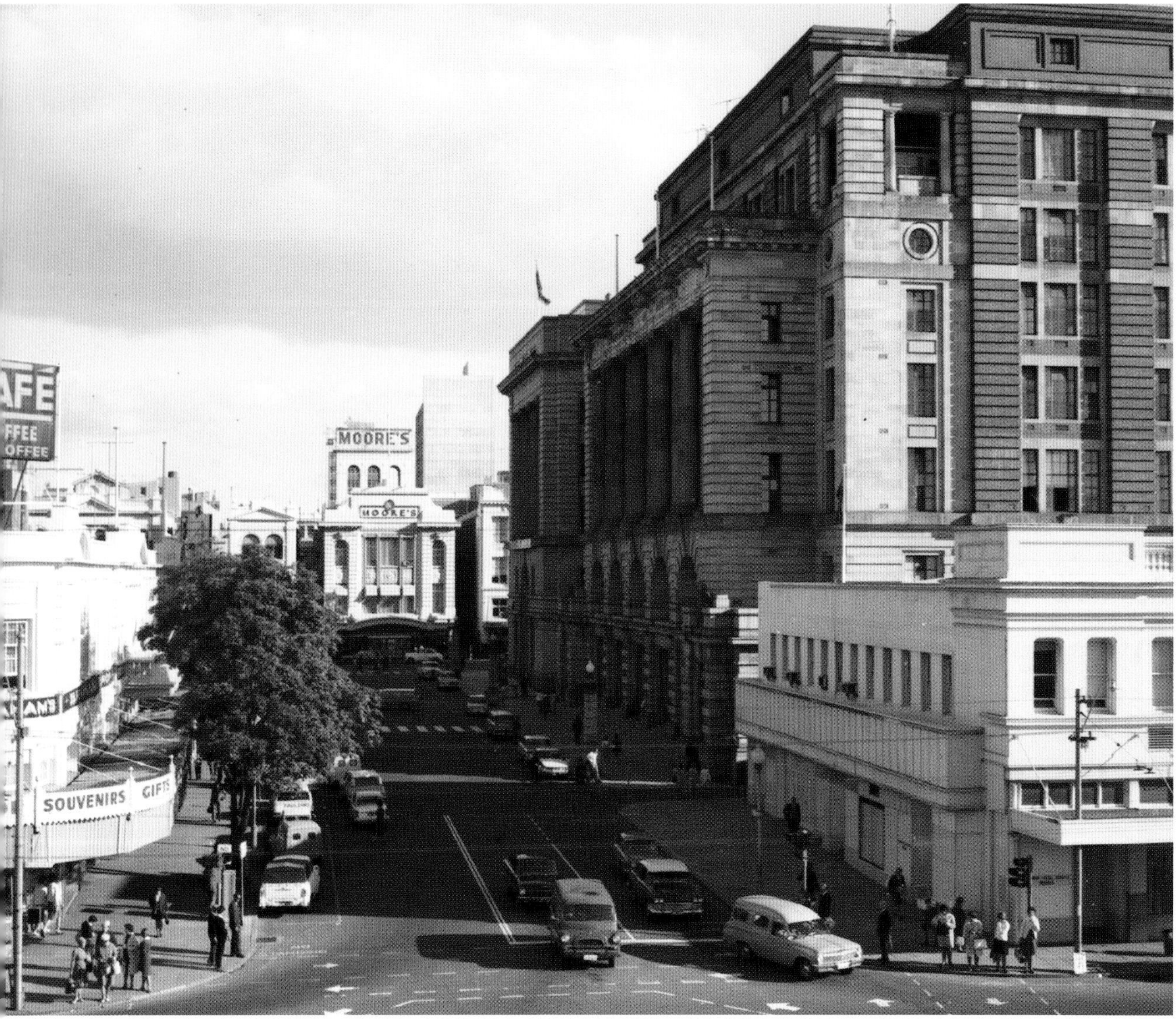


## **Forrest Place** 1968

This photograph of Forrest Place, taken in 1968, highlights different components of the same area. Taken from the roof of the railway station, the photograph not only shows the magnificent GPO and Commonwealth Bank buildings but also, on the right, the former Central Hotel, which appears to have opened some time during the 1880s as the Miners' Arms Hotel. It very often featured in the local newspapers for all the wrong reasons, such as a robbery, obstructing the police, and even a suicide. The hotel was demolished in 1989.

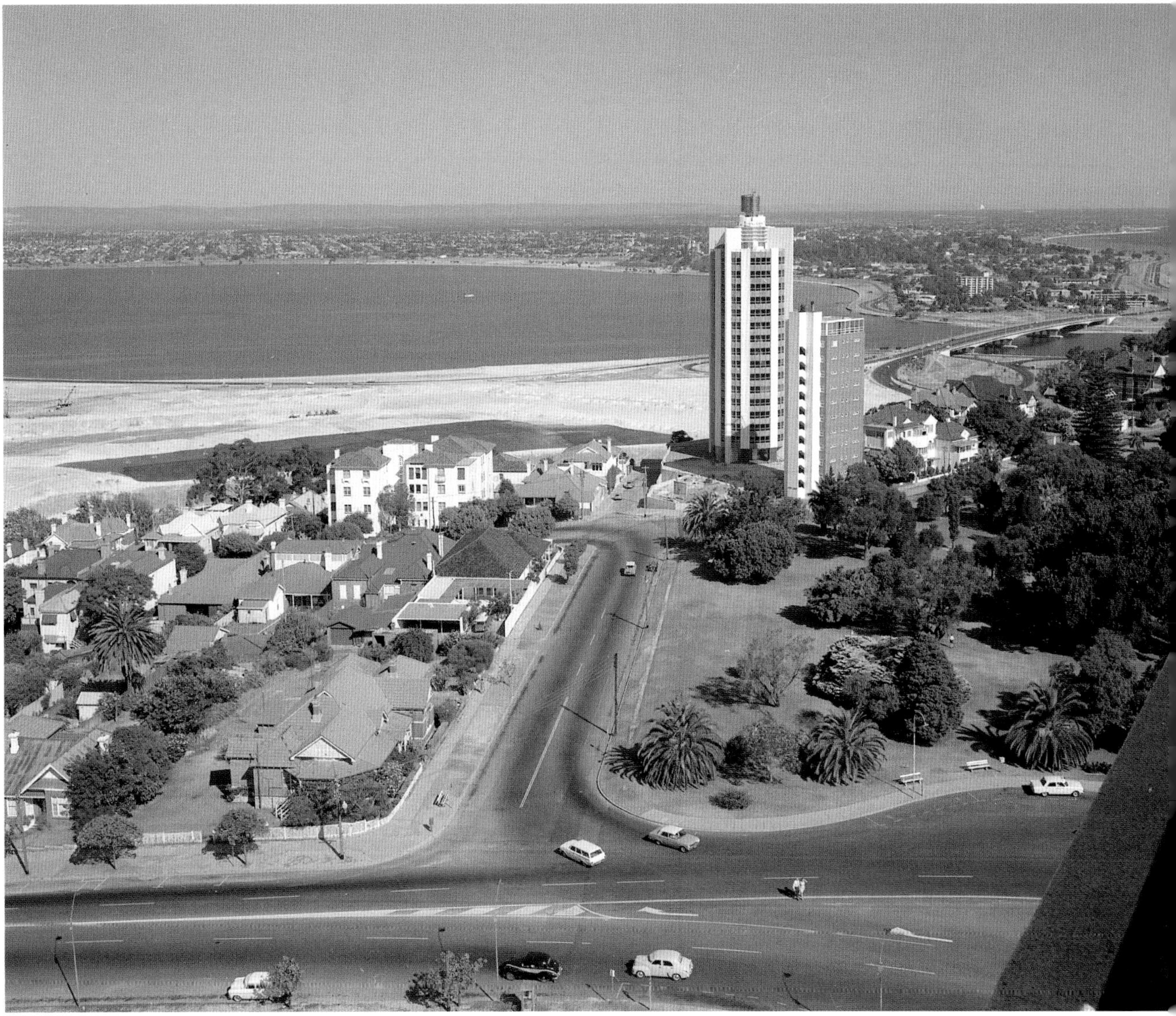

## **Mount Eliza Apartments** 1966

Sometimes affectionately known as the 'Thermos Flask' or occasionally the 'Spark Plug', the Mount Eliza Apartments is one of Perth's most iconic and instantly recognisable buildings. The first circular apartment block to be built in Australia, this building was designed by David Krantz whilst still a student, and completed in 1964. The 16-floor building has two apartments to each floor from 2-11 and one for each of the remaining five floors.

This photograph, taken two years after the completion of the apartments, which are situated on the crest of the Mount Eliza escarpment also shows, in its raw state, the re-profiled river area of Perth Water leading up to the Narrows Bridge.

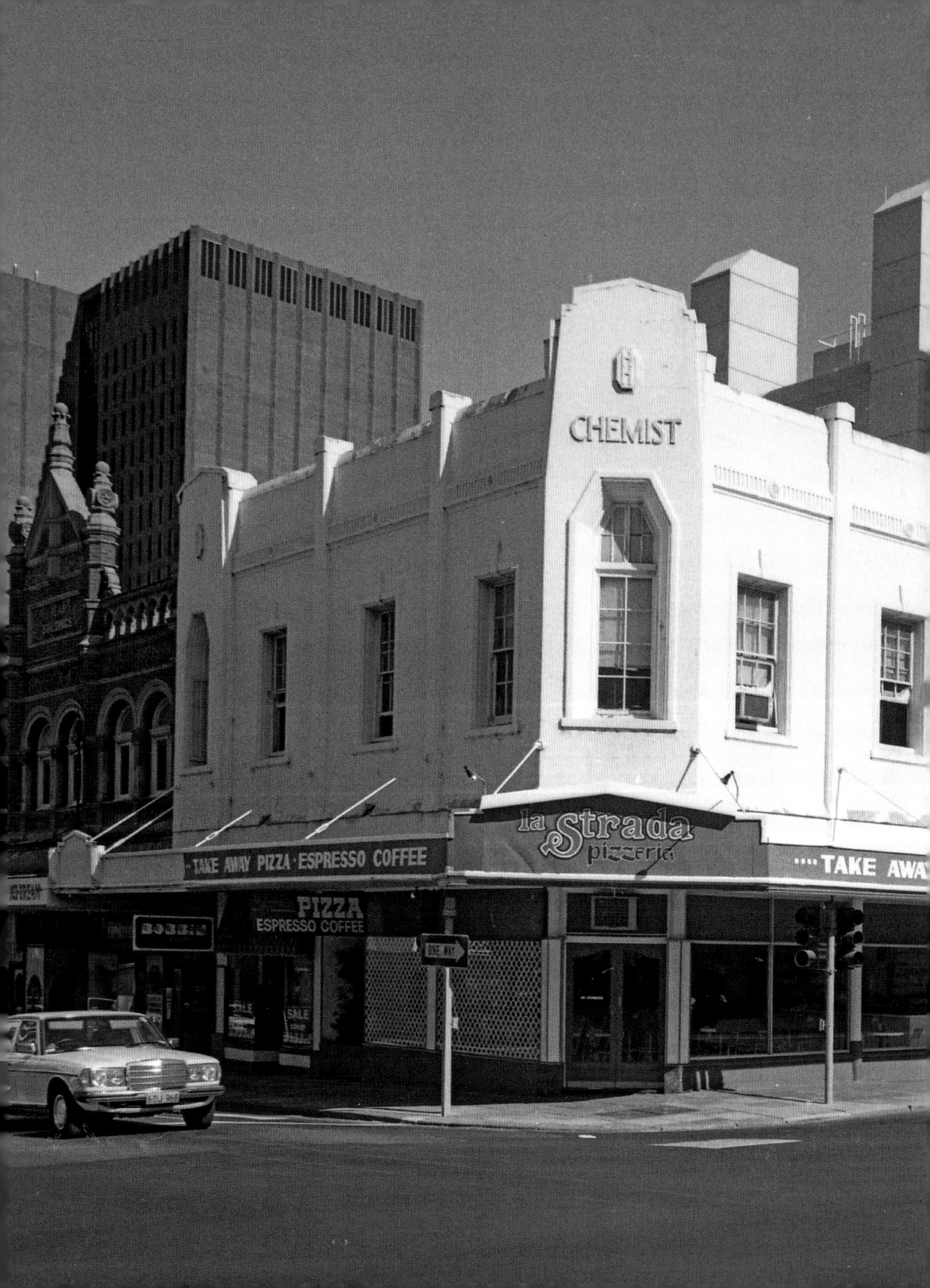
CHEMIST
TAKE AWAY PIZZA · ESPRESSO COFFEE
la Strada pizzeria
TAKE AWA
PIZZA
ESPRESSO COFFEE
ONE WAY
SALE
SALE

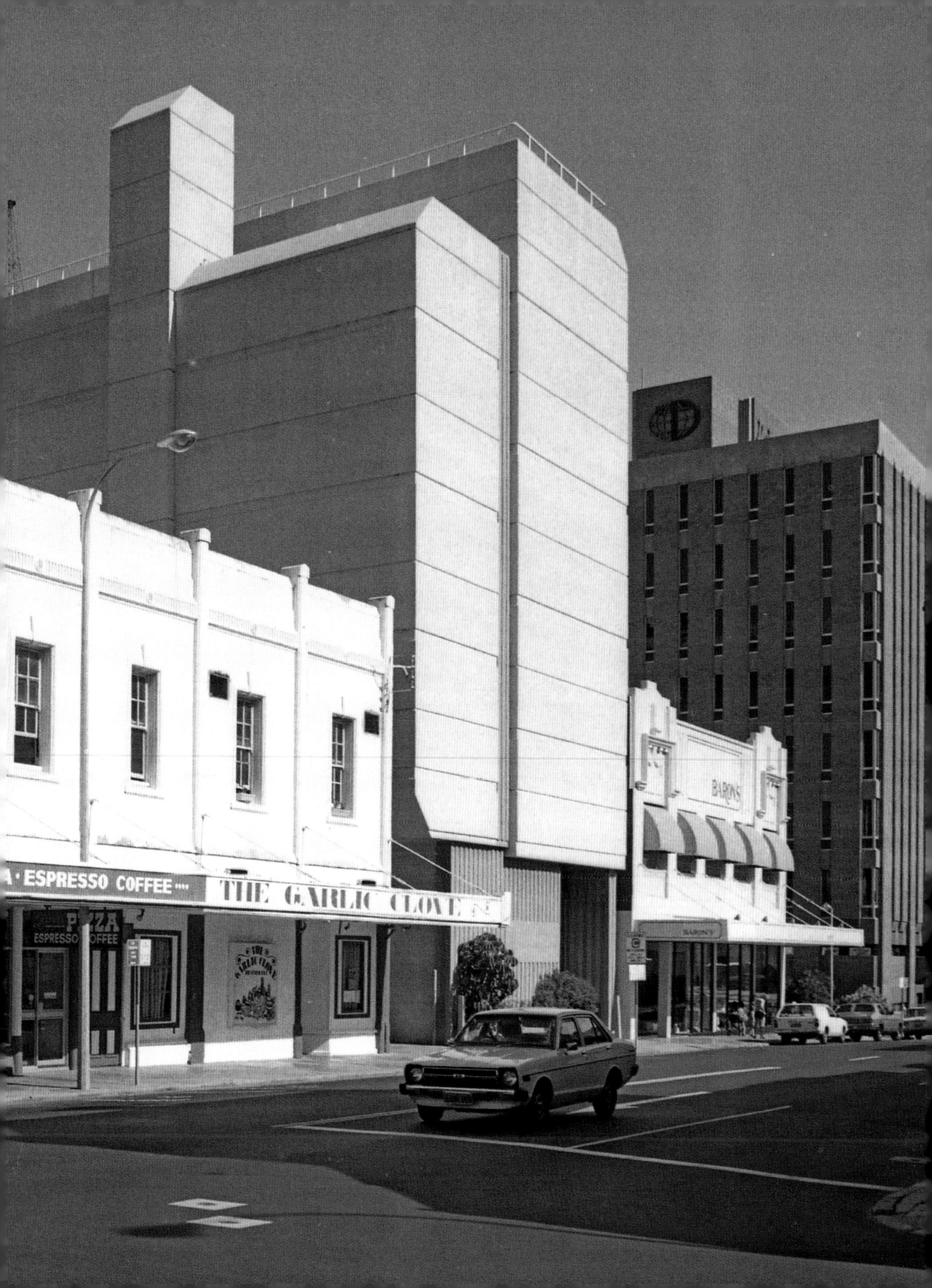
ESPRESSO COFFEE
THE GARLIC CLOVE
PIZZA
ESPRESSO COFFEE
BARONS
BARON'S

## Howling Chemists and Read Building 1982

**PREVIOUS PAGE:** The facades of these two neighbouring buildings, still grace the junction of Hay and Milligan Streets, covering the lower stages of two office blocks.

The origins of Howling's chemist shop date back to 1904, when a new building was constructed on 'Melba Corner' and named after Perth's heartthrob of the time, Dame Nellie Melba. The original design of the facades was classical and described by the West Australian as 'of the Ionic order and forming a pleasing skyline'.

The ground floor was taken over by pharmacist Hugh Howling in 1919 and the Sun newspaper remarked it was, 'A coincidence that the name of Chemist Hugh Howling is painted large on the most operatically-named corner in Perth — Hay and Milligan streets — Melba House.'

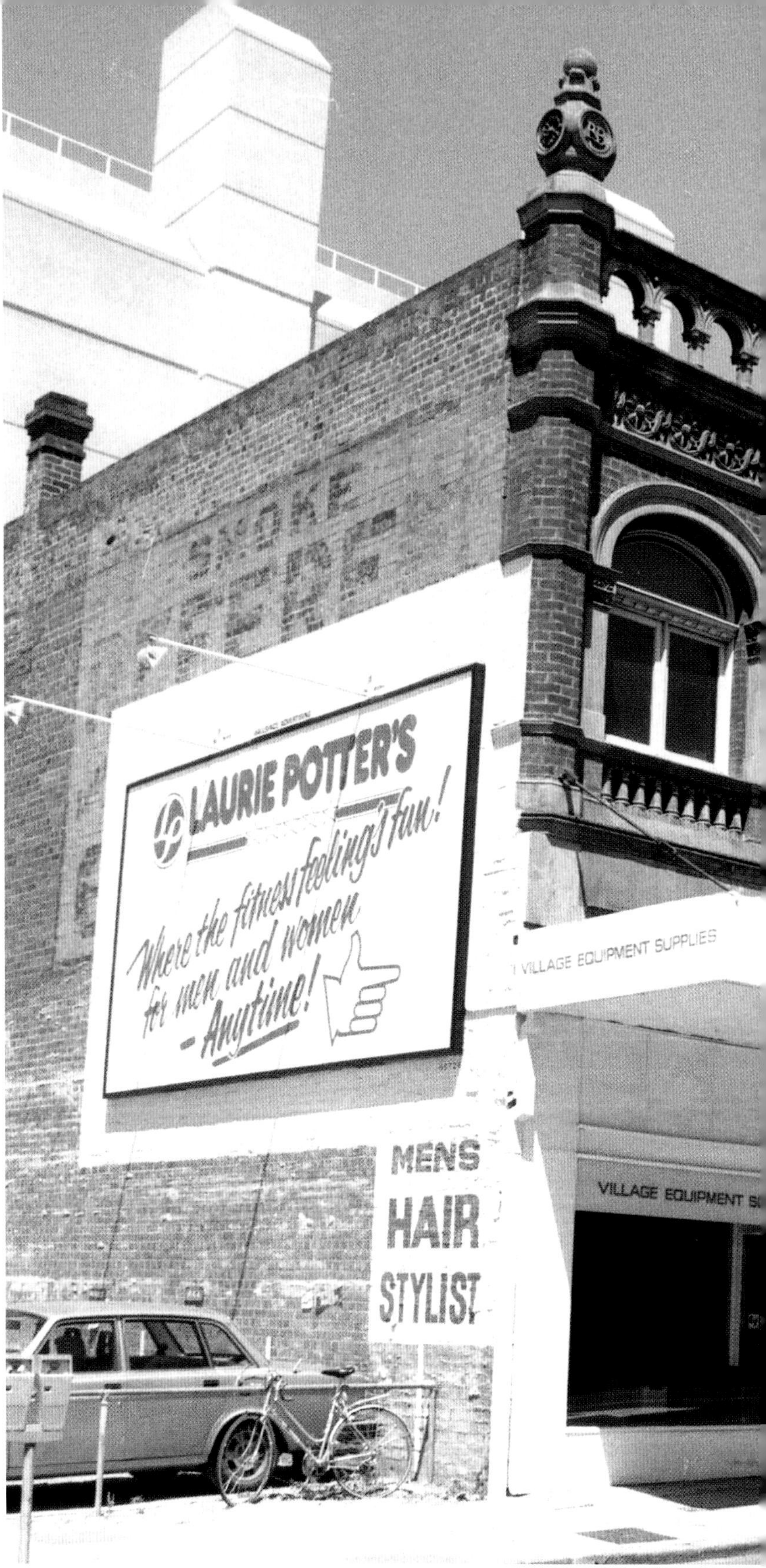


**RIGHT:** In 1934, Melba House was renovated, with the 'old fashioned' ornamental facade replaced by a yellow sanded cement front in Art-Deco style. In 1982 the shop became a pizza bar until the major redevelopment of the site in 2015.

Next door, the history of the very elegant Read Building remains a mystery. The two-storey, Federation Free Classical-style building, was constructed in 1895 and features a brick facade, stucco decoration, arched windows, decorative pediment and colonnaded parapet, but who designed it is unknown. The building underwent major additions in 1924, since when it has housed a number of different commercial tenants.

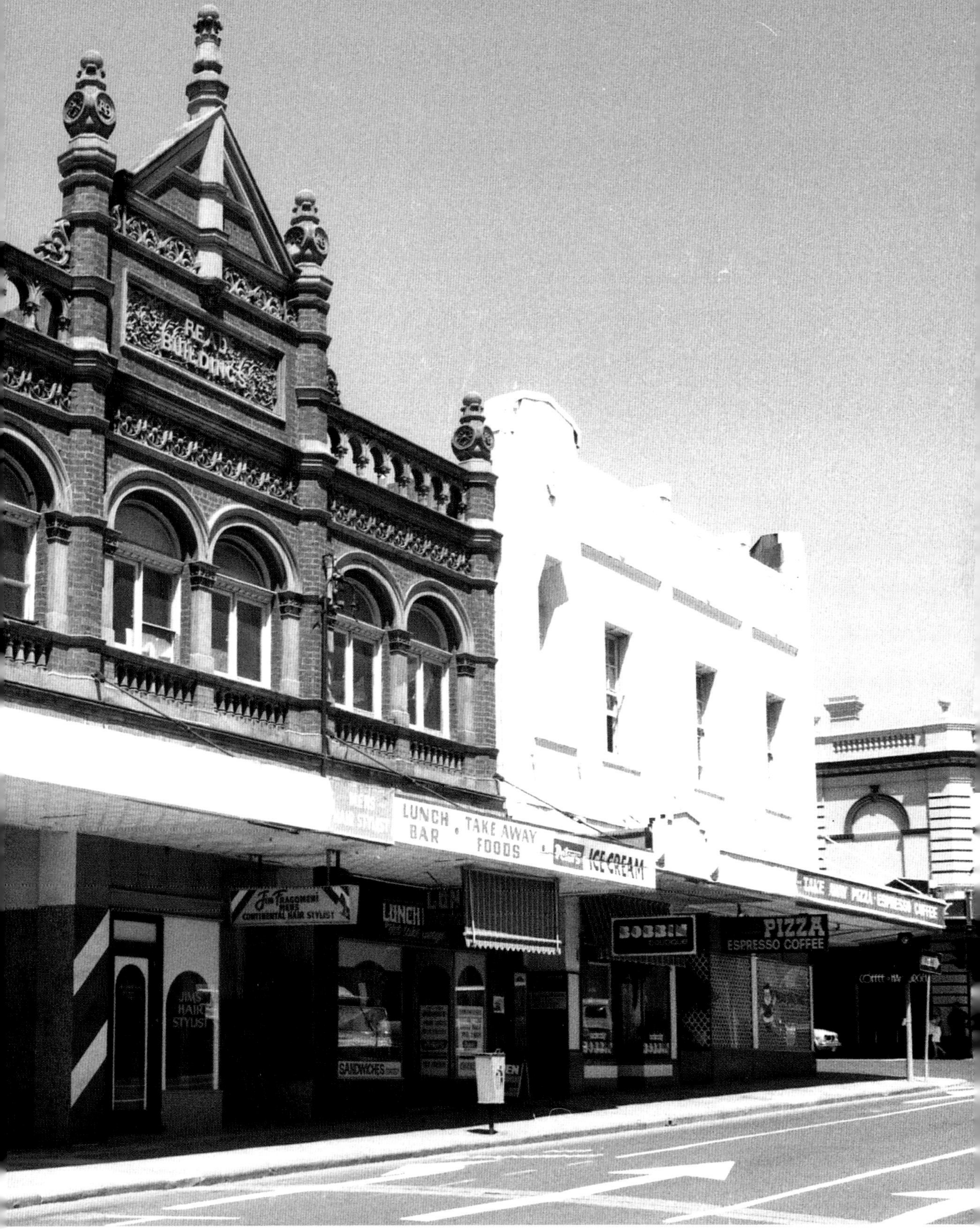
BUILDINGS
LUNCH BAR
TAKE AWAY FOODS
ICE CREAM
CONTINENTAL HAIR STYLIST
JIMS HAIR STYLIST
SANDWICHES
BOBBIN
PIZZA
ESPRESSO COFFEE

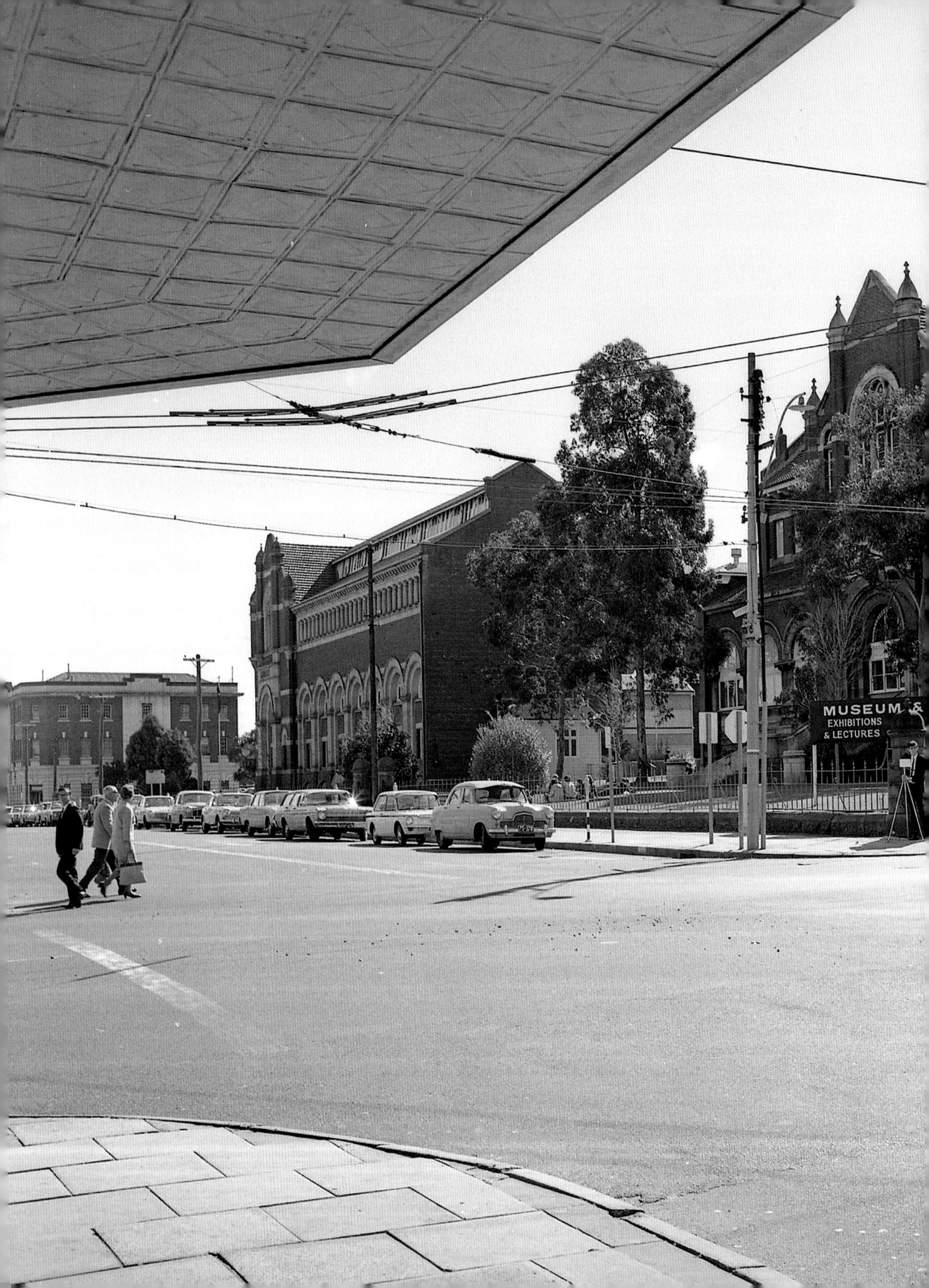
MUSEUM &
EXHIBITIONS
& LECTURES

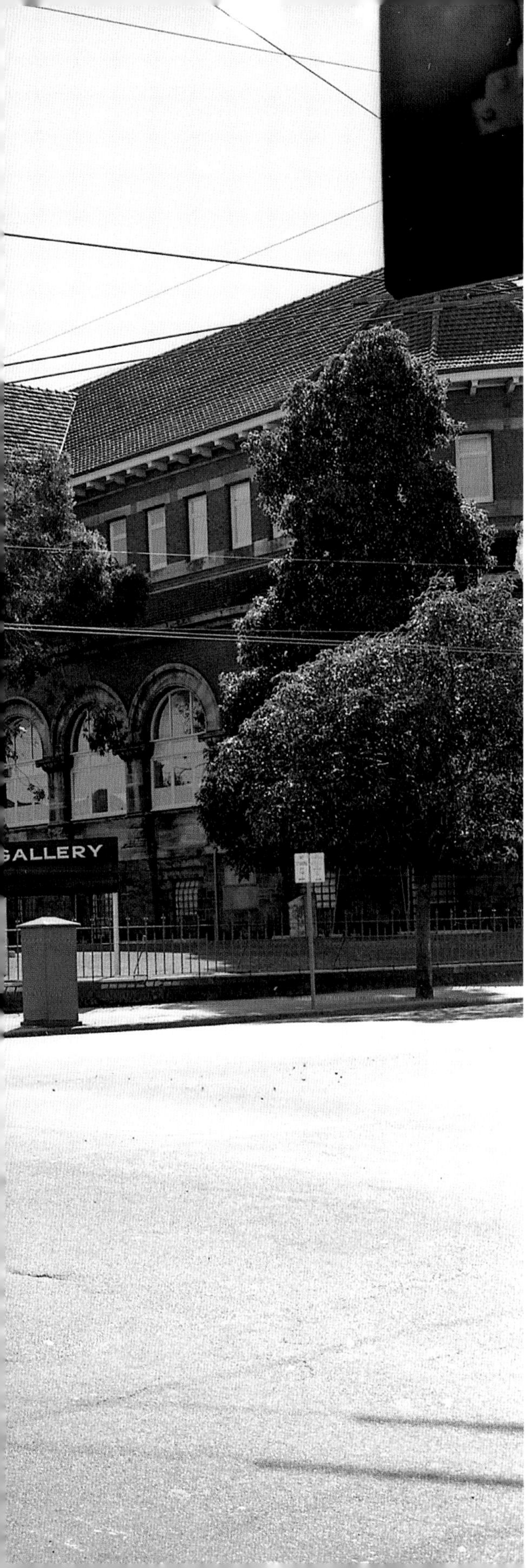


## **Western Australian Museum** c.1970

Originally established in 1891 as a geological museum with a collection housed in the Old Perth Gaol, the Western Australian Museum, as it became known, moved into the Byzantine-style 'Jubilee Building' (seen on the right of this photograph) in 1897.

To the left is the magnificent Hackett Hall, which was built in 1913 as an extension to the Public Library.

In the distance can be seen the Arundale Hall, which was designed by Bill Tracey and built for the Theosophical Society in 1929. This building was demolished to make way for the new Western Australian State Library building in about 1982.

Below the museum sign can be seen a gentleman with a tripod/surveyor's pole. He appears in several of Ernie's photographs in this book and it is assumed these photographs were taken during Ernie's surveying work for the City Council, with his assistant captured in the shot.

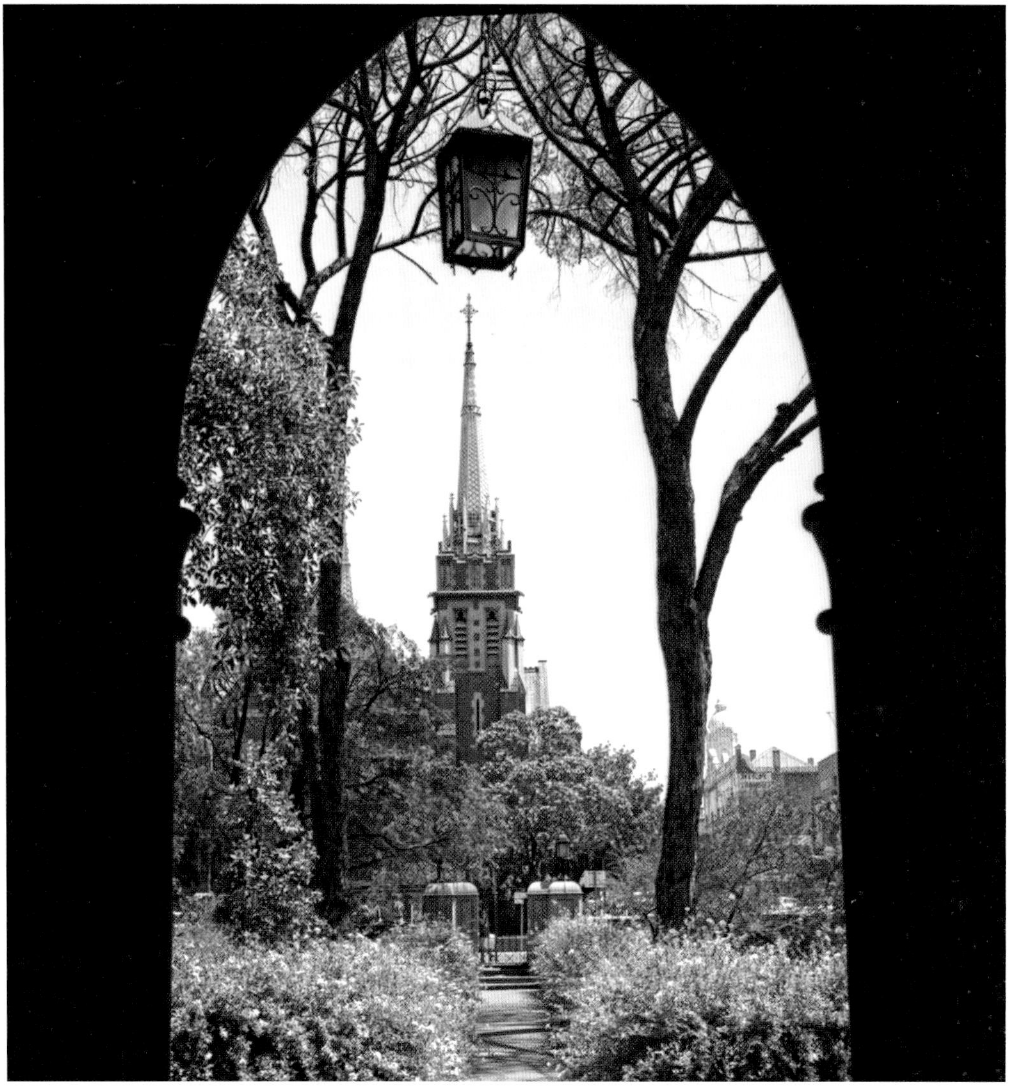

## St Andrew's Presbyterian Church 1960

This atmospheric shot of the tower of St Andrew's Presbyterian Church was taken from the colonnade of Government House.

The church we see today is the second church, the original St Andrew's, built in 1882 on a site slightly north of the present building, being the first Presbyterian Church in Western Australia.

During the 1890s Gold Rush, the Presbyterian congregation quickly grew and it was decided to build a bigger church. An architectural competition was held with prizes of £75 for the winner and £25 for the second-best design. Although first prize was awarded, insufficient building funds were available and the plans were abandoned. A second competition also failed to find an affordable design. Eventually a design for a smaller church was utilised and the foundation stone was laid in June, 1905.

The heritage listed church is closed and is expected to be adapted to form part of a new development on the site.

## St Georges Terrace 1960s

The main street of Perth seems to have originally been named King Georges Terrace after King George IV, but he was probably one of England's least liked and respected monarchs, so the name may not have been a popular choice. The King died in 1830 and by 1833 the street was being called St Georges Terrace, after the patron saint of England. Even so, 'King George's Terrace' crops up in official documents until 1834.

In the early days of the Colony, St Georges Terrace and Adelaide Terrace were fashionable residential streets and a regulation was passed in 1833 that required owners to build homes costing at least £200. This was presumably to ensure those of lower social status could not afford to build on this affluent thoroughfare. From the first Gold Rush onwards, however, it became, as it is today, the central business district of the city.

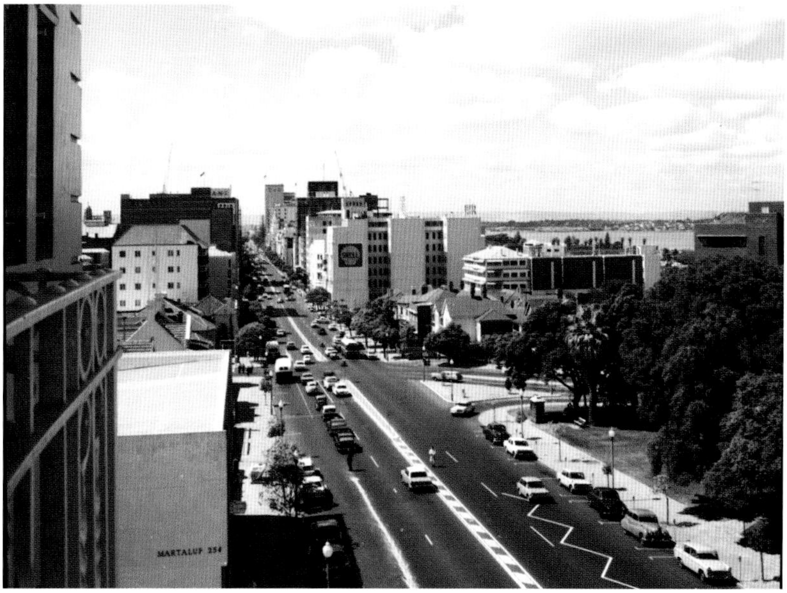

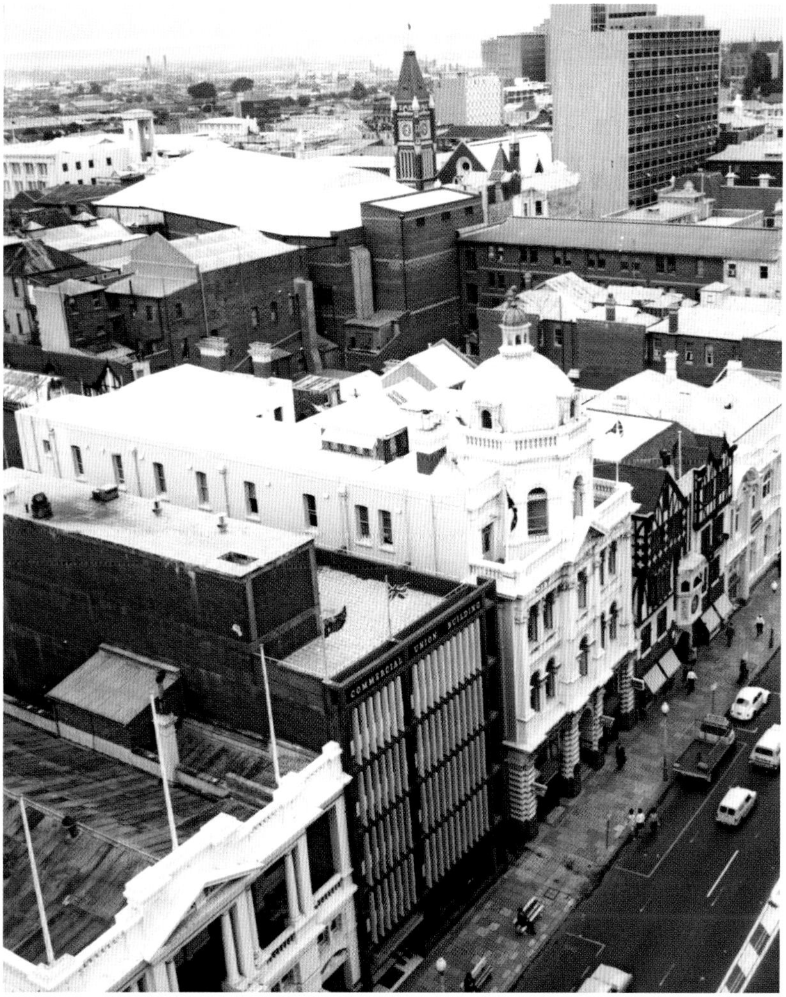


**RIGHT:** Of the buildings shown in this 1960s picture, the only one still standing is London Court. To the right of it can be seen the old National Bank building and to the left the very fine Forrest Chambers, built for Sir John Forrest. The building was designed by local architect Edwin Summerhayes and opened in 1905. At the time of opening the Western Mail wrote, the building 'will stand, as a monument to the enterprise of the owners, who have shown their unbounded faith in so many different ventures in the interests of Western Australia.' Sadly this monument to enterprise only lasted about 70 years before being sent to a landfill site.

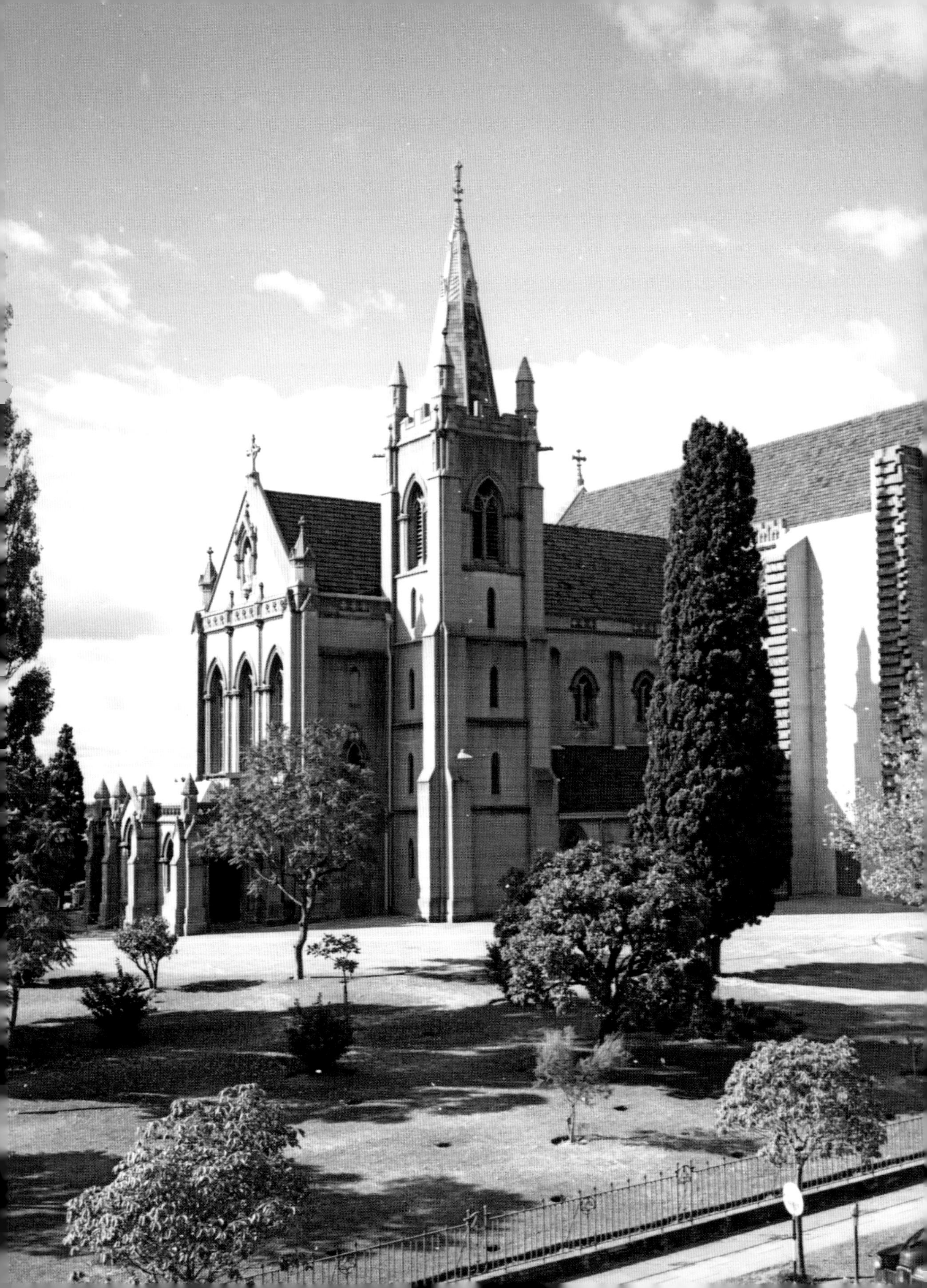

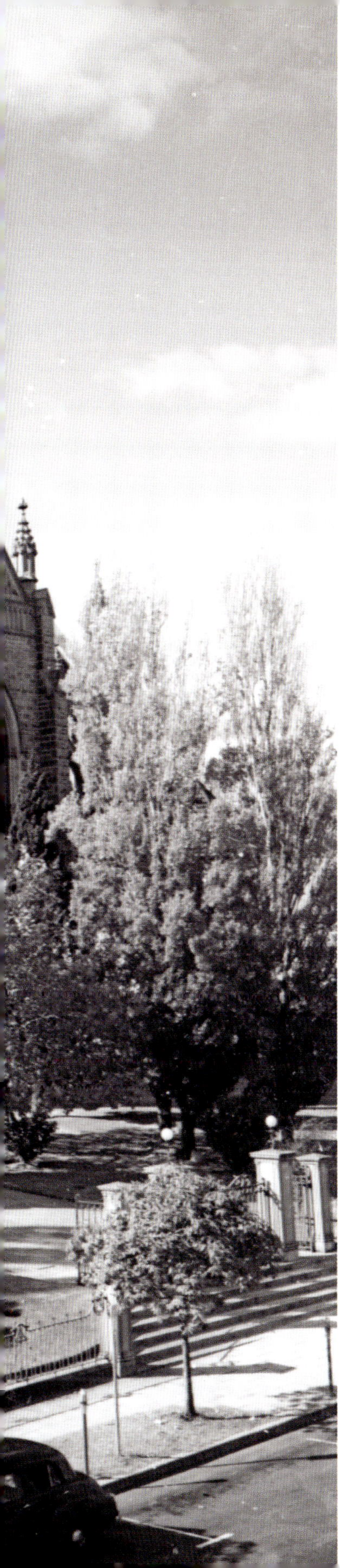

## St Mary's Cathedral c.1960 and 1979

During its early year, there were only a few Catholics living in the Swan River Colony and it was not until 1843 that there were sufficient to justify a full-time priest in Perth. In that year, Father John Brady was sent to minister to the Catholic settlers and by December enough funds had been found to build the first Catholic church in Western Australia. St John's Church still remains and is the oldest church in the city centre.

By the early 1860s, the increasing size of the Roman Catholic population in the colony necessitated the construction of a larger cathedral. The area known as Church Square, just up the hill from St John's, originally reserved for the Anglican Church, was acquired as a site for a larger church. Building work began in 1863, with the foundation stone being laid by Bishop Rosendo Salvado of New Norcia in February.

By early 1864 the building was complete to the height of the walls but the bell tower had still to be built. After further fundraising, the completed building was opened as the Cathedral of the Immaculate Conception in January 1865.

**BELOW:** Alterations to the building in 1905 included the addition of a slate-clad steeple, pinnacles and gargoyles to the bell tower.

In the early 1920s, plans were formulated to complete the cathedral by the addition of a new sanctuary, transepts and east end for the cathedral. This work was blessed by Archbishop Patrick Clune on 4 May 1930, and this is how it was when Ernie photographed the Cathedral in the 1960s and 70s.

Since then a major programme of works to conserve and once again enlarge the Cathedral culminated with its re-consecration in December, 2009.

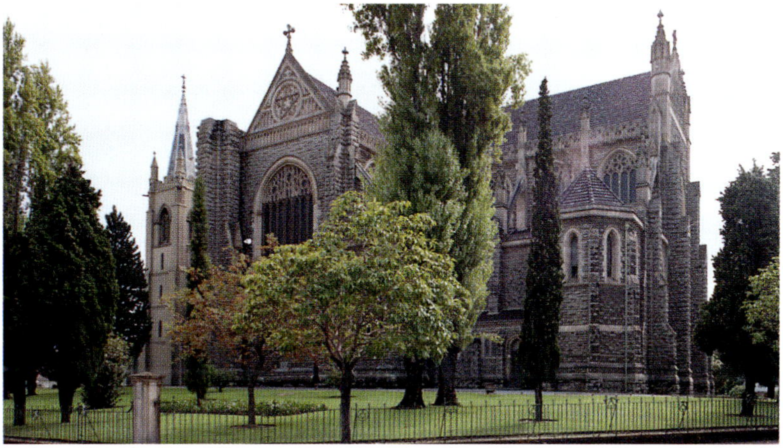

# Automatic Telephone Exchange 1982

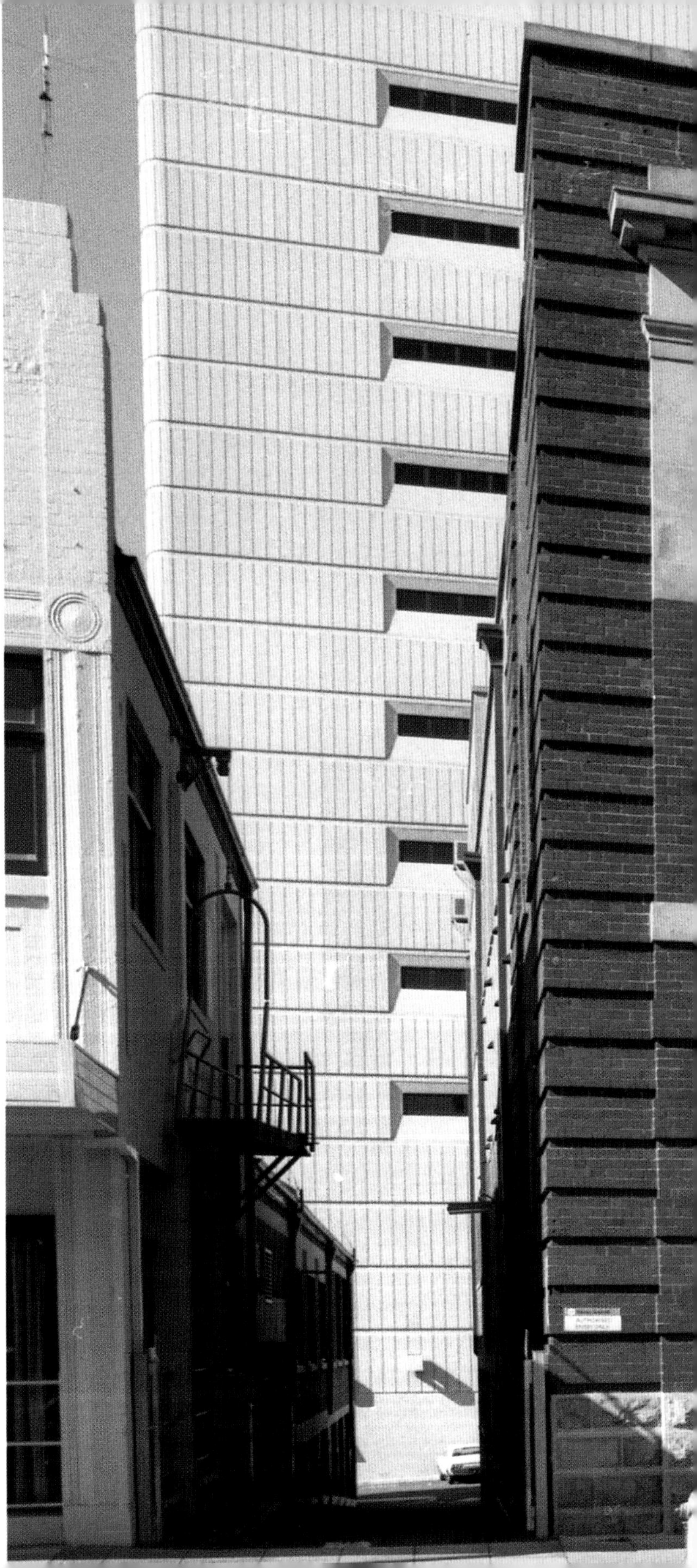

Perth's first telephone exchange was established in 1887 in a small cottage in Wellington Street. The 17 subscribers only had a service between Perth and Fremantle. The Fremantle end of the line opened in a small room in the Town Hall with nine subscribers.

By 1910, the Perth manual exchange was overloaded with customers and thoughts turned to a new exchange, which opened in Murray Street in September 1914. This was the second automatic dial telephone exchange in Australia and, with 3,200 subscribers, the largest.

Initially, the exchange had two major problems. Firstly customers were unfamiliar with dial telephones and much preferred the helpful voice of a telephonist asking, "number please". More seriously, insufficient switch gear was provided by the US suppliers for the predicted number of subscribers, leading to many complaints from customers. After a lot of legal wrangling, the equipment was upgraded.

The exchange was finally decommissioned in 1987 and the building converted to offices. The replacement exchange forms the backdrop to this photograph.

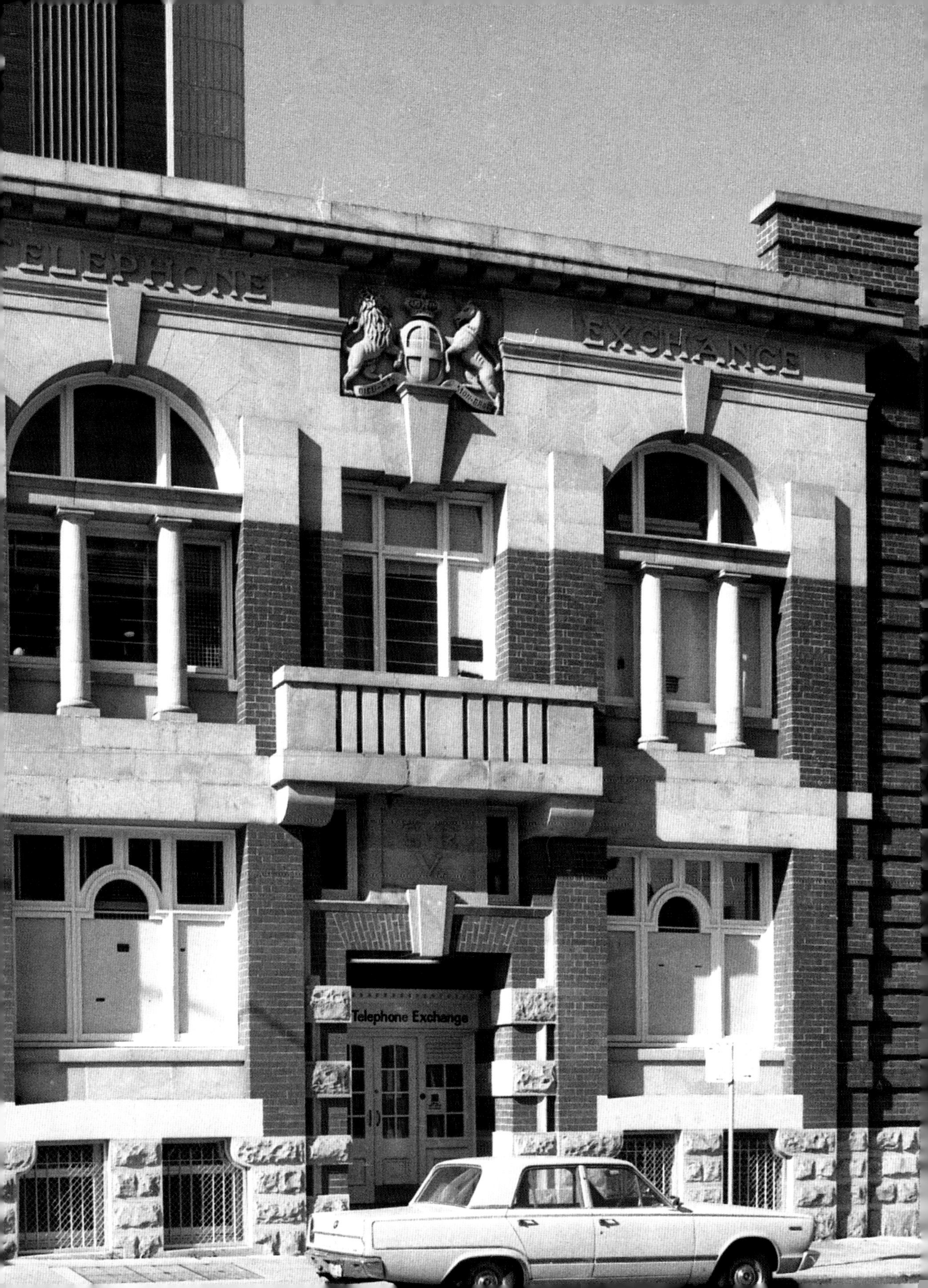
TELEPHONE
EXCHANGE
Telephone Exchange

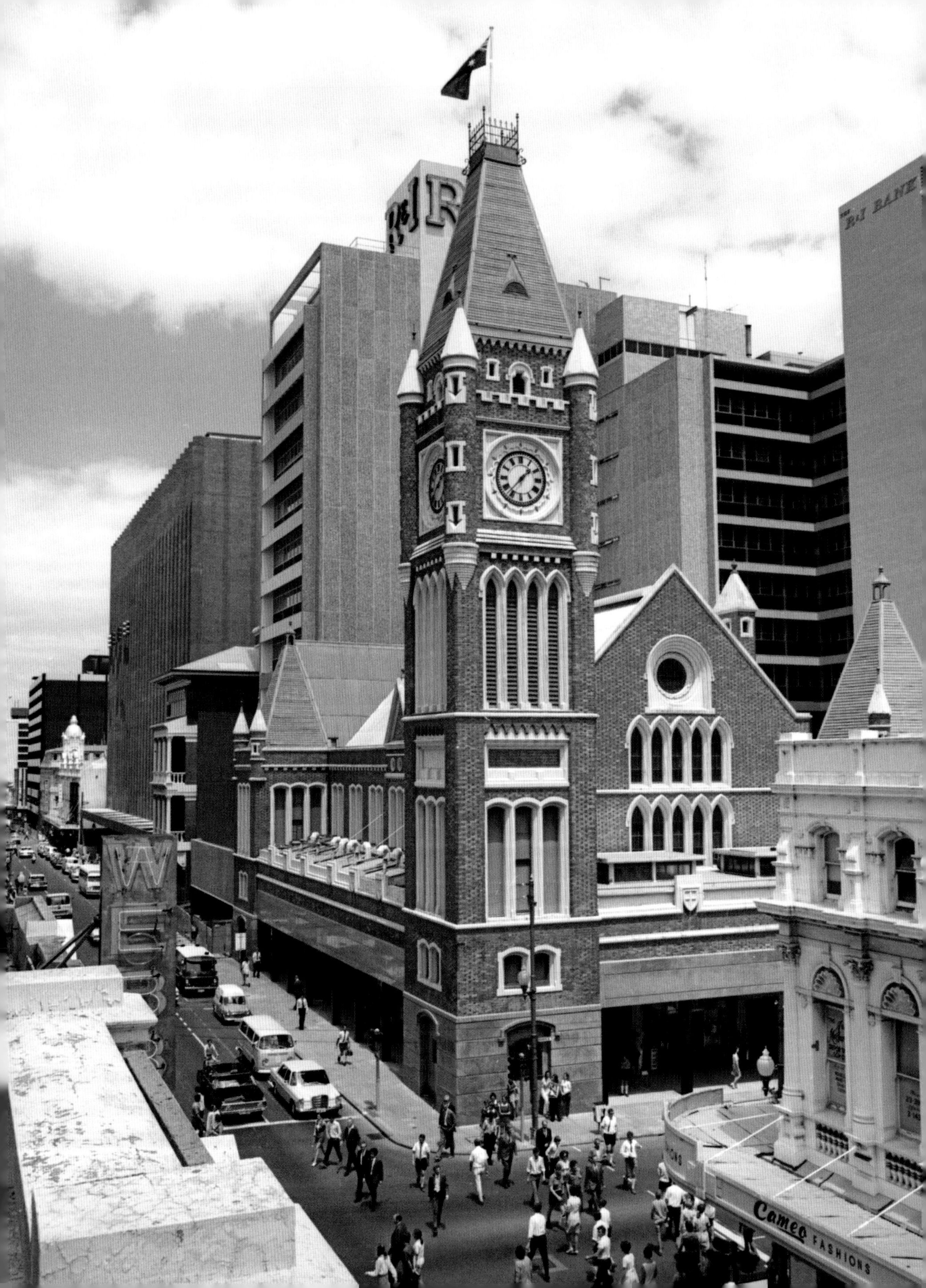
Cameo FASHIONS

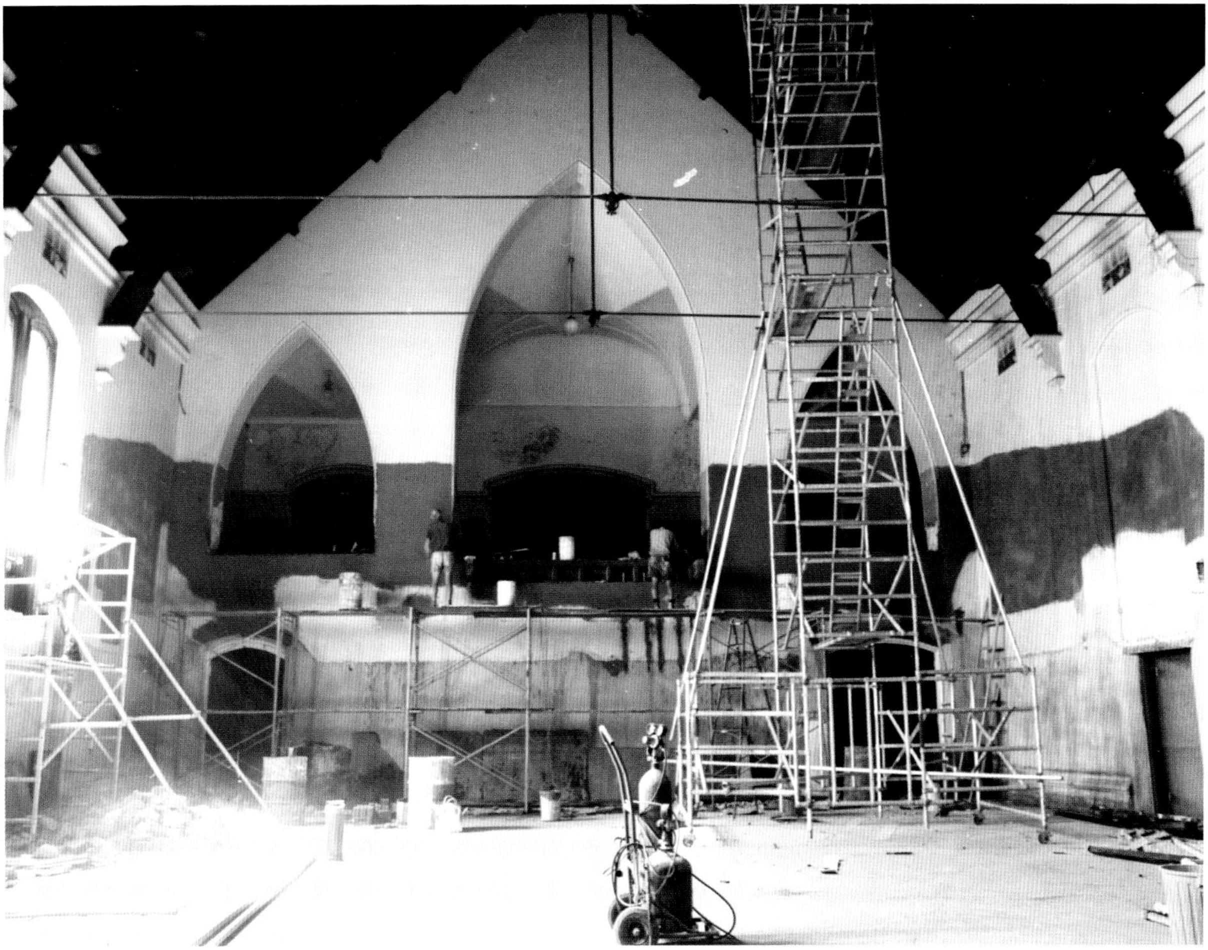

## Perth Town Hall 1972

**LEFT:** Perth Town Hall is a distinctive and much-loved icon of the centre of Perth. Architecturally it would probably feel at home in almost any European city.

In 1866, Governor John Hampton announced a town hall for Perth would be part of the programme of public works being undertaken by the convict force. This did not meet with universal approval, many considering it unnecessary, too big and a waste of public funds, which would be far better spent on improving the roads around Perth.

The building was designed by the Supervisor of Public Works, Richard Roach Jewell, who based his design on the medieval town halls of Europe. Construction started in 1867, using mainly convict labour. The expected completion time of 12 months was a gross under-estimate and the building eventually took three years to complete.

The official opening took place on 1 June, 1870, when Governor Weld formally handed over responsibility for the building to the City Council.

**ABOVE:** Over the years many alterations and restorations have been carried out to the Town Hall. The radical building surgery shown in this photograph took place in 1972.

The work included cutting new archways through the north-east tower to extend the colonnade eastwards past the newly built R & I Bank tower next door. The old main staircase was completely removed, the foyer floor was rebuilt and the remaining staircase in the south-east corner widened by 300mm to satisfy Public Health regulations. In the first floor main hall, the east end windows were bricked up, the front portion of the gallery – added in 1935 – was removed to eliminate the two supporting columns which reduced seating capacity.

Two further restorations ( 1993 and 2005) later, the Town Hall continues to be an important community hub.

# Perth Railway Station c.1960 and 1987

**RIGHT:** One of the unique features of Perth Station is its horseshoe-shaped bridge at the western end. Originally, the railway had a gated level-crossing at the line's intersection with William Street. Sixteen years later, for the convenience of pedestrians, a timber footbridge was added. As road and rail traffic in the growing city increased, the level-crossing became a constant source of congestion and strong representation was made to the government for the crossing to be replaced with a bridge.

Initially, a conventional bridge was contemplated, but this was abandoned when it was realised how much would need to be paid out in compensation to private land owners in the vicinity for its construction. To avoid this, a bridge in the shape of a horseshoe was designed, thus minimising the encroachment on private property.

When it opened one disgruntled pedestrian calculated it added an extra three miles a week to his walk to work!

**BELOW:** After much debate about the need and route, the first leg of the Fremantle to Guildford railway started operating in August 1880 between Fremantle to North Fremantle. In March the following year the line was opened to Guildford, later being extended to Midland Junction and eventually on to Northam.

The Fremantle to Midland line was closed in September 1979, but, following public uproar and a vigorous campaign, the line re-opened in 1983. Four years later, a large redevelopment at the station site took place adding a steel and glass roof to cover the central platforms, and the construction of the Citiplace Centre above the platforms at the eastern end of the station.

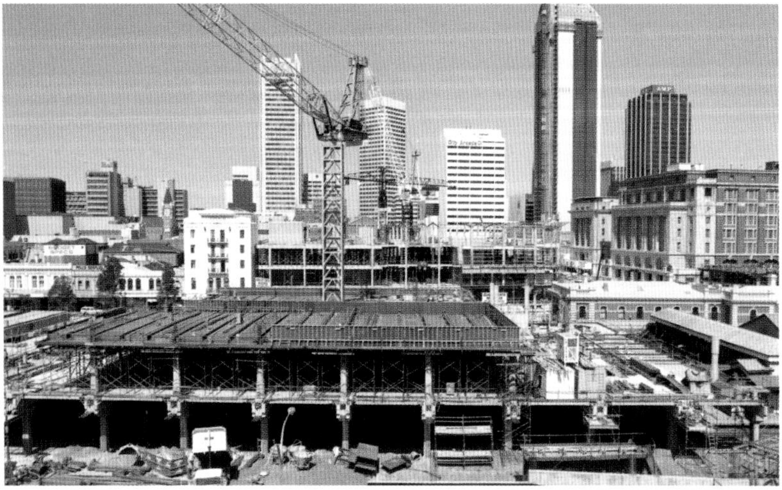

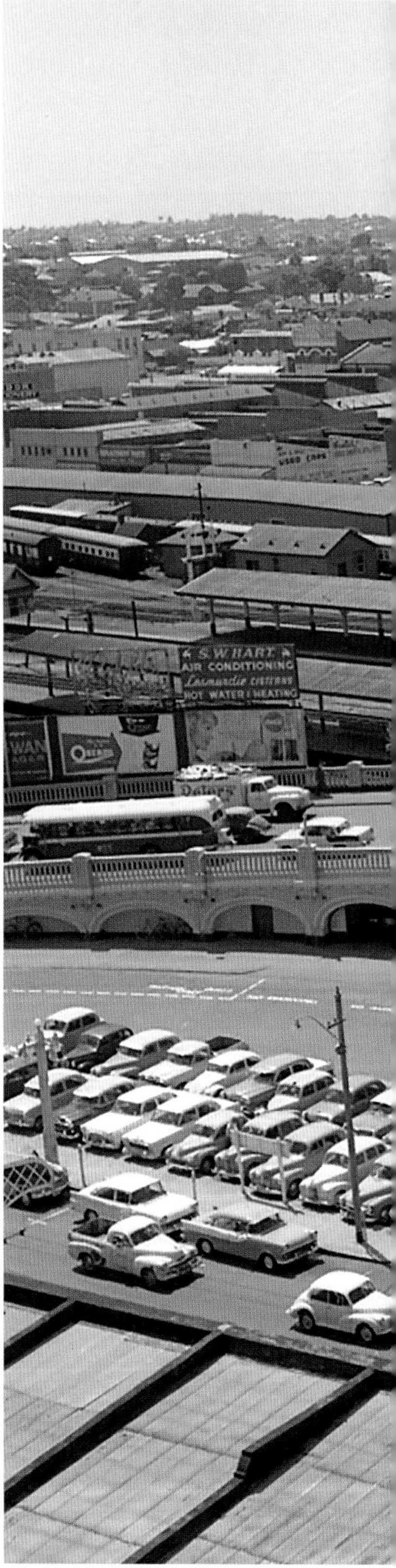

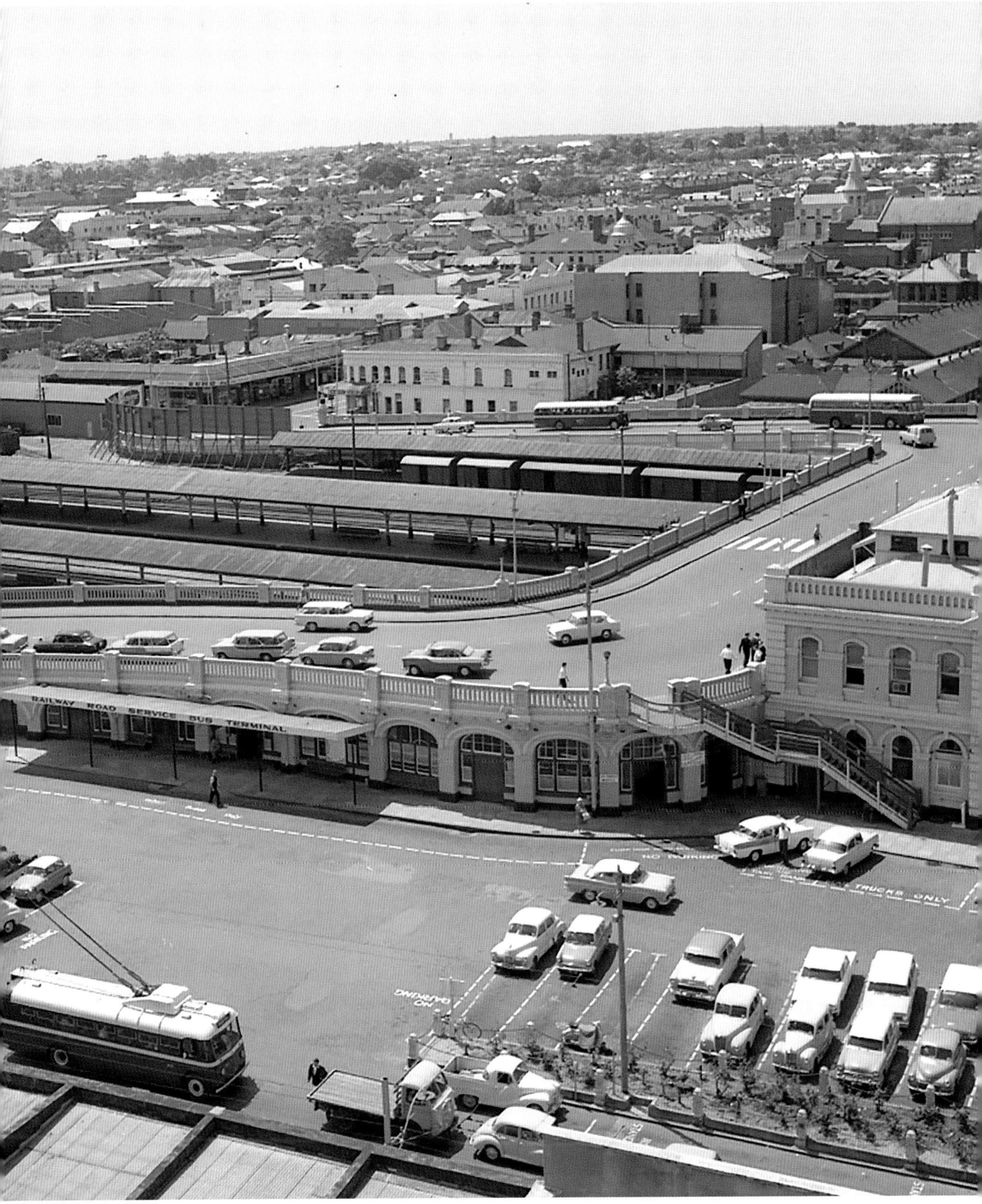
RAILWAY ROAD SERVICE BUS TERMINAL
NO PARKING
TRUCKS ONLY

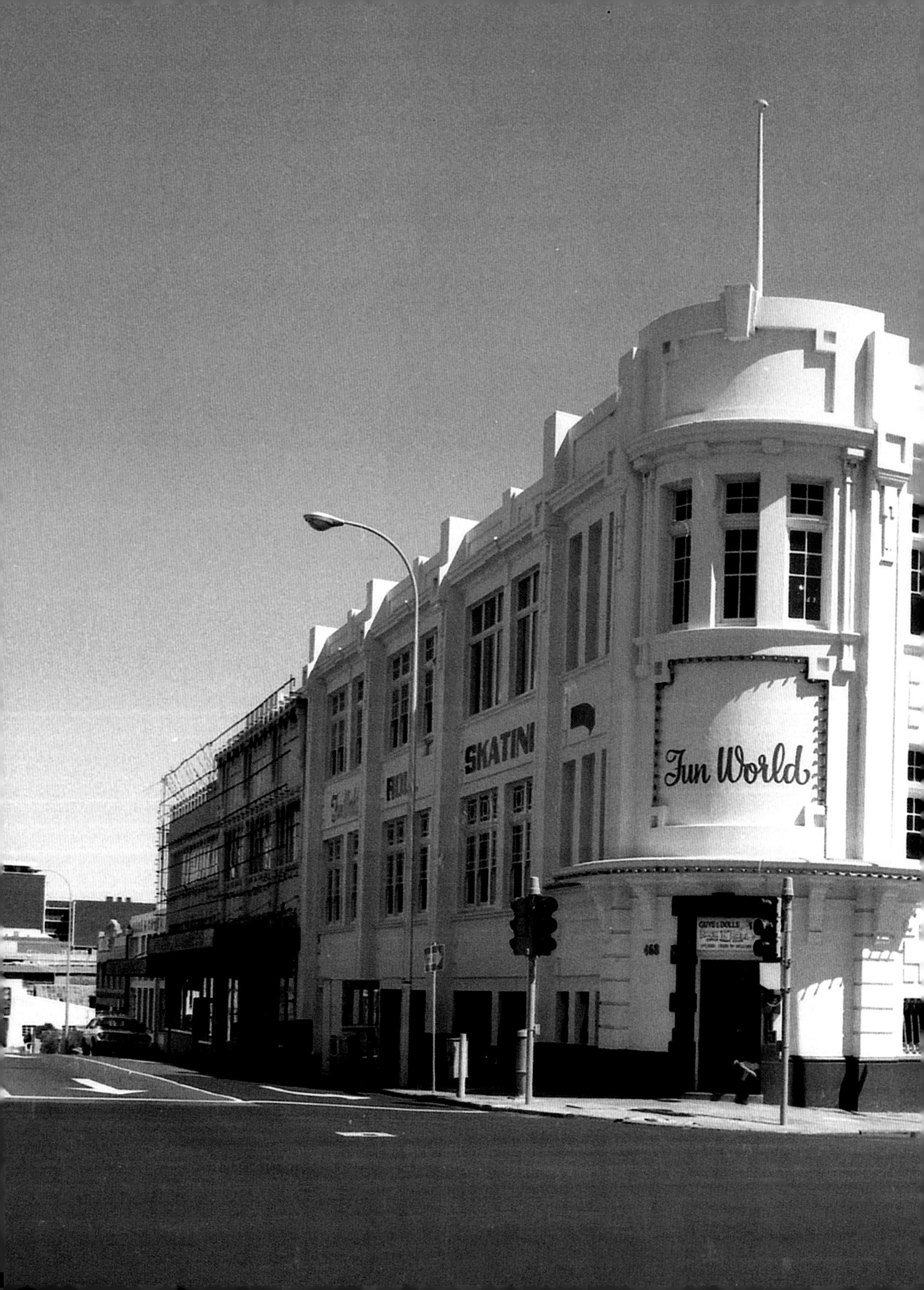

SKATIN
Fun World
468

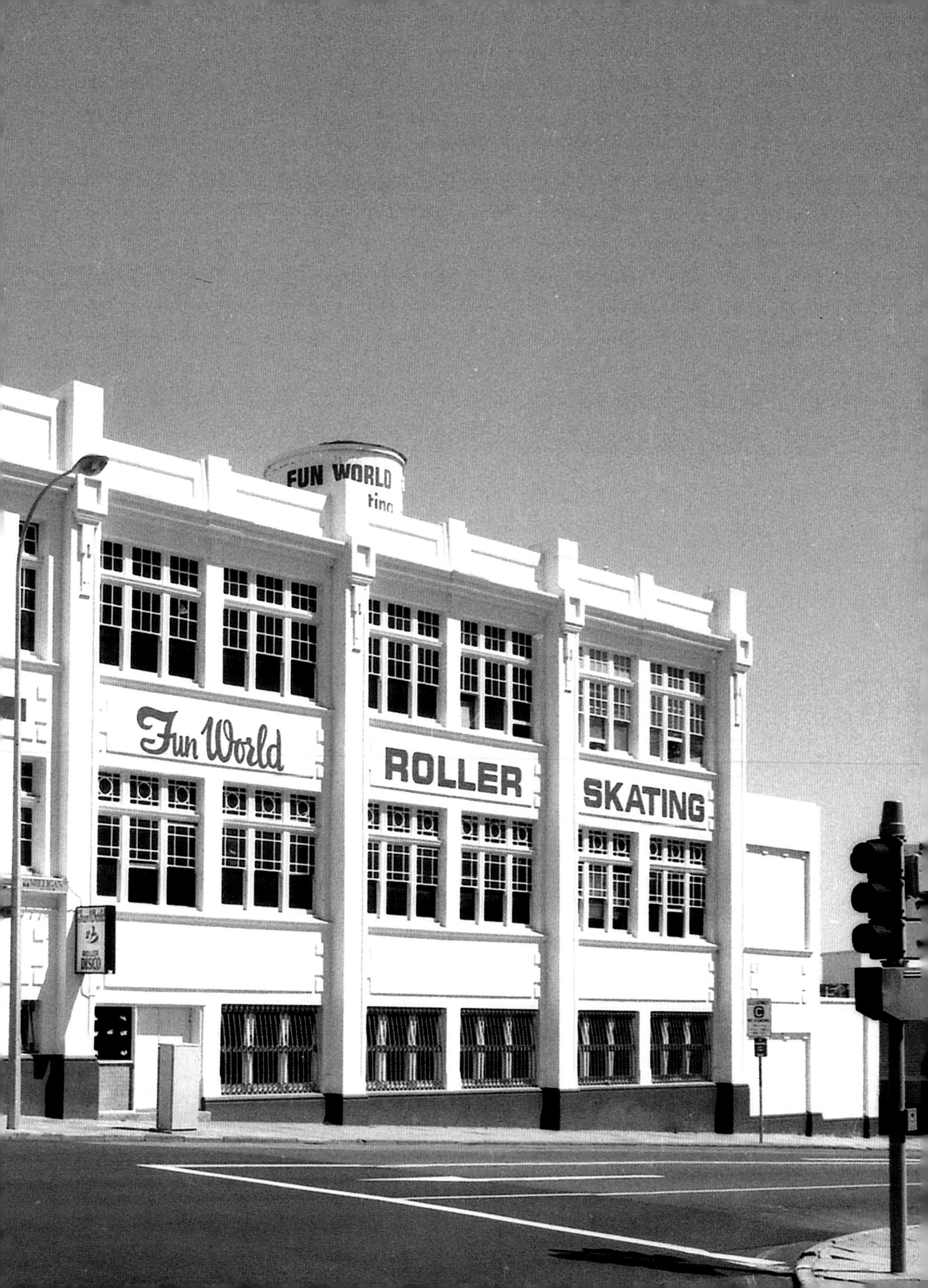
FUN WORLD
Fun World
ROLLER
SKATING

## W. D. & H. O. Wills Building 1982

**PREVIOUS PAGE:** When smoking was fashionable and not considered a health hazard, W. D. & H. O. Wills was probably one of the best known tobacco companies in the world. In 1901, the Wills Company realised that Australia had one of the highest tobacco consumptions in the world and registered an Australian company to market their brands.

A new office and warehouse complex on the corner of Milligan and Murray Streets was built for the company in 1927. In order to save space, the building's designers, Oldham, Boas & Ednie-Brown utilised a revolutionary new technique employing concrete 'mushroom' columns, the broad tops of which merged into and supported the reinforced concrete floor slab above, thus saving space normally filled with steel beams supporting the floor slab.

The warehouse remained the Wills base until 1967. Since then, it has been a night club and even a roller-skating rink. More recently, three storeys were added and the building converted into offices and apartments.

## Wesley Church c.1960s

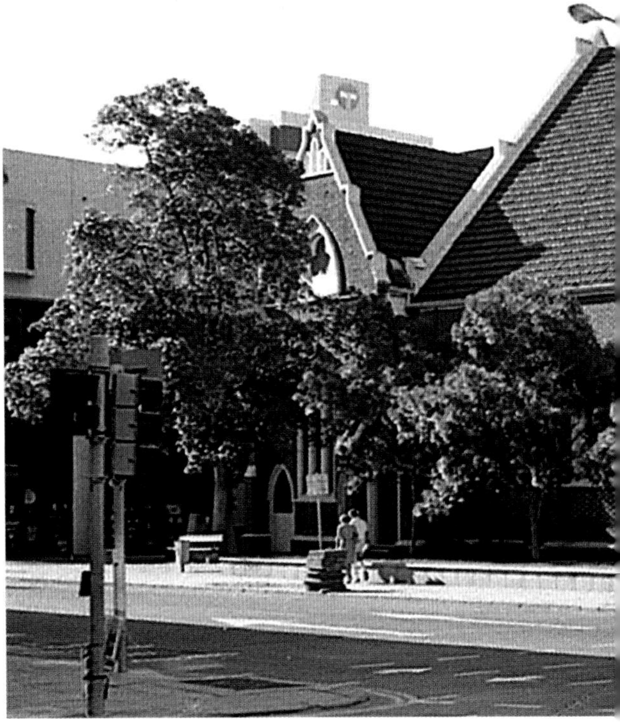

**RIGHT:** Wesley Church, clearly in 1960s wedding mode judging by the ribbon-clad cars parked outside.

The first Methodists arrived in the Swan River Colony in February, 1830 to found a small Wesleyan community on what is now the Maylands Peninsula. The first public Methodist service in Perth was held under a tree in June 1830, and in 1834 a small chapel was built on the corner of William and Murray Streets. A second, larger chapel was constructed in 1841, but within 30 years, this building was also proving too small.

A fundraising campaign was launched to help raise the £3,000 required to build a new church; a large sum for a congregation of 138 to raise. To encourage donations, a pew incentive scheme was developed, by which the best seats in the church were allocated to those who donated the most money.

The church was completed in 1870 and remains an active city-centre church to this day.

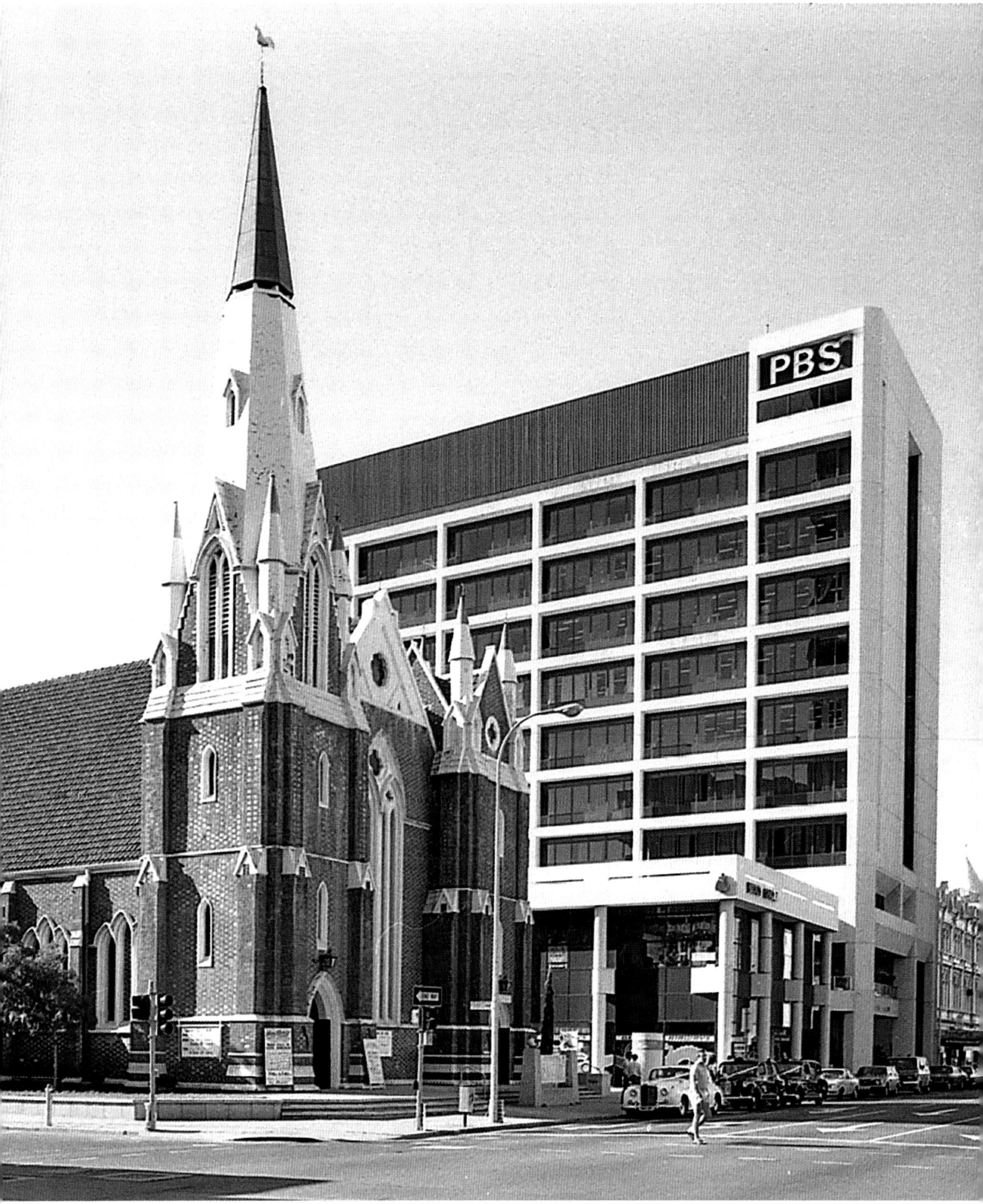
PBS

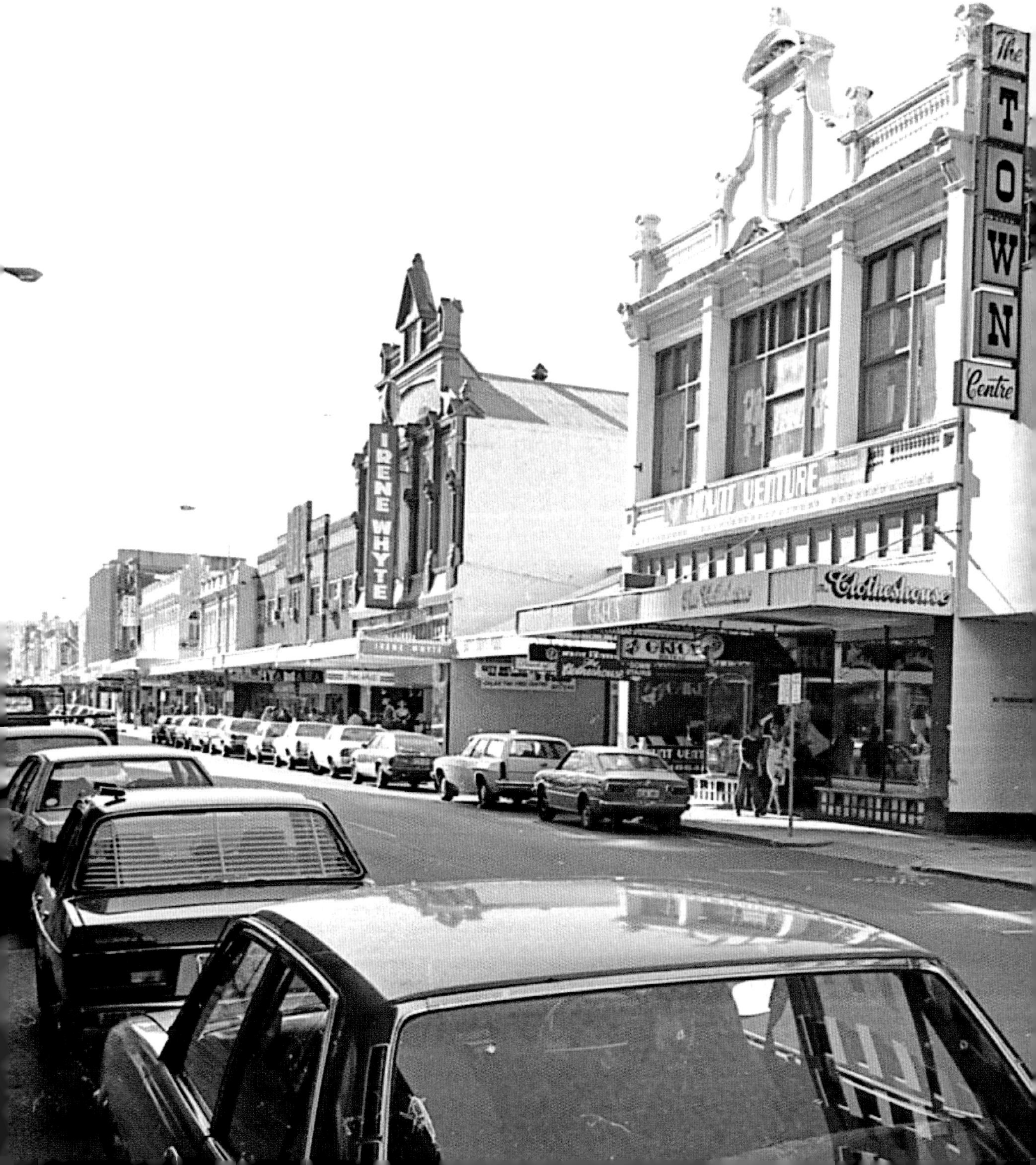
The
TOWN
Centre
IRENE WHYTE
Clotheshouse

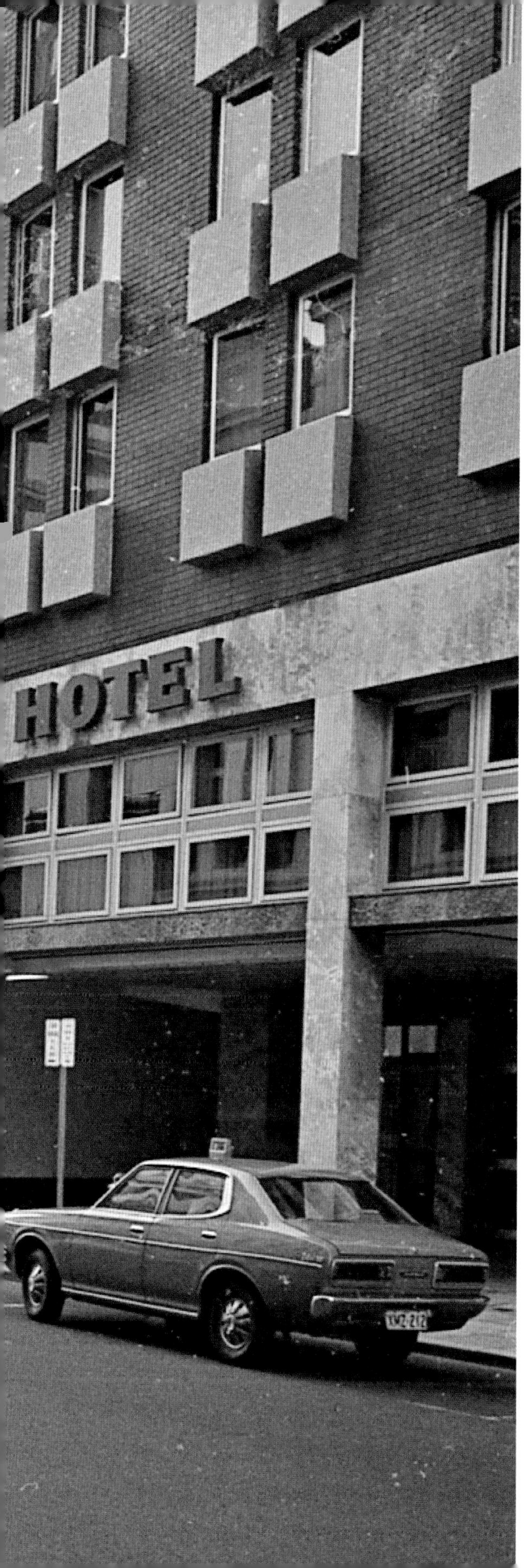


## Hay Street 1982

**LEFT:** The Town Centre building to the left of the hotel was enlarged and given its facade in 1910 when it was the home of the Metropolitan Dental Company. Established in 1908, this company advertised extensively in newspapers, claiming to, 'have been inaugurated in order that persons of the most limited means can avail themselves of the most skilful dental specialists in the Southern Hemisphere.' The business thrived and continued into the second half of the 20th century.

The Dobbie Building can be seen next but one shop to the left, occupied at this time by Irene Whyte ladiesware. Alexander Dobbie, at the age of 19, set up his own business in Adelaide, selling anything from sewing machines to milk separators. Alexander established a branch in Perth around 1900, selling musical instruments and later manufacturing some of the first radio sets in WA.

In August, 1906, the firm announced in a newspaper advertisement that it was, 'now comfortably installed in new premises at numbers 580-82 Hay Street, where a splendid stock of pianos has been laid down'.

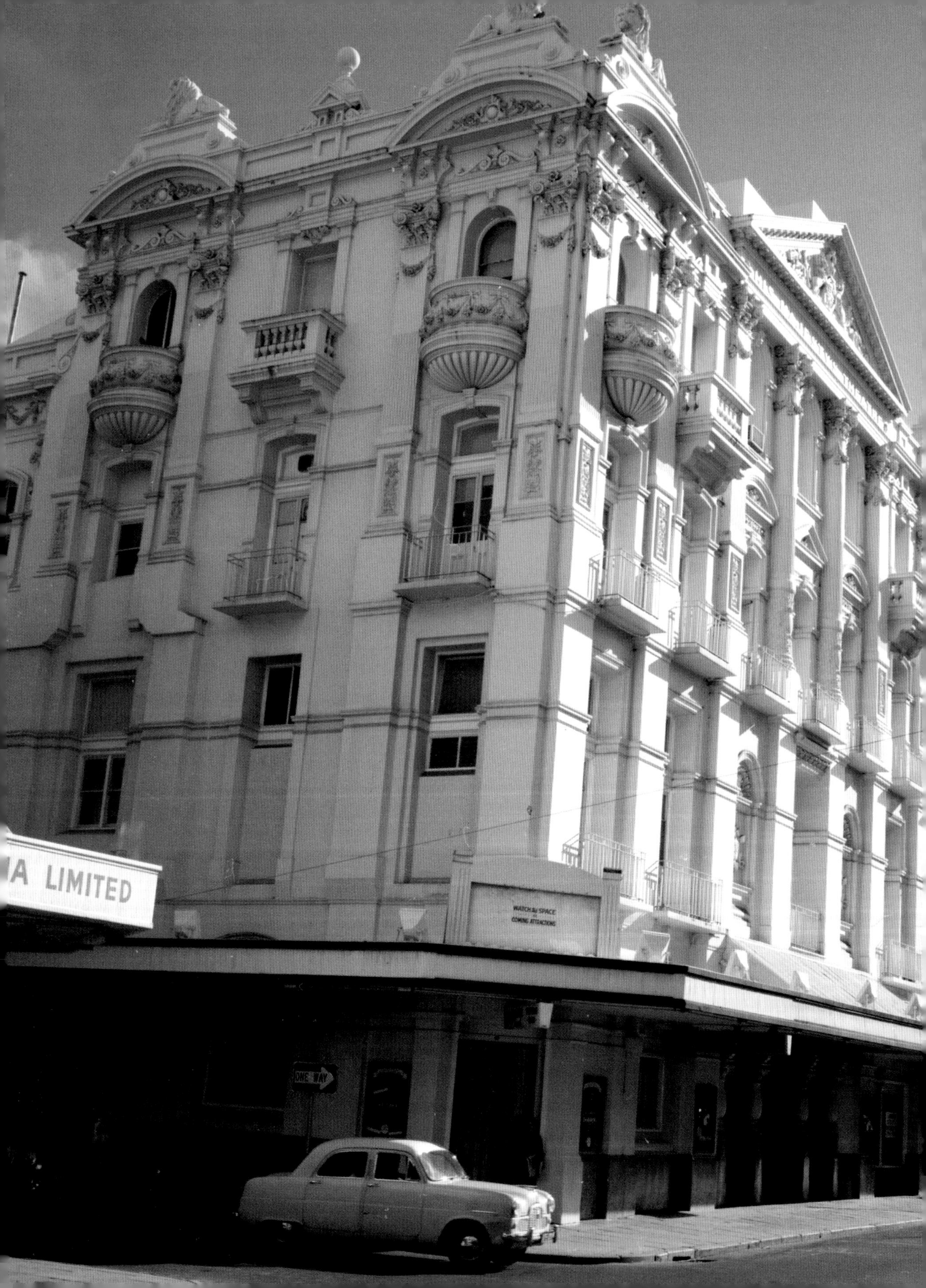
A LIMITED
ONE WAY

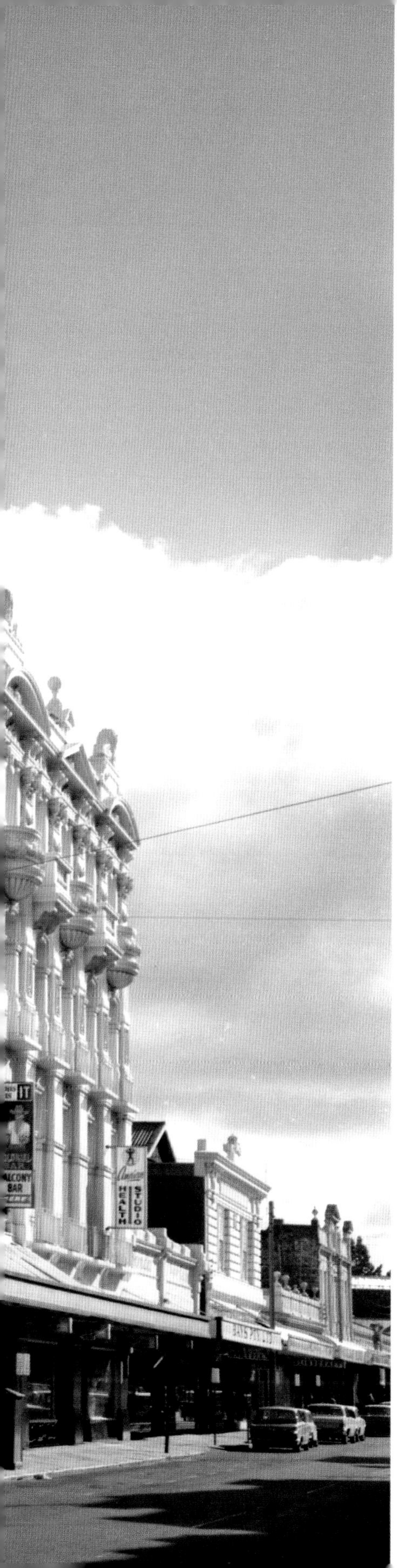


## His Majesty's Theatre c.1969

The plot on which His Majesty's Theatre now sits had been a popular outdoor entertainment venue for fairs and outdoor theatre since the 1870s and on 21st November, 1896 it was where the people of Perth got their first glimpse of moving pictures; a film of that year's Melbourne Cup.

In 1902 Thomas Malloy, one of the wealthiest men in Perth, acquired the plot in order to give Perth its second theatre – Malloy's Theatre Royal in Hay Street had opened in 1897. Taking around two years to complete, the opening of the theatre in 1904 was postponed several times because the building was not ready. On Christmas Eve, the opening was again delayed for a few minutes because the lock on the main gates had jammed and workmen had to prize them open before anyone could get in!

Since that ignominious start, the theatre has endured many trials and tribulations, but today remains one of Perth's favourite theatre venues.

## **Economic Stores** c.1960s

Economic Stores was a department store which had a long association, from the 1860s, with its site on the corner of Hay and William Streets.

In 1907, new premises designed by architects Hobbs, Smith and Forbes were built on the site. Sadly, that building was completely destroyed by fire in January 1921. In order to continue trading after the fire, the firm hired the Queen's Hall from the Methodist Church and set up a temporary department store, which they used for about a year.

In the meantime, a much larger store was designed in the 'Inter-war Art Deco' style by J. J. Talbot Hobbs and opened in 1923. Since then the building has continued to be used as retail and office space. During the latter part of the 20th century the ground floor was occupied by Walsh's Menswear store. In the 1950s, a new floor was added to the building and in 2012 major renovations and refurbishments took place.

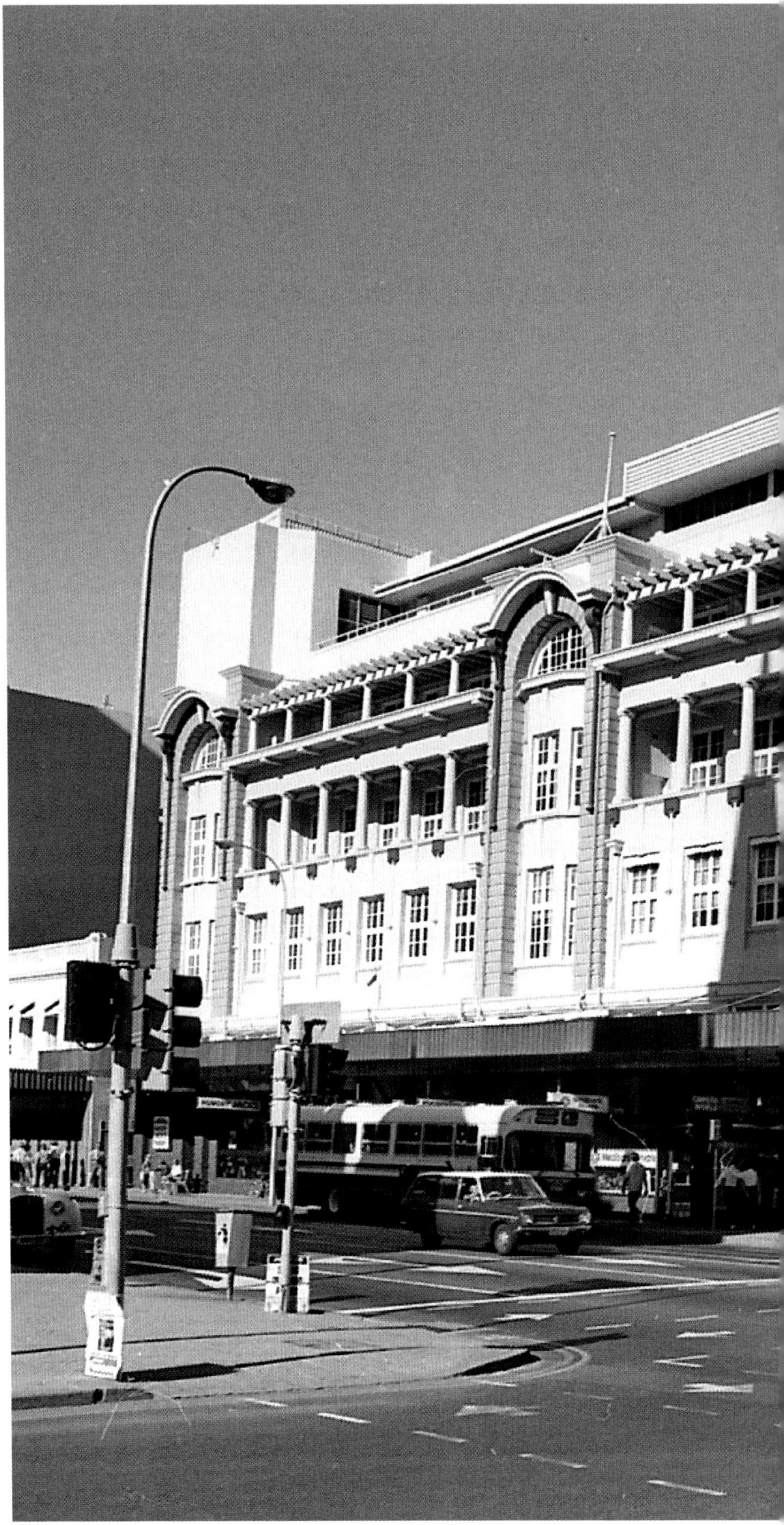

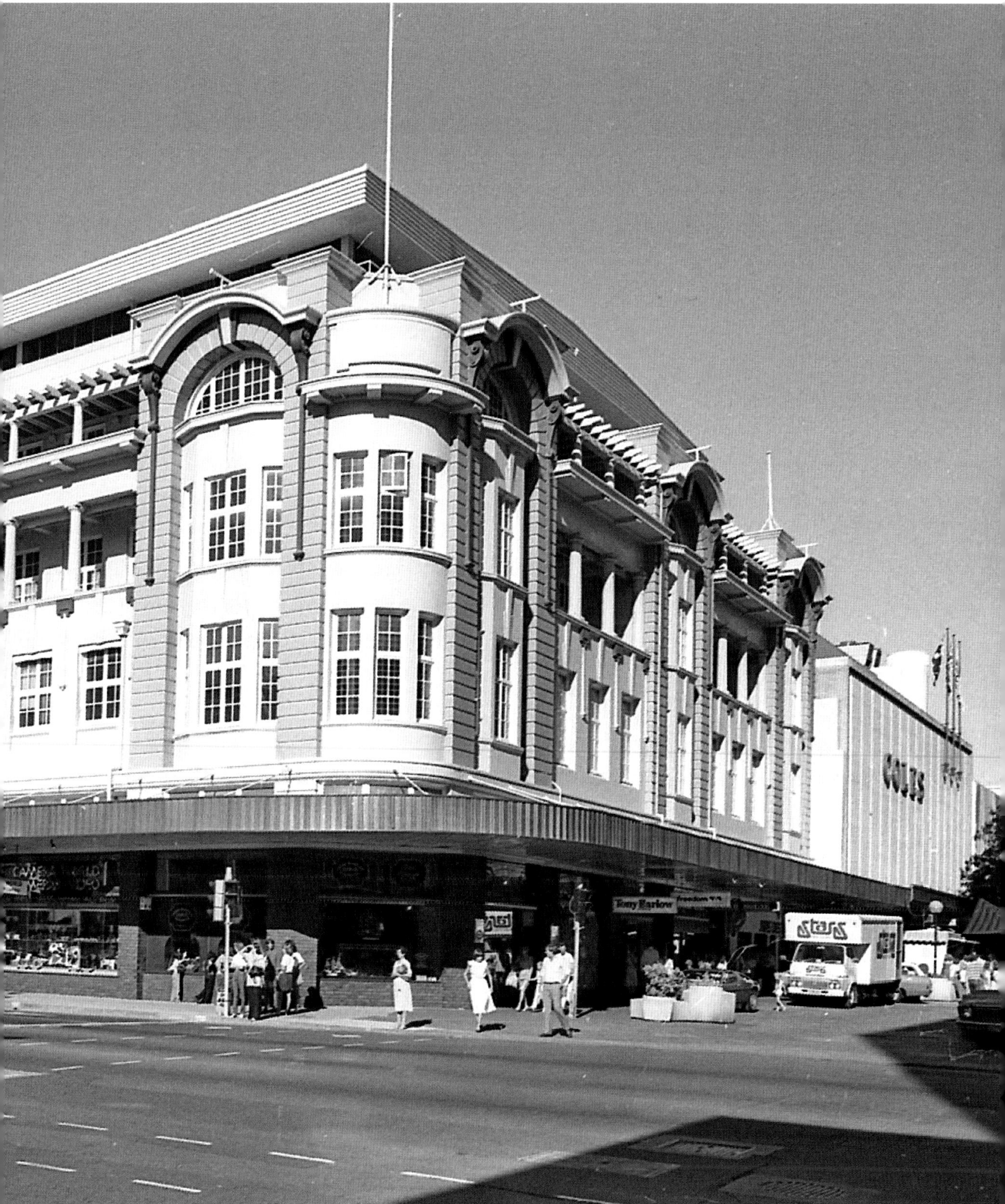
Tony Barlow
stars

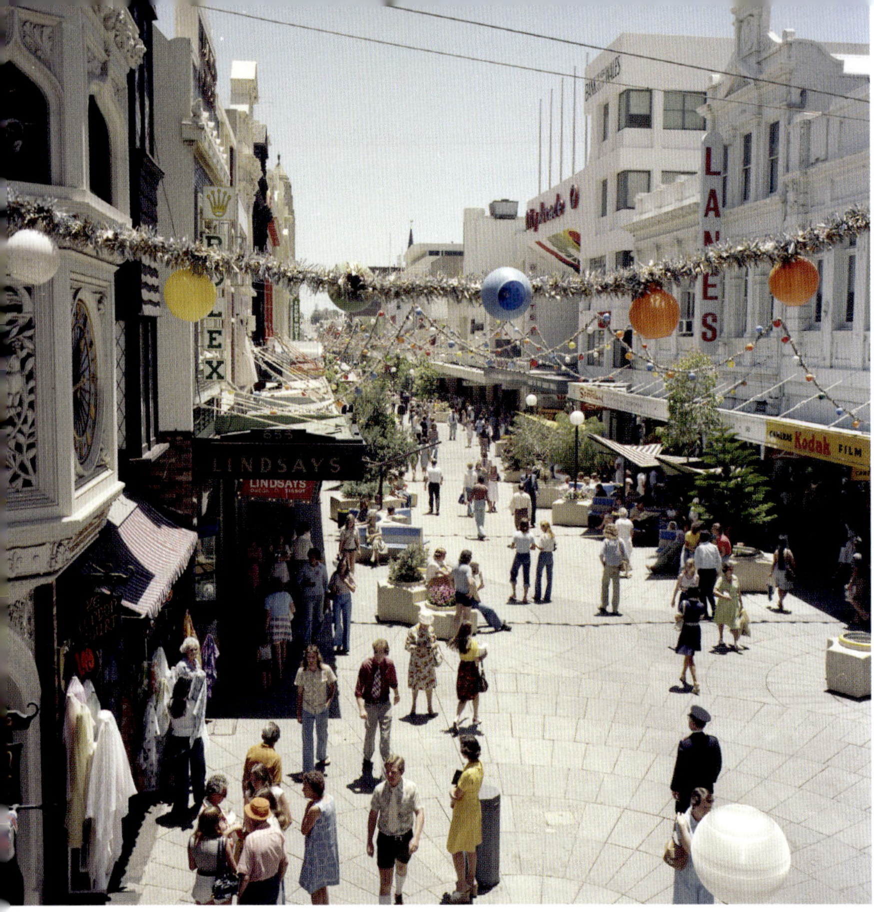


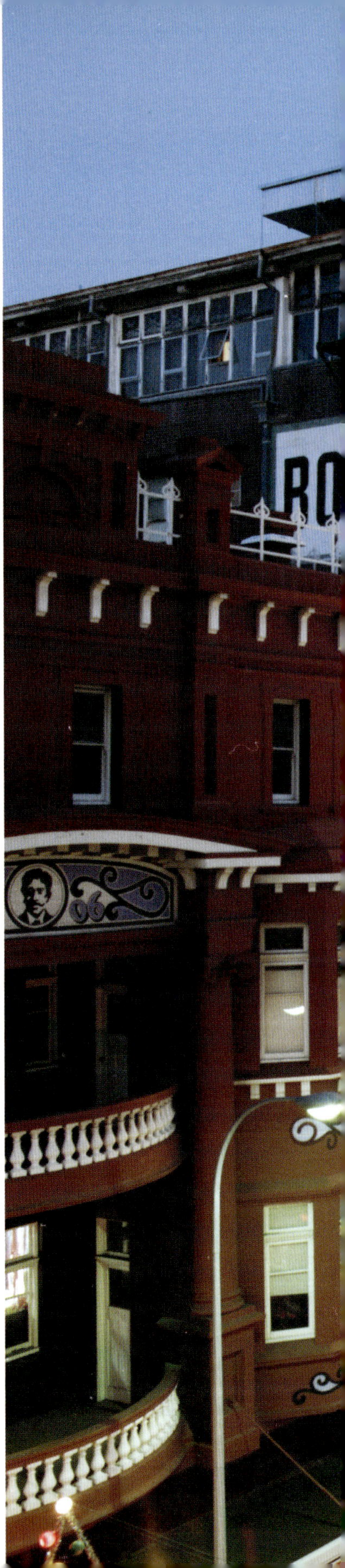

## Christmas in Perth c.1975

Some parts of Perth city centre were decorated for Christmas, including a Christmas tree, as early as the 1880s. After World War I, many of the city's department stores, particularly Boans and Foy & Gibson, started using electric lamps as part of their special Christmas window displays. One newspaper correspondent described the Boans window display in 1921 as, 'Boans Limited, have a very creditable window display replete with every toy the childish mind could fancy, the dolls and teddy bears being very artistically arranged.'

During the 1950s, the City Council started putting up Christmas decorations in the city centre and out of this developed the City's Festival of Christmas. In 1979, the Christmas decorations reflected the 150th anniversary of the foundation of the Swan River colony, under the banner of 'A Year of Excitement'.

Ernie captured these photographs of the Perth Street decorations during the 1970s, by which time the custom of decorating the Perth streets for the Christmas shoppers was well established.

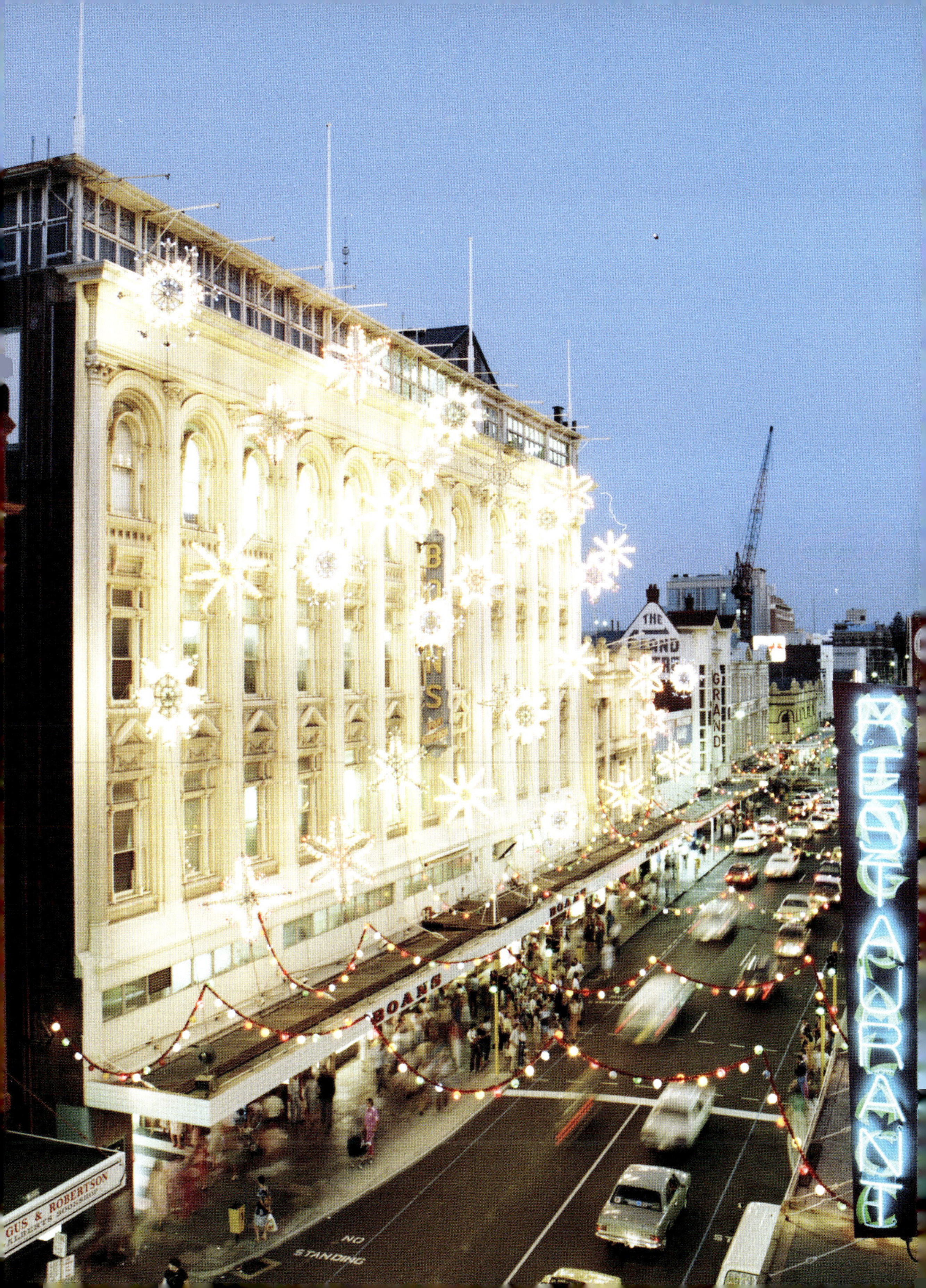
BOANS
BOANS
BOANS
GRAND
GUS & ROBERTSON
NO
STANDING

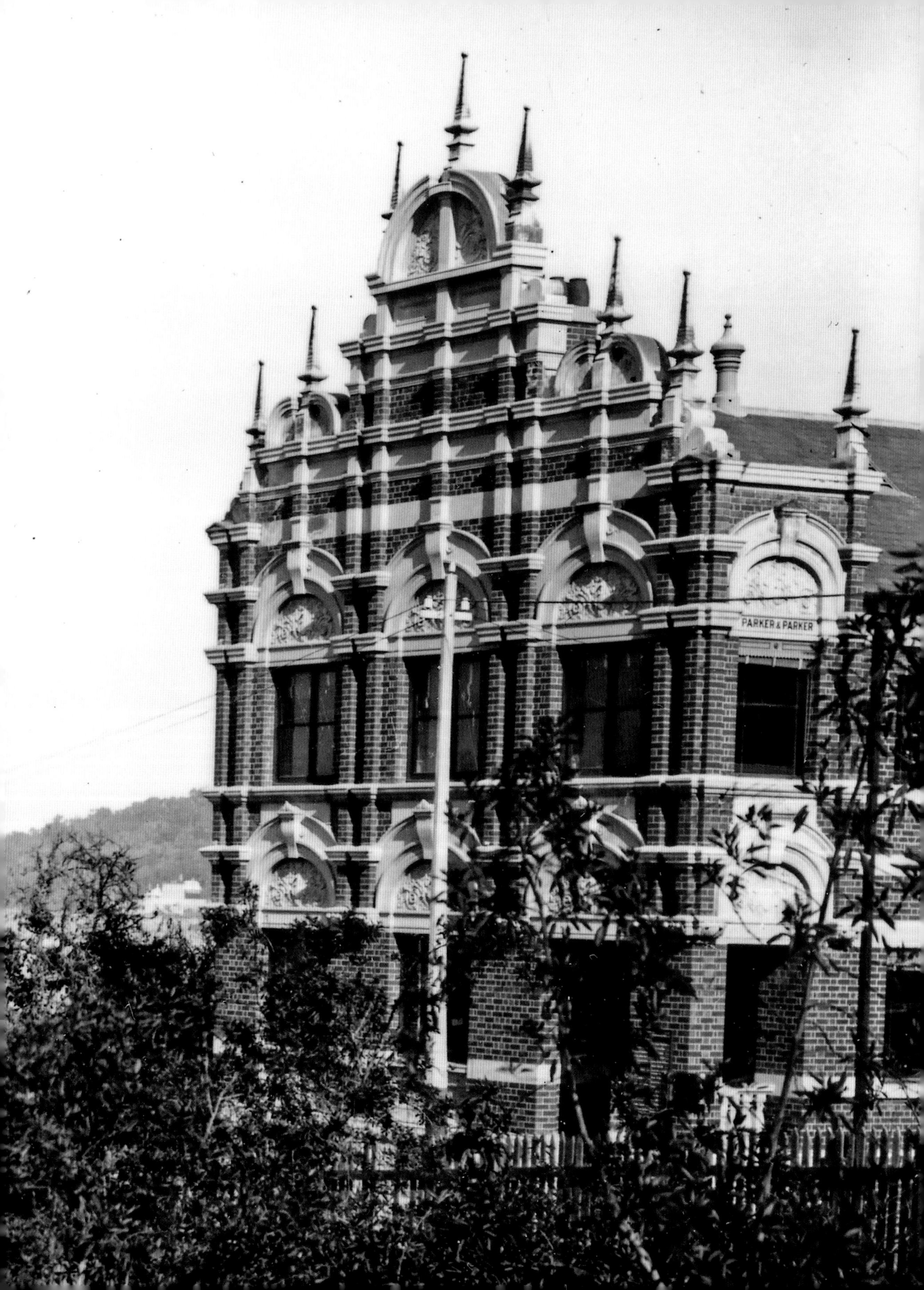
PARKER & PARKER

## 21 Howard Street 1974

**LEFT:** The first Western Australian Gold Rush of the 1890s brought about a significant expansion of the commercial centre of Perth. Howard Street, with its close proximity to the Supreme Court and Government Offices, became the heart of the financial and legal district of the city.

In 1905, the West Australian newspaper announced that architects, 'Oldham and Cox have just completed a building, consisting of office premises in Howard Street'. The cost of the building was reported as £8,000. Soon after its completion Parker and Parker Solicitors relocated their chambers from William Street to the new building; an association which lasted until 1964 when the firm relocated to St Georges Terrace.

Ernie's image captured the office from a view made possible by demolition work occurring along St Georges Terrace in 1974 to make way for Allendale Square. It also shows the building in its original state, before later renovations removed its elaborate pediment.

## Melbourne Hotel c.1973

**FOLLOWING PAGE:** Like the Palace Hotel, the Melbourne Hotel was another of John de Baun's luxury establishments, built in 1896 to capitalise on the excitement of Perth's first Gold Rush.

By the 1970s, when this photograph was taken, the hotel became a regular platform for emerging live artists and bands. A decade later, it had morphed into a nightclub, trading under various names such as the Pink Galah Cabaret, Tiffany's Nightclub and The Firm. According to the hotel's website, these clubs were so popular that the number of patrons often exceeded the licenced capacity of the building.

In 1993, yet another change was planned, this time to become an exclusive, and expensive, private gentlemen's club. Over 200 businessmen paid the joining fee, only to have it returned to them when the entrepreneur for the venture was forced to sell the hotel for economic reasons.

After several more iterations, the Melbourne Hotel is once again a thriving city-centre hotel, bar and restaurant.

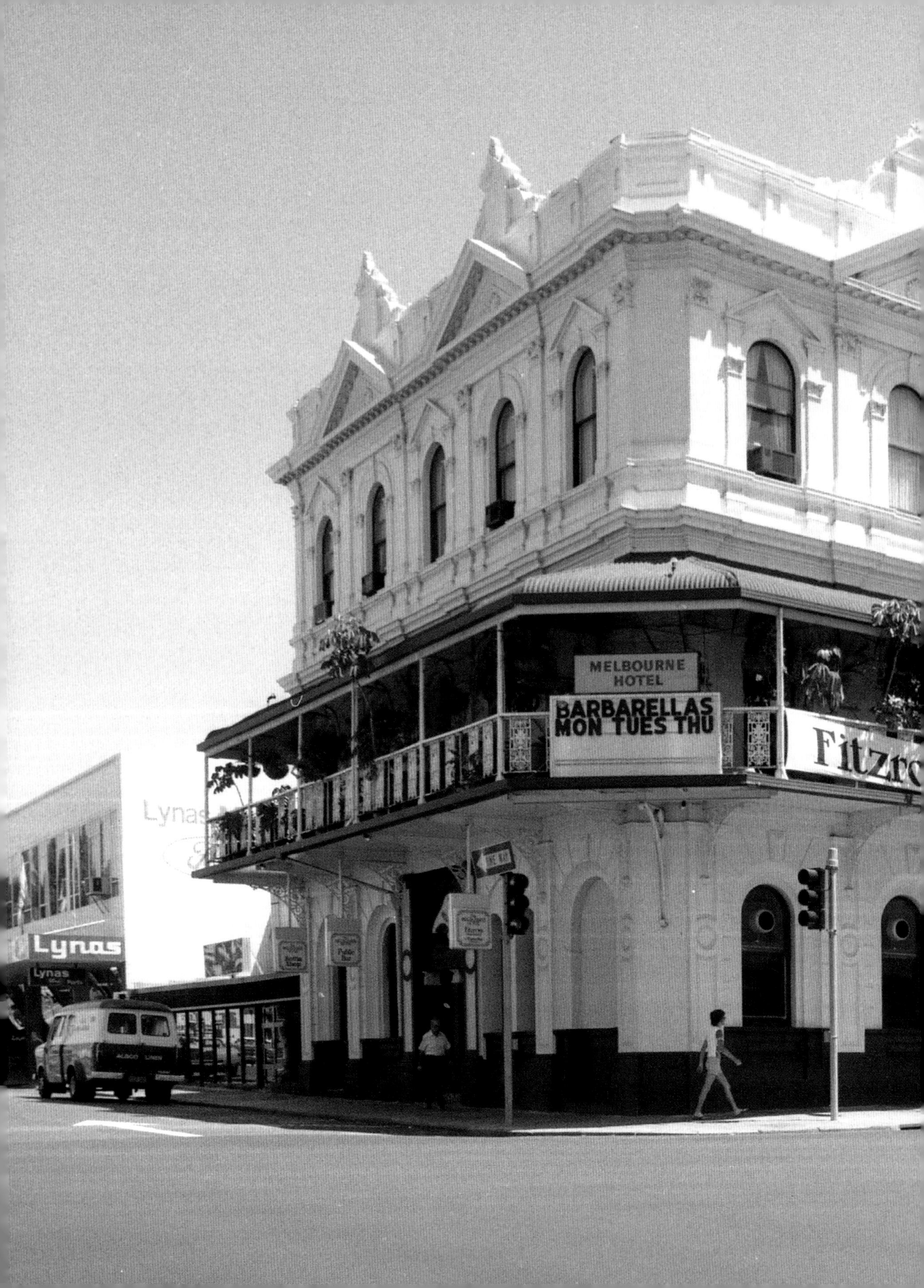
MELBOURNE HOTEL
BARBARELLAS
MON TUES THU
Lynas
Lynas

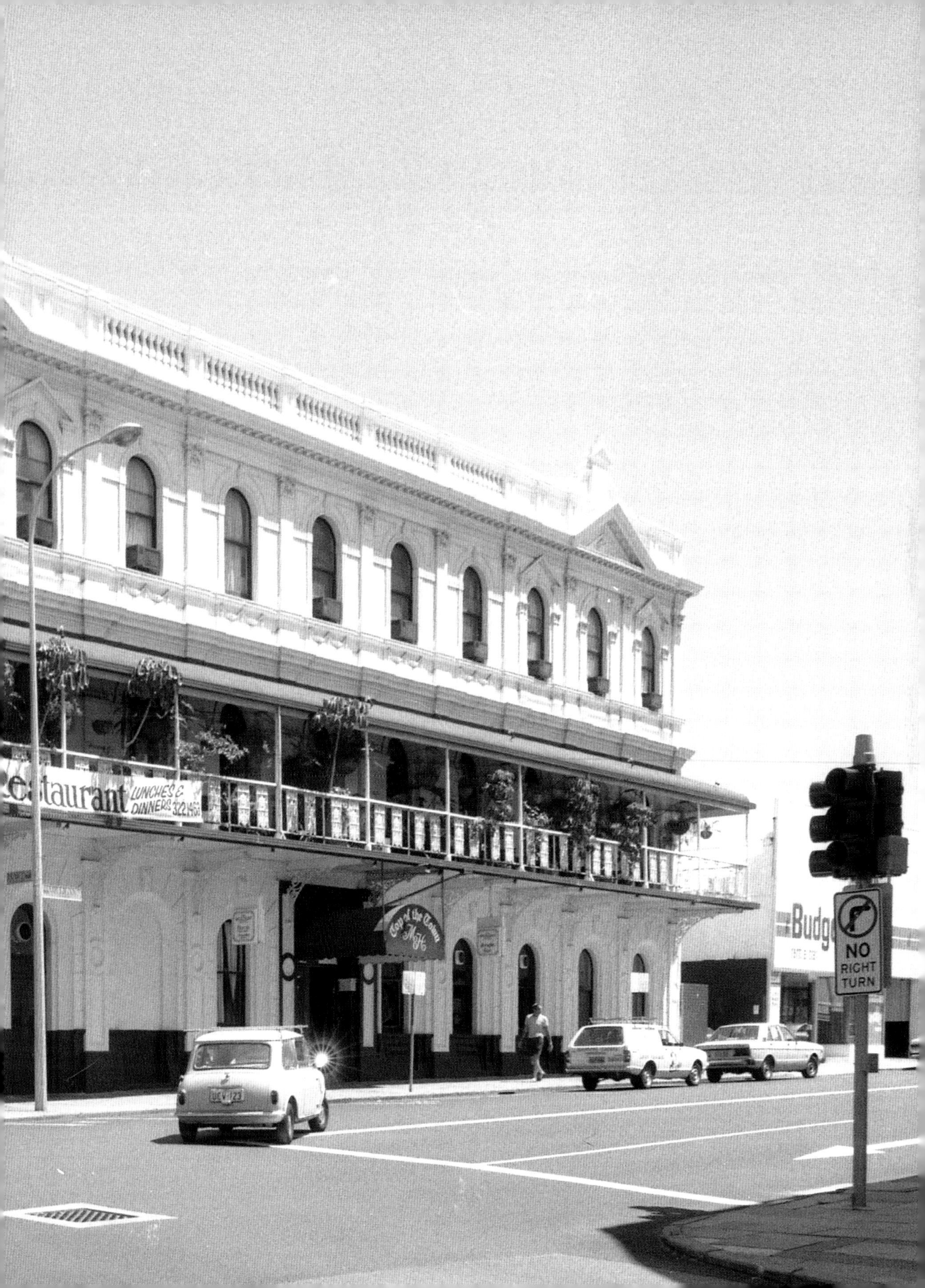
estaurant
LUNCHES &
DINNERS
Top of the Town
NO
RIGHT
TURN

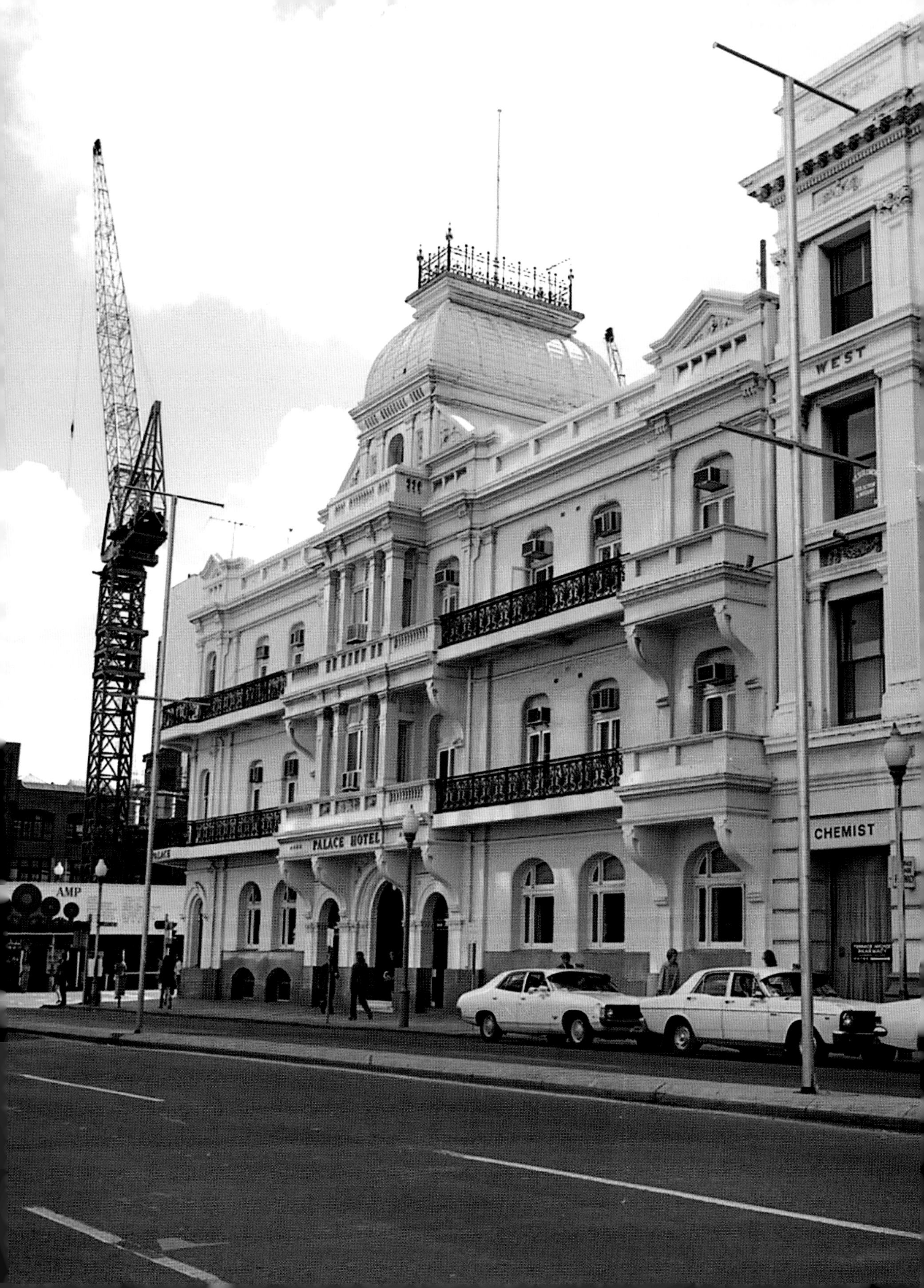
AMP
PALACE
PALACE HOTEL
WEST
CHEMIST

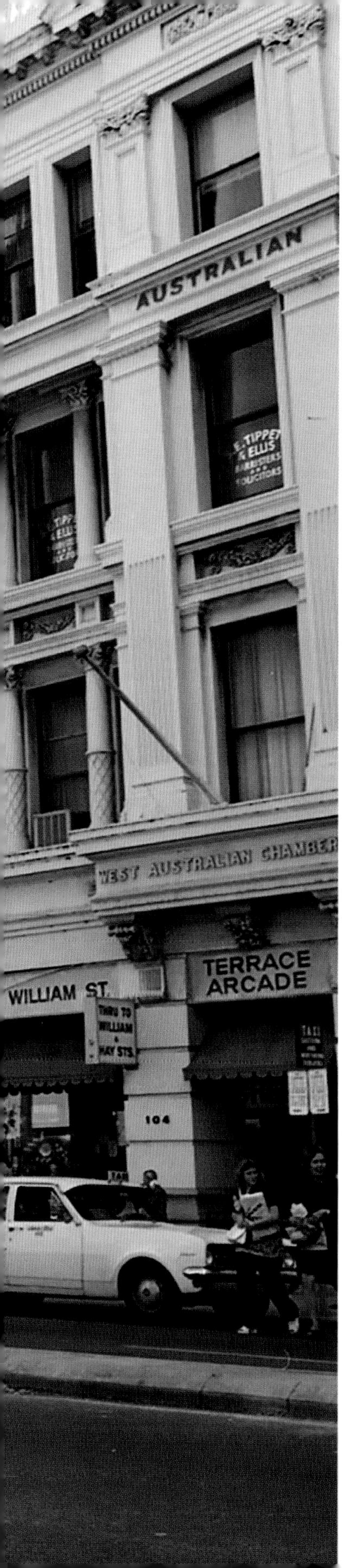


## Palace Hotel 1978

**LEFT:** The Palace Hotel was one of Perth's first luxury hotels, catering for what would now be called the 'high-end market': those who had found wealth in Western Australia's first Gold Rush.

Built on the site of The King's Head, one of the first licenced hostelries in central Perth, the Palace Hotel was the brainchild of American hotelier John De Baun. He ensured that no expense was spared to create a luxury establishment.

Marble for the fireplaces and mosaic floor tiles for the main entrance and bar-room floors came from Italy. Imported cedar was used for the central staircase, the doors of the main entrance, bar and wall panelling, and ceilings were covered in pressed metal in a variety of patterns.

Opening its doors for business in March, 1897, it was described by one correspondent as 'one of the most beautiful and elegant hotels in Australia'.

**BELOW:** A favourite watering hole for the journalists at the nearby offices of the Western Australian newspaper, the Commonwealth Bank purchased the property in 1972 and announced it was to be demolished. This caused a public outcry, not least from the journalists, who mounted a campaign for the building's preservation, led by a group known as 'The Palace Guards'.

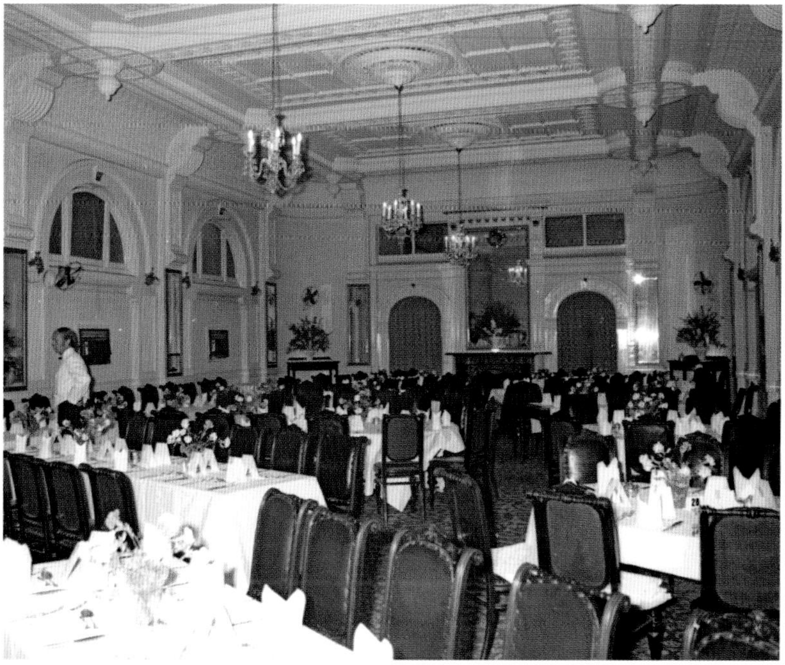

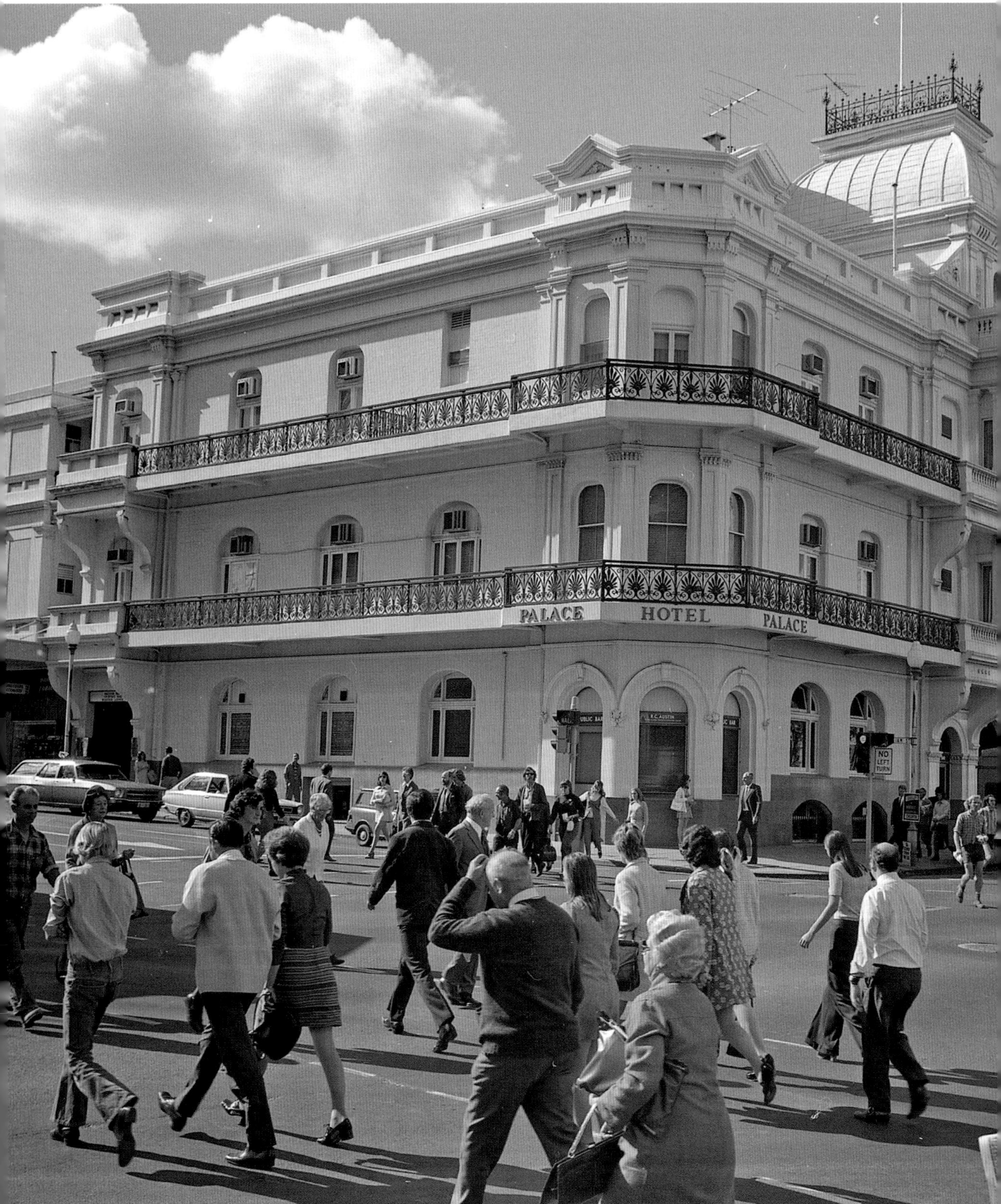
PALACE
HOTEL
PALACE
NO LEFT TURN

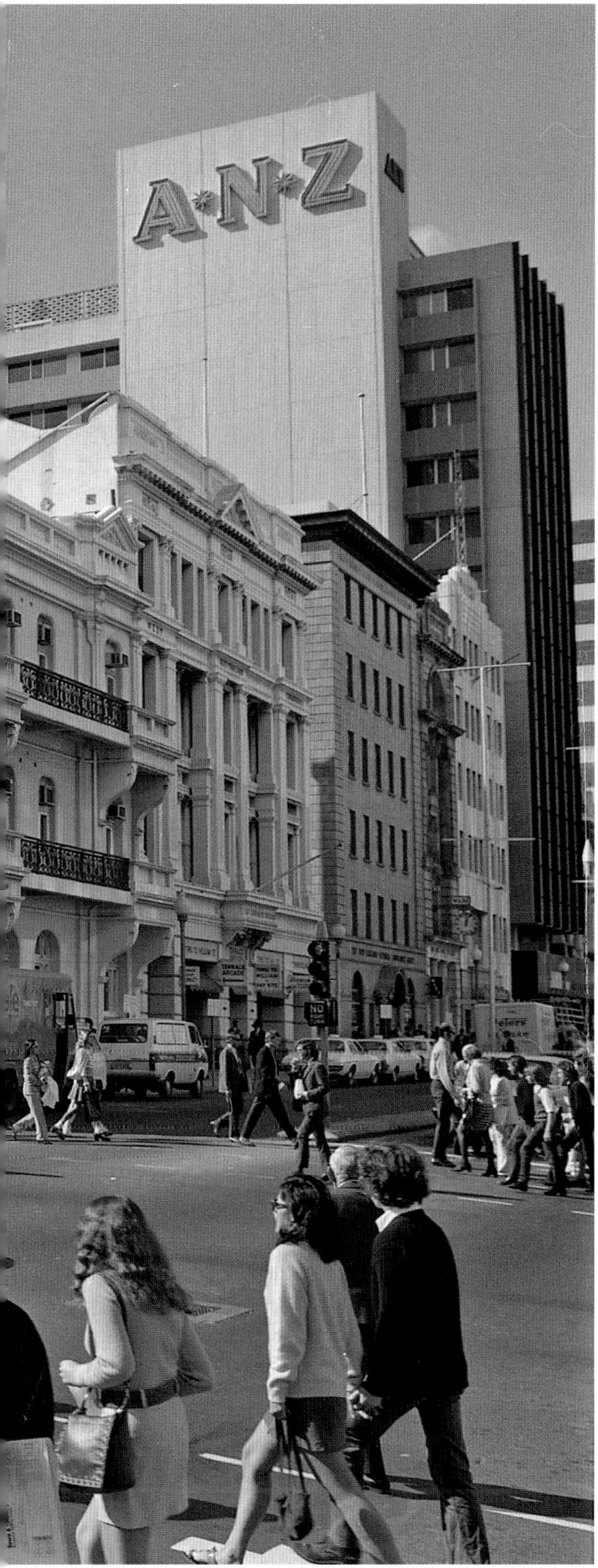


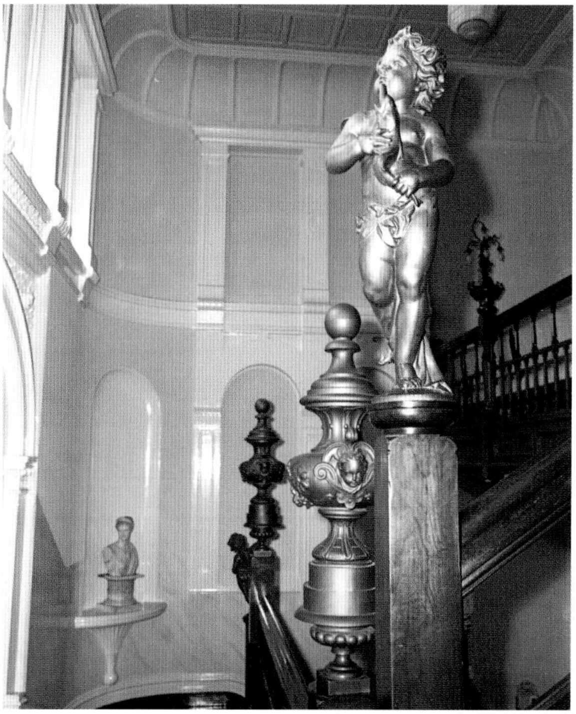

## Palace Hotel 1978

In 1978, the Bond Corporation purchased the property and those adjacent, building the 50-storey office block which sits on the North-East corner of the building. This photograph was taken soon after work commenced on the new building.

Much of the original hotel did, however, survive this addition and was used as a bank until 2015, when the bank vacated the building.

The Palace hotel then underwent an extensive programme of renovation and was adapted for use as an architect's studio, bar and a restaurant. Thus part of the building has now returned to its original purpose, although probably not as many snappy news headlines are being composed by journalists over a lunchtime pint as in its former days!

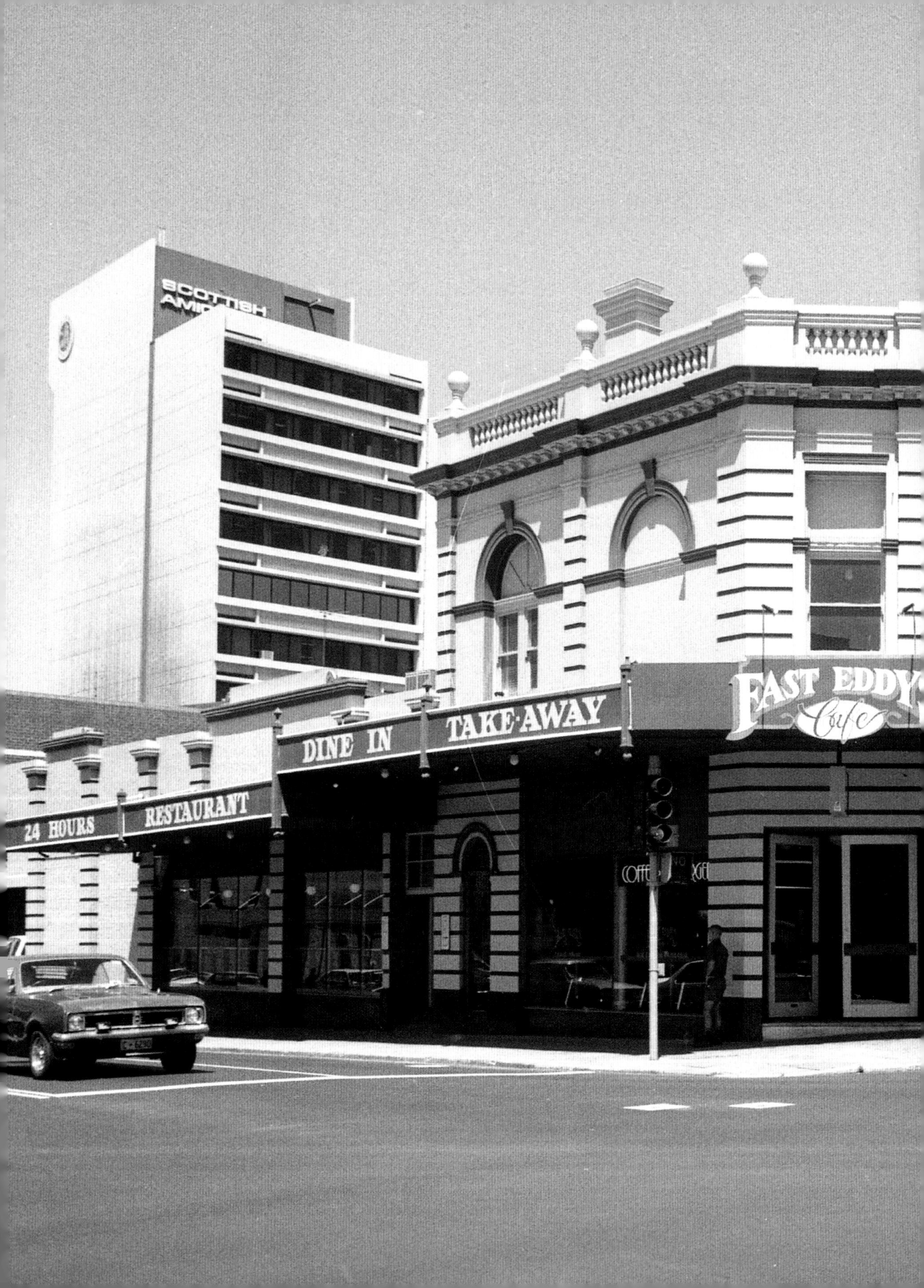
SCOTTISH
24 HOURS
RESTAURANT
DINE IN
TAKE·AWAY
EAST EDDY
Cafe

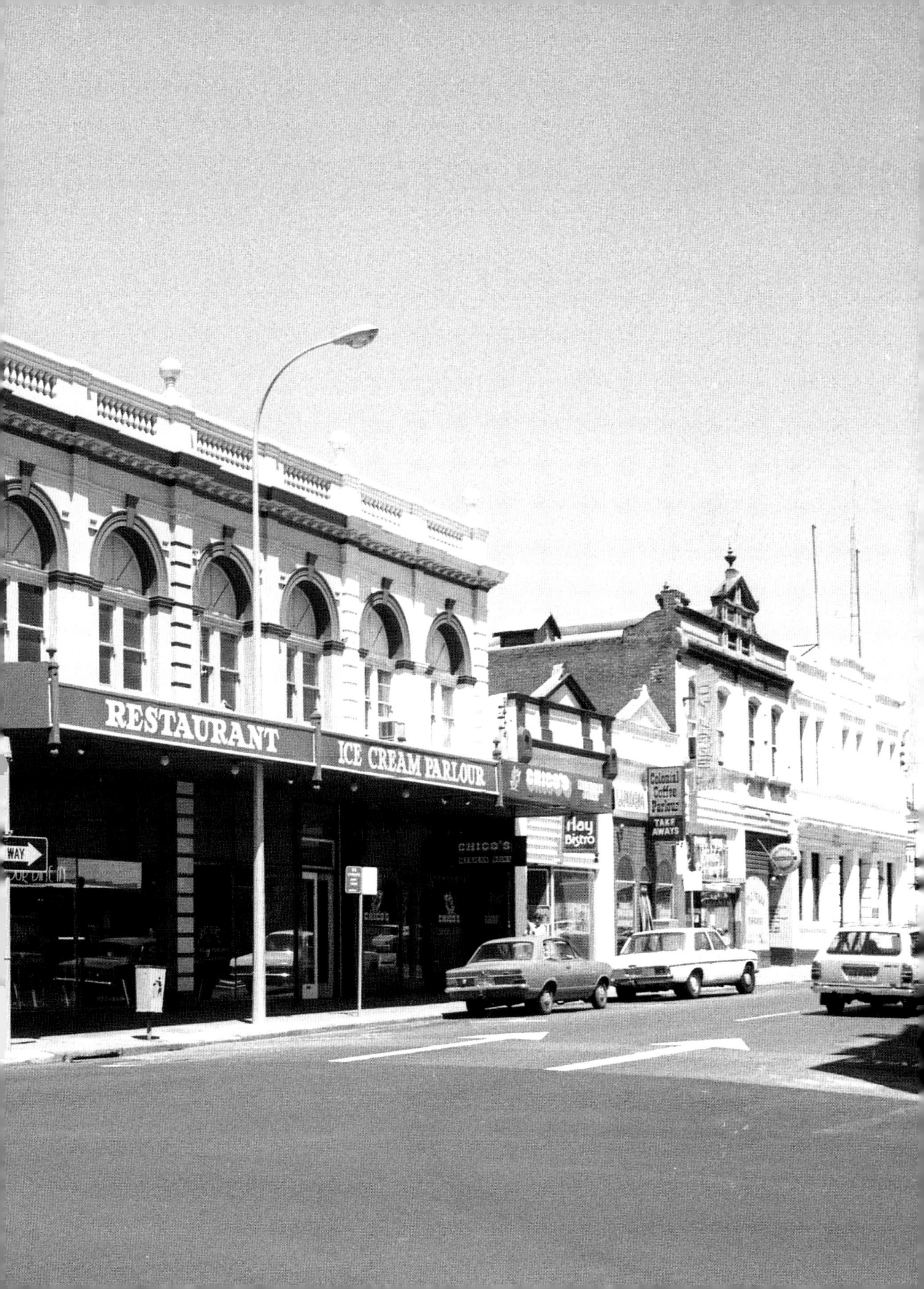
RESTAURANT
ICE CREAM PARLOUR
CHICO'S
Hay Bistro
Colonial Coffee Parlour
TAKE AWAYS
WAY

## Fast Eddys c.1982

**PREVIOUS PAGE:** Fast Eddys was the first restaurant in Perth to open 24 hours a day, seven days a week. This iconic Western Australian institution was a gastronomic revolution when it was opened on the corner of Hay and Milligan Streets by Christopher and Con Somas in 1979. Never before had Perth citizens been able to dine out on egg and chips at 3:30 in the morning!

It is said that the restaurant took its name from the fictional character (Fast) Eddie Felson, featured in the 1961 film 'The Hustler', although no sources have been found to prove this.

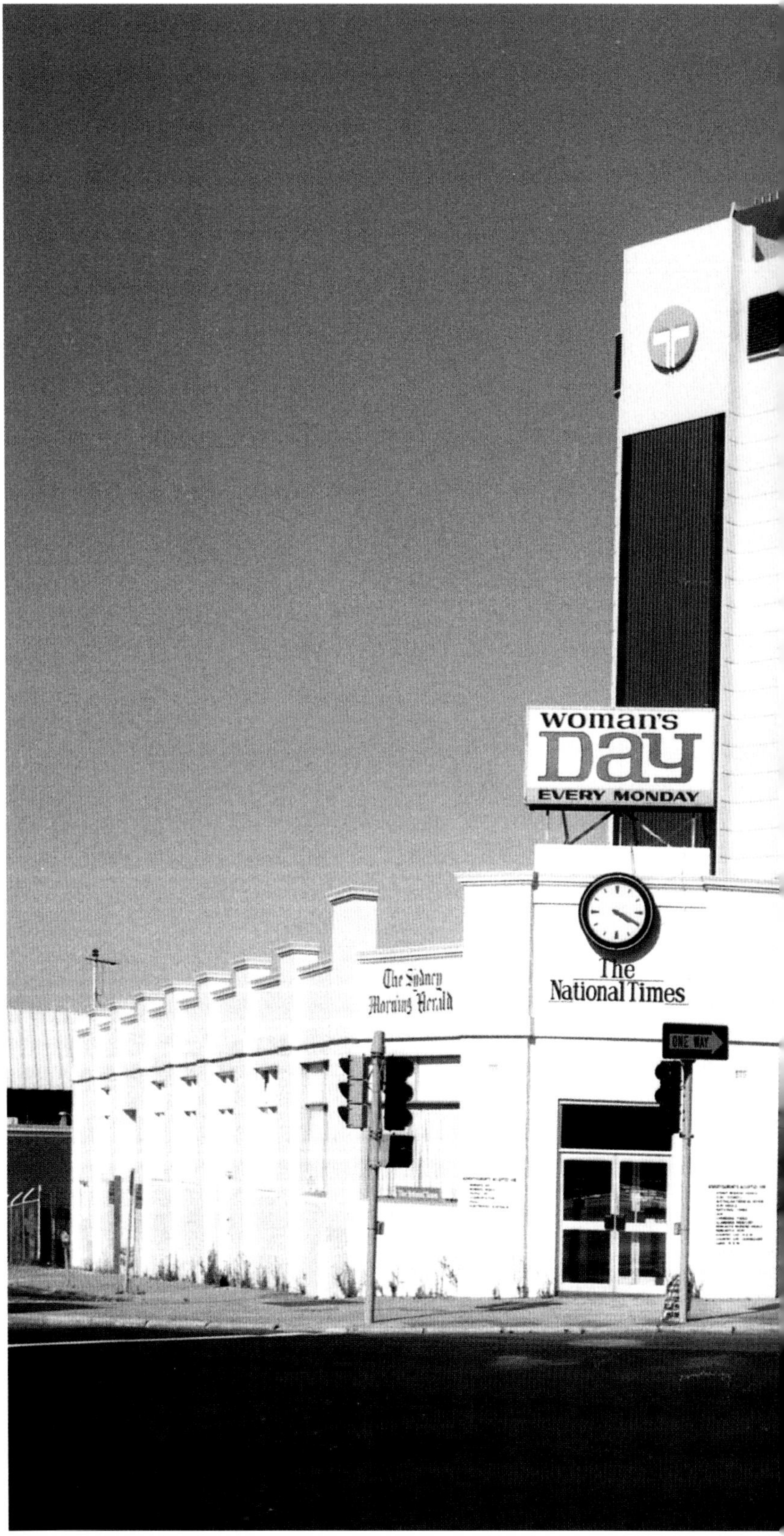


**RIGHT:** In the early 1990s, the restaurant moved to 454 Murray Street, which had been built in 1989 for the Fairfax Media company, where it remained until 2019 when it made its own news headlines by closing the ever-open doors and thus ending a Perth fast food tradition.

Towering above the building in this photograph is the Telstra telephone exchange, which was completed in 1979. Constructed of concrete and seeming to have no windows, in order to maintain a constant temperature inside the building, it had the strange distinction at the time of its completion of being the heaviest building in Perth.

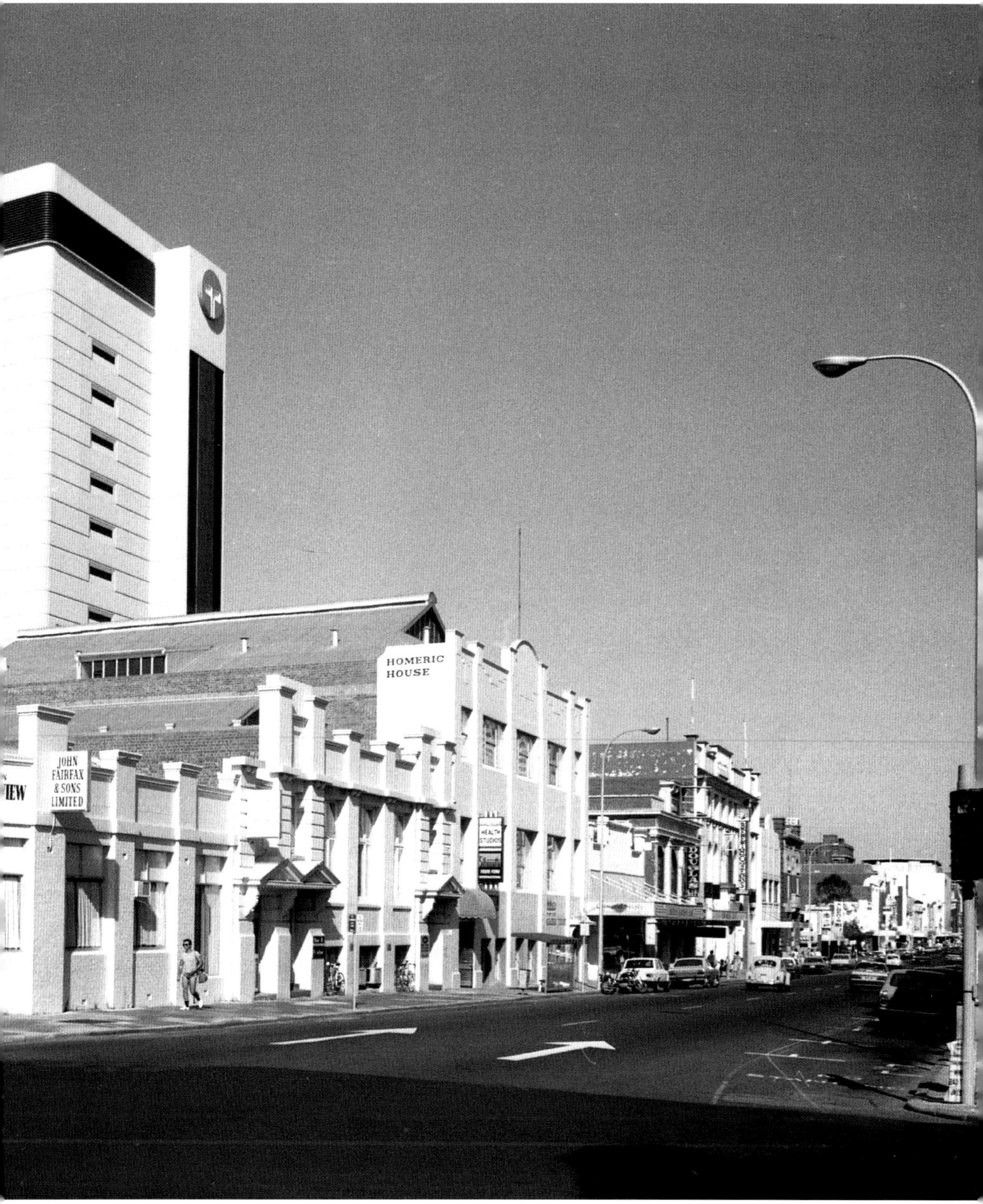
HOMERIC
HOUSE
JOHN
FAIRFAX
& SONS
LIMITED

# 3

# The Freeway is Coming

The construction of Perth's first freeway in the late 1950s not only heralded a transport revolution, but also caused a considerable upheaval in the layout of the city. Once again Ernie was on hand to record the changes that took place, including the long-wished-for bridge across the Narrows.

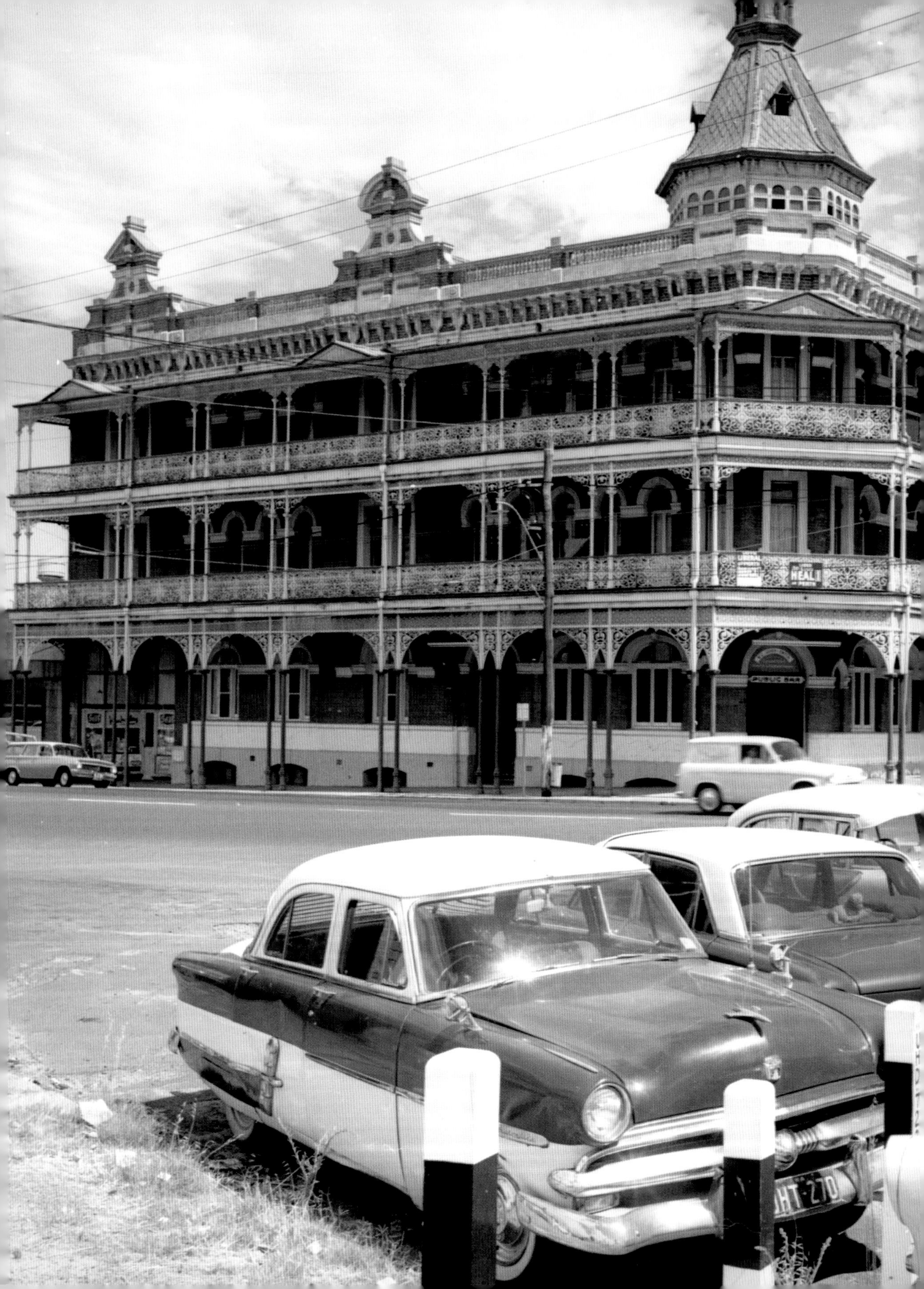

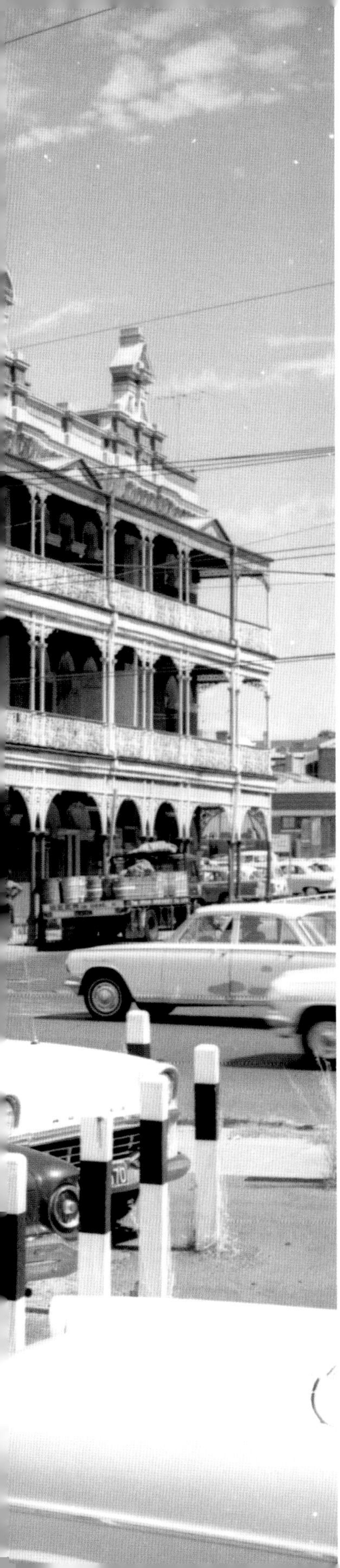

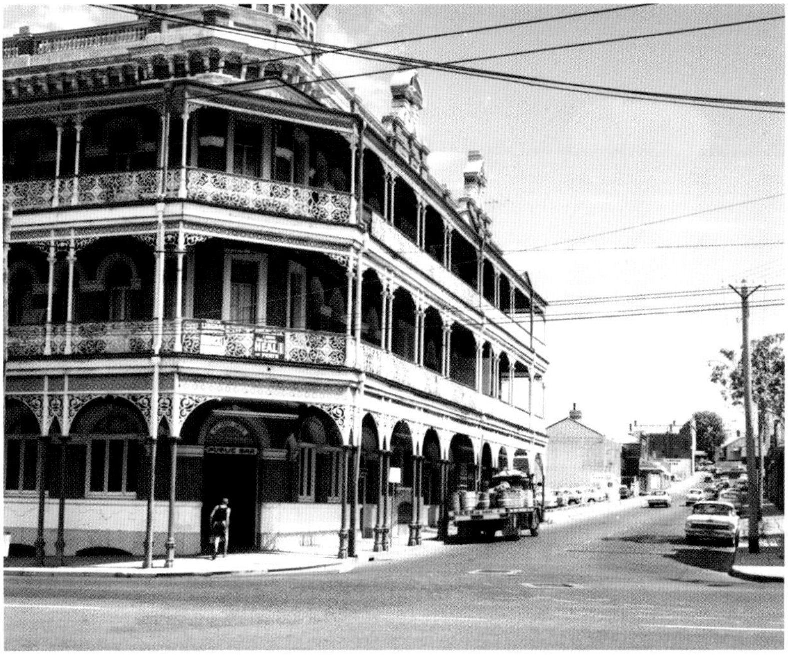

## Federal Hotel c.1960s

The Federal Hotel started its life in 1897 as 'Stein's Coffee Palace', a temperance hotel, on the corner of George and Douro (later Wellington) Streets in West Perth. It was built for ex-convict Bernard Stein, who may well not have been allowed to hold a liquor licence because of his criminal record.

History shows that temperance enterprises have never been hugely popular in Western Australia and this could well have been why the lessee of Stein's Coffee Palace, Michael Daly, applied for and obtained a licence to sell alcohol, reopening the establishment as the Federal Hotel in January, 1898.

The Federal became a popular Perth watering hole, which offered both short and long-term accommodation until the early 1960s when it was acquired in preparation for what was to become the construction of the Mitchell Freeway. The building was demolished in 1972, but its inscribed foundation stone was rescued and is now in the possession of the Royal Western Australian Historical Society.

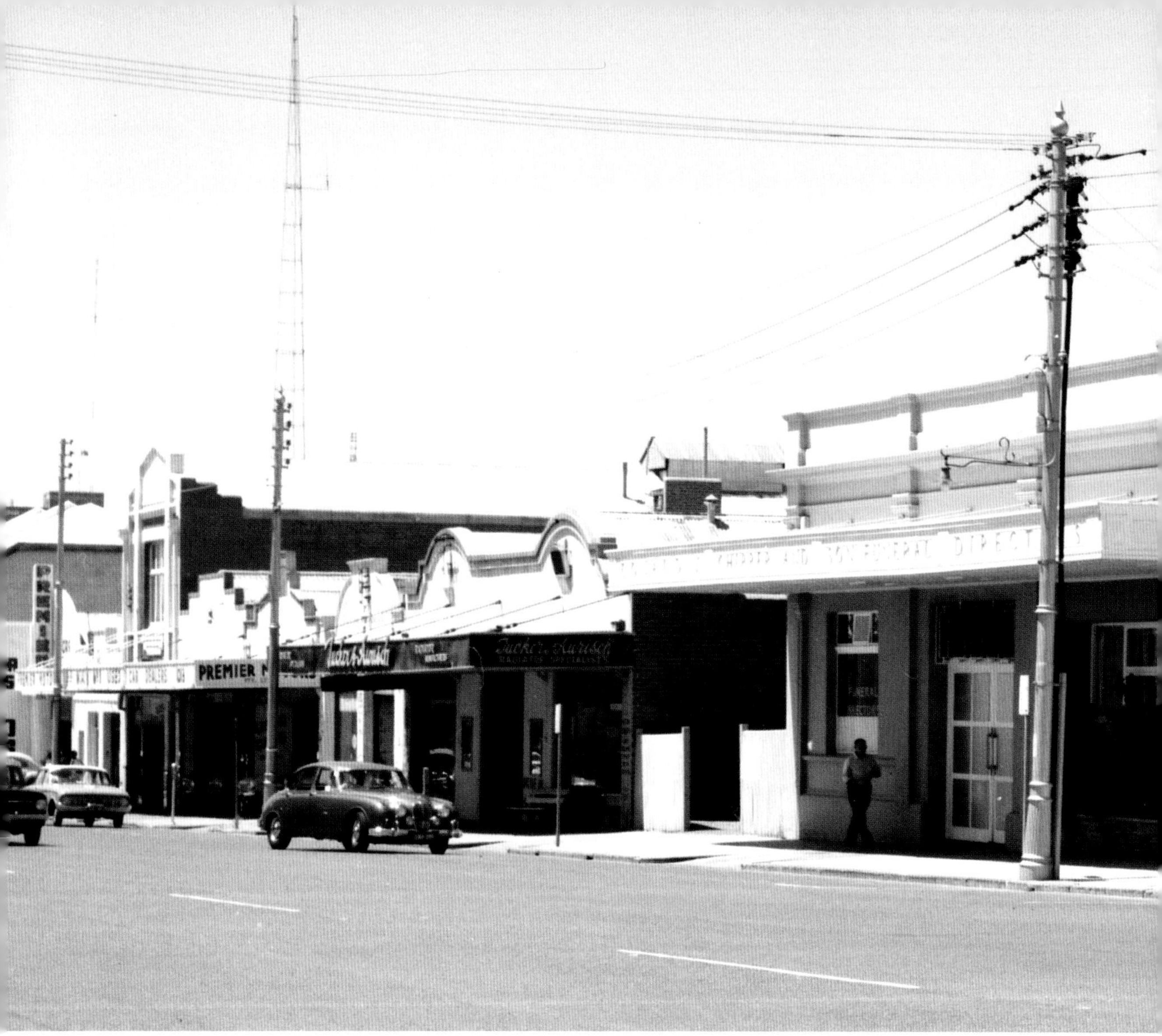


## Chippers Funeral Directors 1953

**ABOVE:** Situated on the corner of Hay and George Streets in West Perth, Donald J. Chipper and Son Funeral Directors was one of the buildings lost when the first section of freeway was constructed.

The Chipper family business can be traced back to the 1860s when Stephen James Chipper and his brother John Charles gained government rights for the burial of destitute paupers. At the age of 16, Stephen's fourth son, Donald, started an apprenticeship as a coach builder, wheelwright and undertaker. Five years later, having been left property as part of his father's estate, Donald established his own business at 385 Murray Street, Perth. By 1929, the business had grown to such an extent that Chipper was able to build the larger premises seen in this photograph.

A seemingly unlikely subject for photography, this image demonstrate Ernie's aim of capturing ordinary streetscapes that would be lost in Perth's redevelopment.

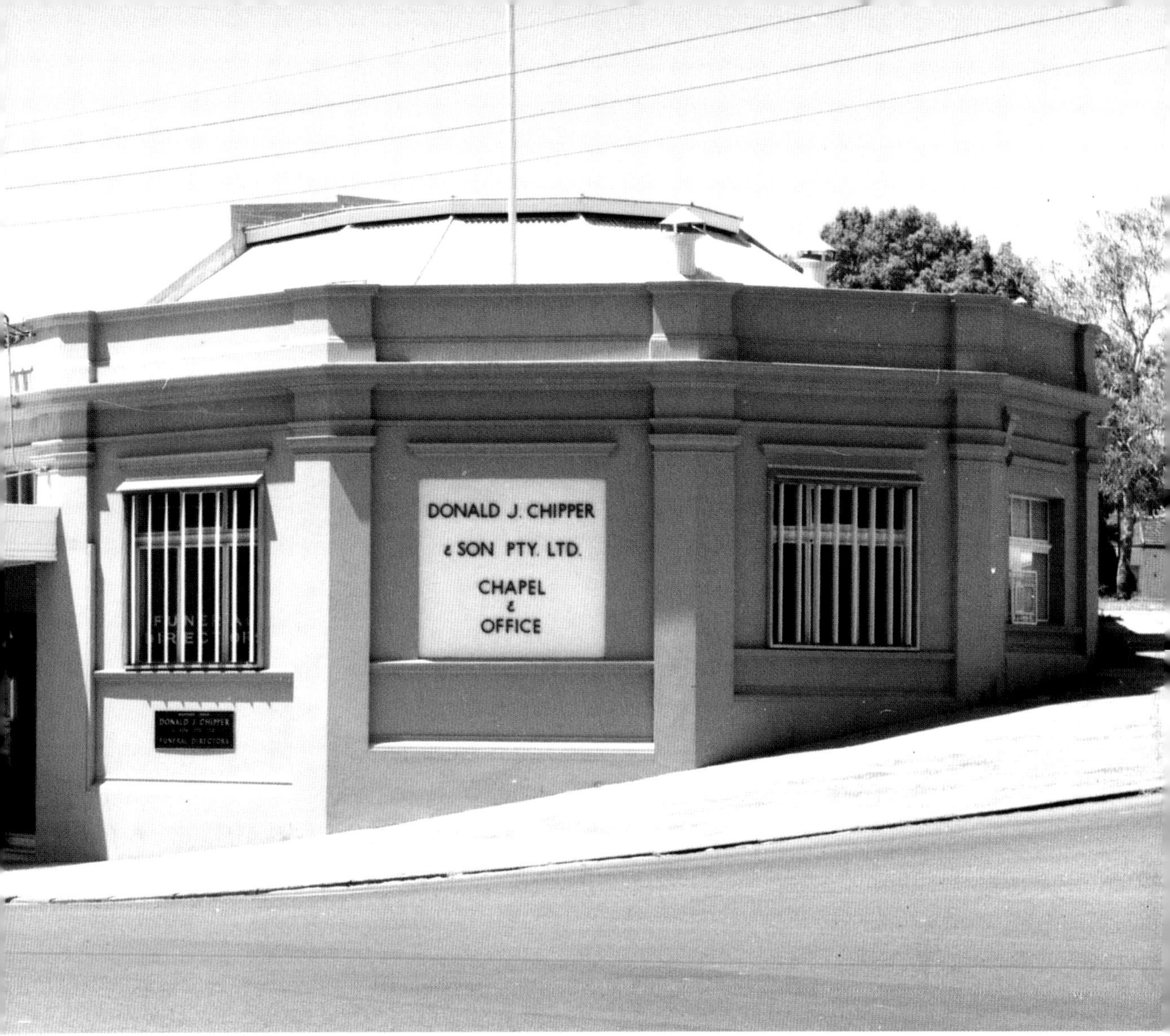
DONALD J. CHIPPER
& SON PTY. LTD.
CHAPEL
&
OFFICE
DONALD J. CHIPPER
FUNERAL DIRECTORS

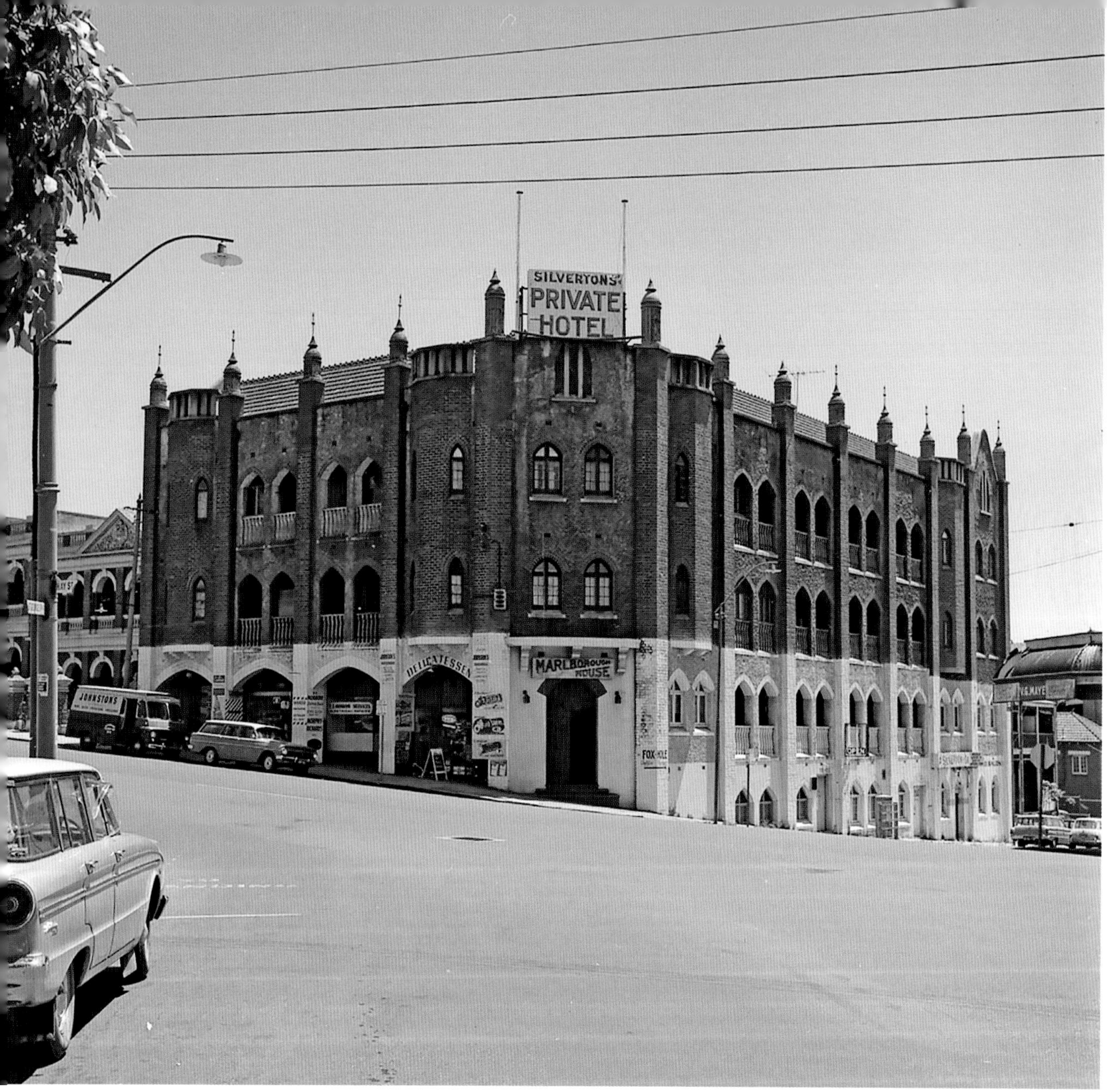


## **Marlborough Hotel** 1963

Marlborough House or 'Marlborough Mansions' as it was originally called, has the architectural air of a fortified citadel. When built in 1923, the West Australian described it as 'an Art Deco hotel with arcade, its arches and balconies a reflection of Federation Gothic architecture, like Perth Girls' Orphanage on Adelaide Terrace.'

Designed by the Perth firm of Oldham and Cox, it continued as a hotel, changing its name in the 1950s to Silverton's Private Hotel until it was demolished in 1964.

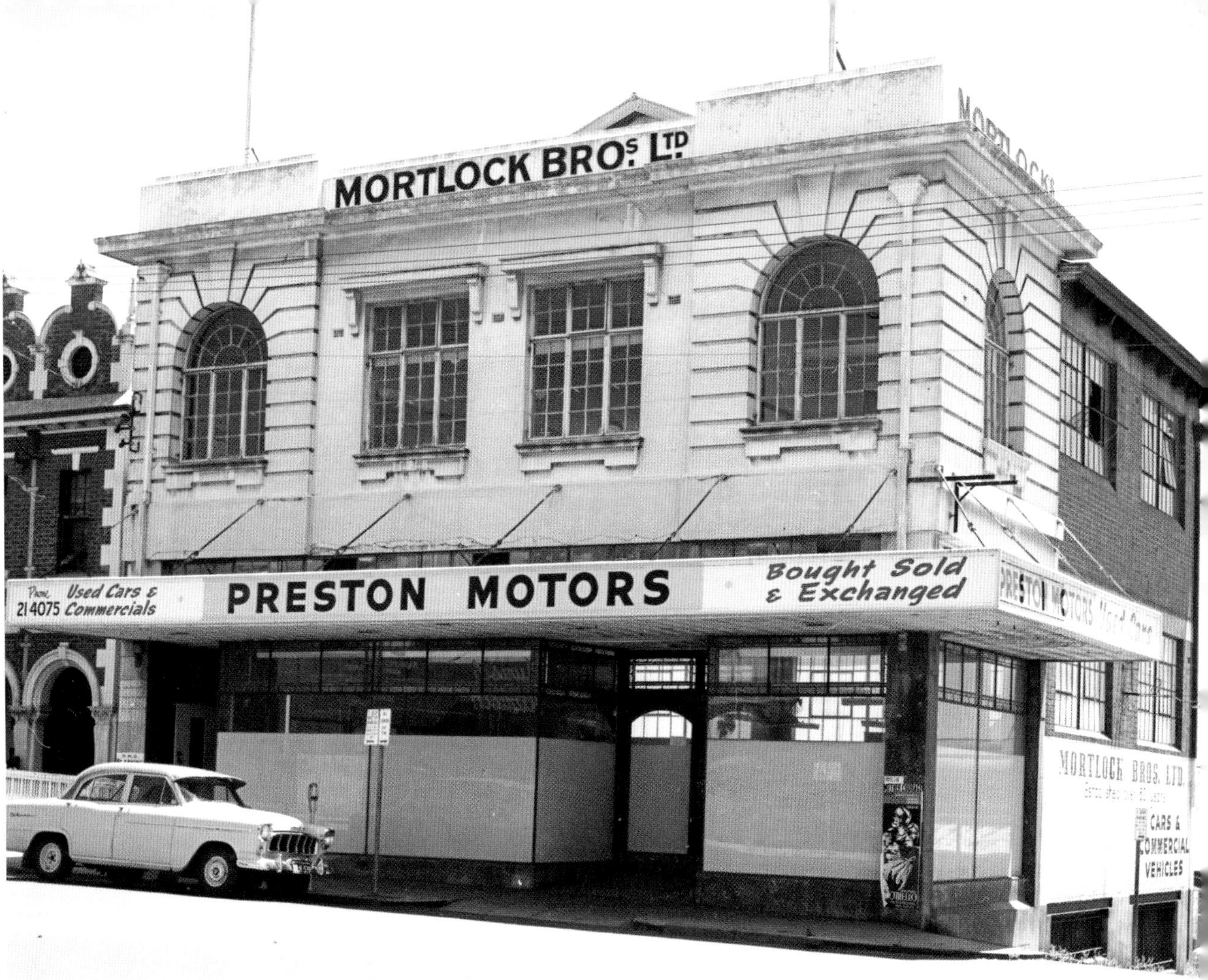


## Mortlock Brothers 1963

In 1929, Mortlock Bros, a firm established in 1896 by three brothers, opened a new showroom on the corner of Hay and Elder Streets in West Perth. Designed by local architects Powell and Cameron, the elegant building shows how the brothers' company had grown from one which originally importing motorcycles and agricultural machinery to a business that catered for just about every aspect of the motor trade.

Ernie captured this photograph of the building, already vacated, just before it was demolished along with the neighbouring buildings to make way for the freeway. The Mortlock firm continued to serve Perth until it was bought out in the 1980s.

## 1018 and 1070 Hay Street 1963

**RIGHT:** During the first 40 years after settlement in 1829, the developed area of Perth was generally confined to the area around St Georges Terrace and Barrack Street in the city centre. However, with an increase in population from the 1870s onwards, development began to creep west in the vicinity of Mount and Malcolm Streets.

By the beginning of the 20th century, as a result of the huge increase in population brought about by the first gold boom, West Perth became one of the more prestigious residential addresses in Perth, with its elevated position and convenient location, making it a much sought-after place to live. In 1906, the area between Hay Street and Kings Park was described as 'a very fashionable resort'.

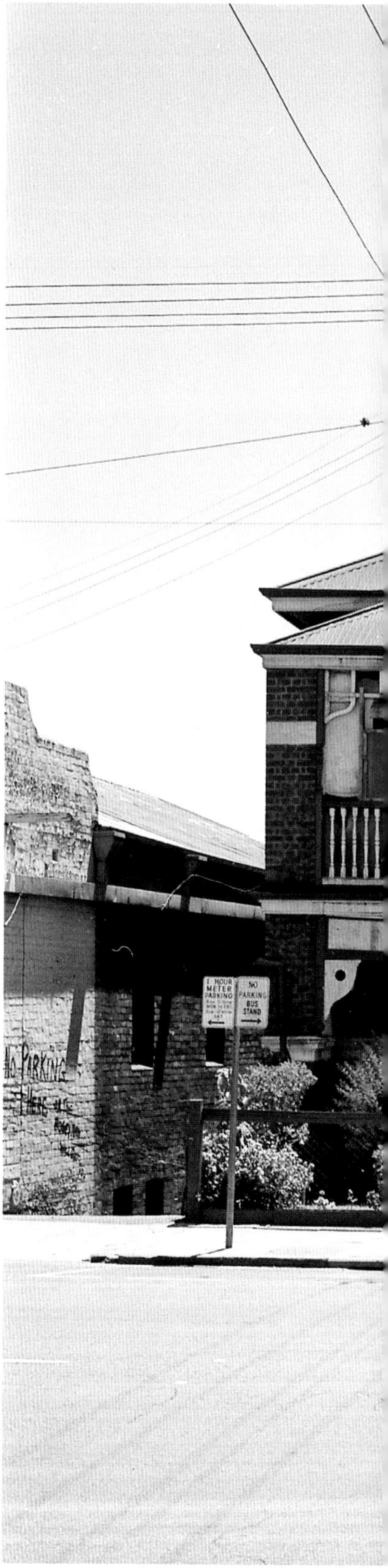


**BELOW:** These two houses on Hay Street, built around the beginning of the 20th century, are very typical of that affluent period in Perth's history. Today, they would be classed as 'very desirable' residences, but in the 1960s, they were considered to be 'old fashioned' and not worthy of preservation.

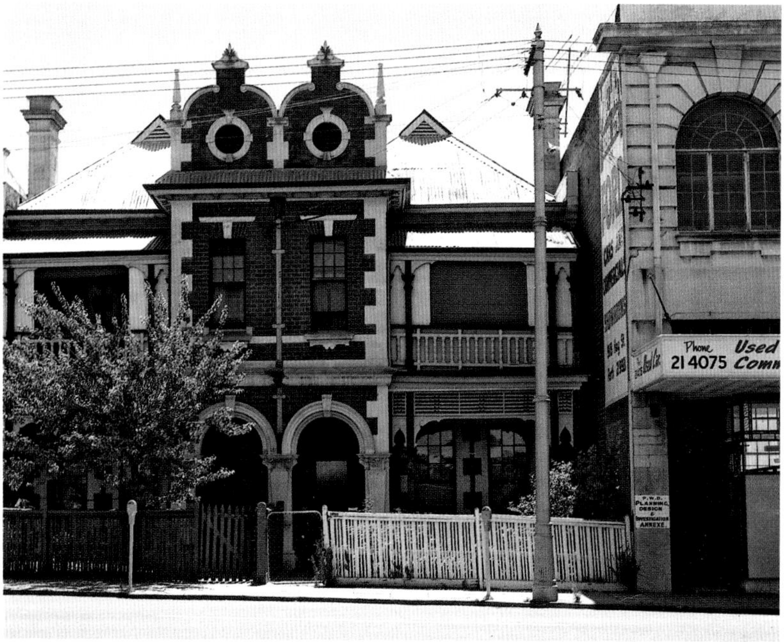

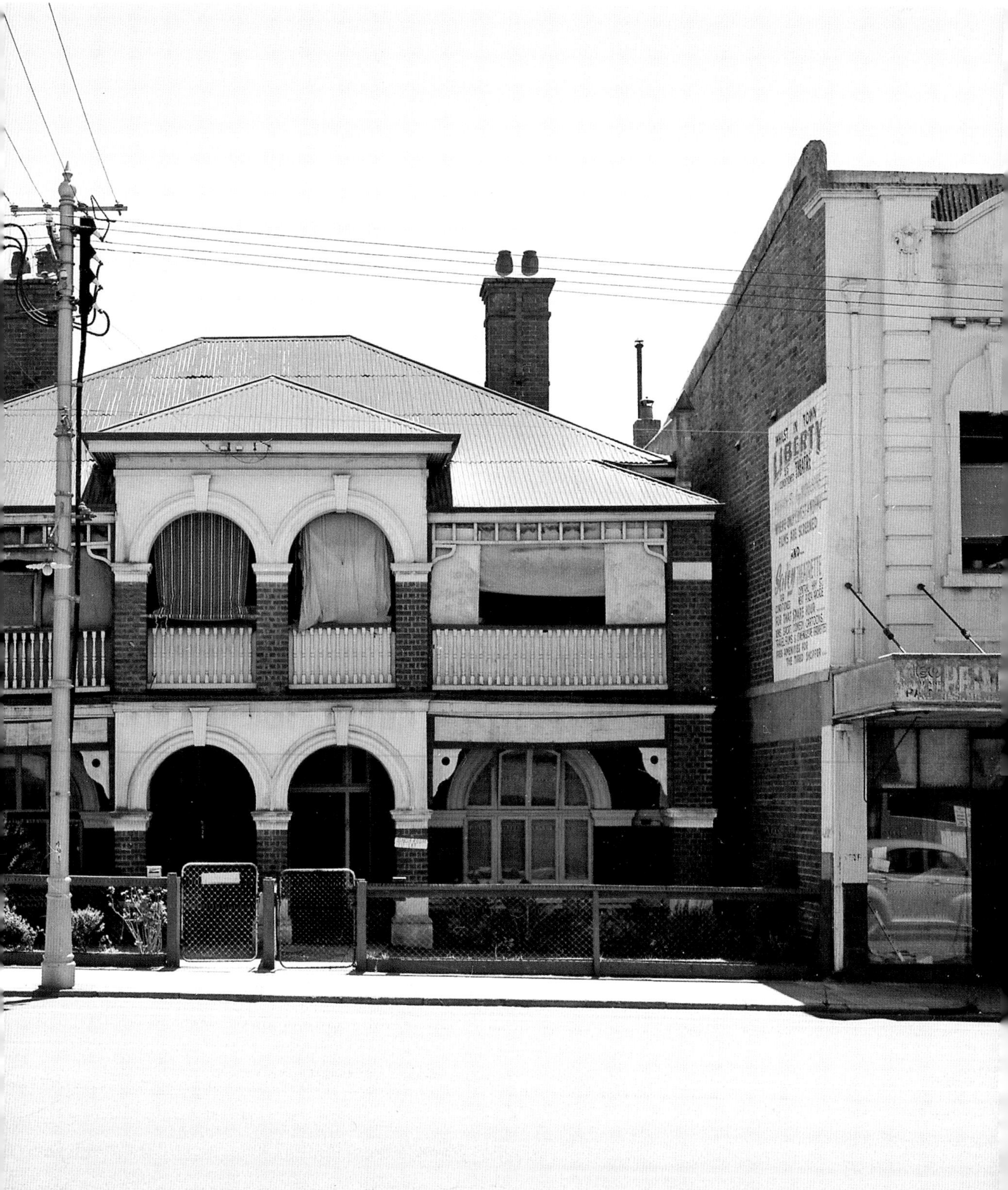
WHILST IN TOWN
LIBERTY
THEATRE
FILMS ARE SCREENED
AND...
FOR THAT SPARE HOUR...
THE TIRED SHOPPER...

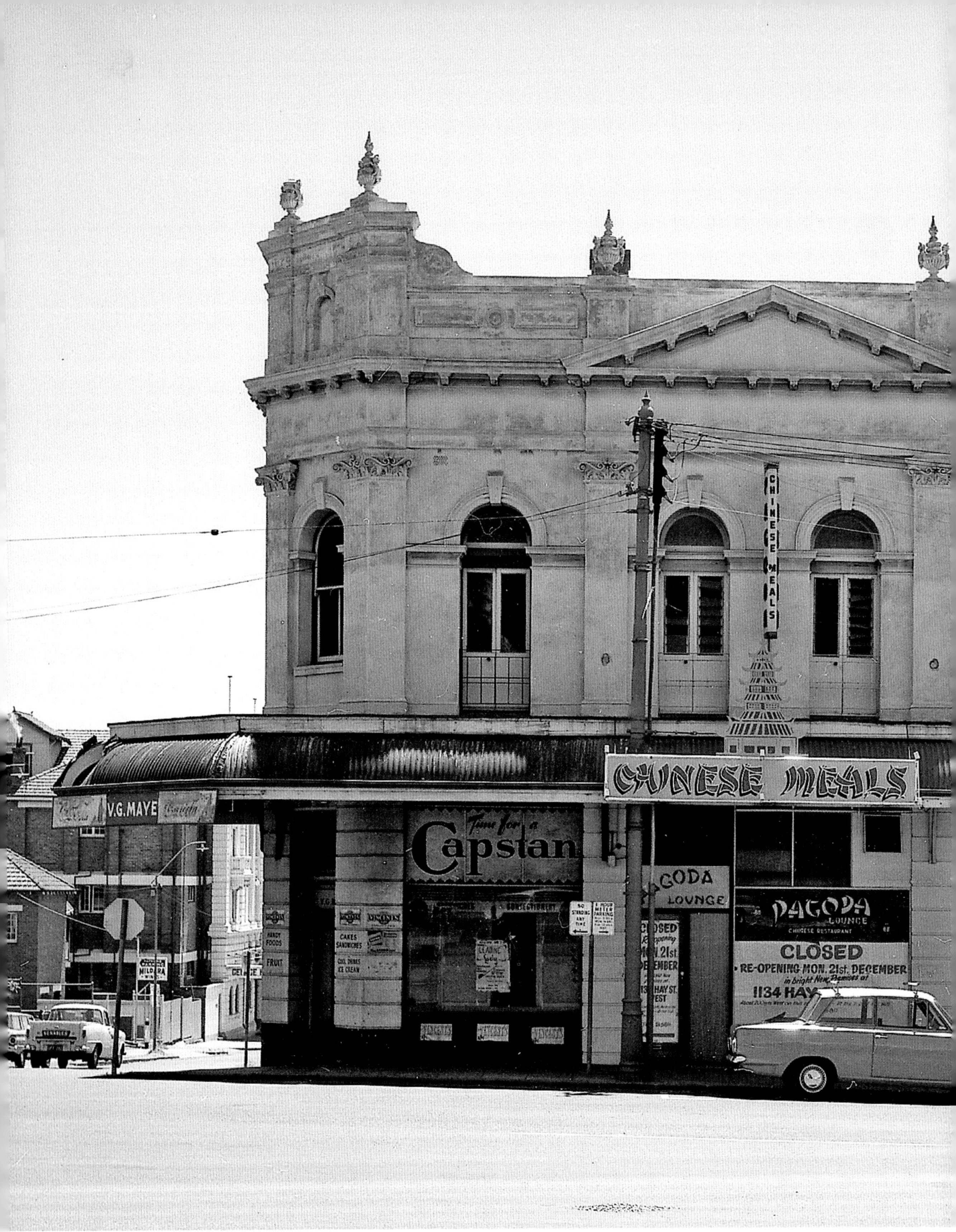
V.G.MAYE
Time for a Capstan
CHINESE MEALS
CHINESE MEALS
LOUNGE
CAKES SANDWICHES
HANDY FOODS
FRUIT
COOL DRINKS ICE CREAM
CONFECTIONERY
PAGODA LOUNGE
CHINESE RESTAURANT
CLOSED
RE-OPENING MON. 21st. DECEMBER
in bright New Premises at
1134 HAY

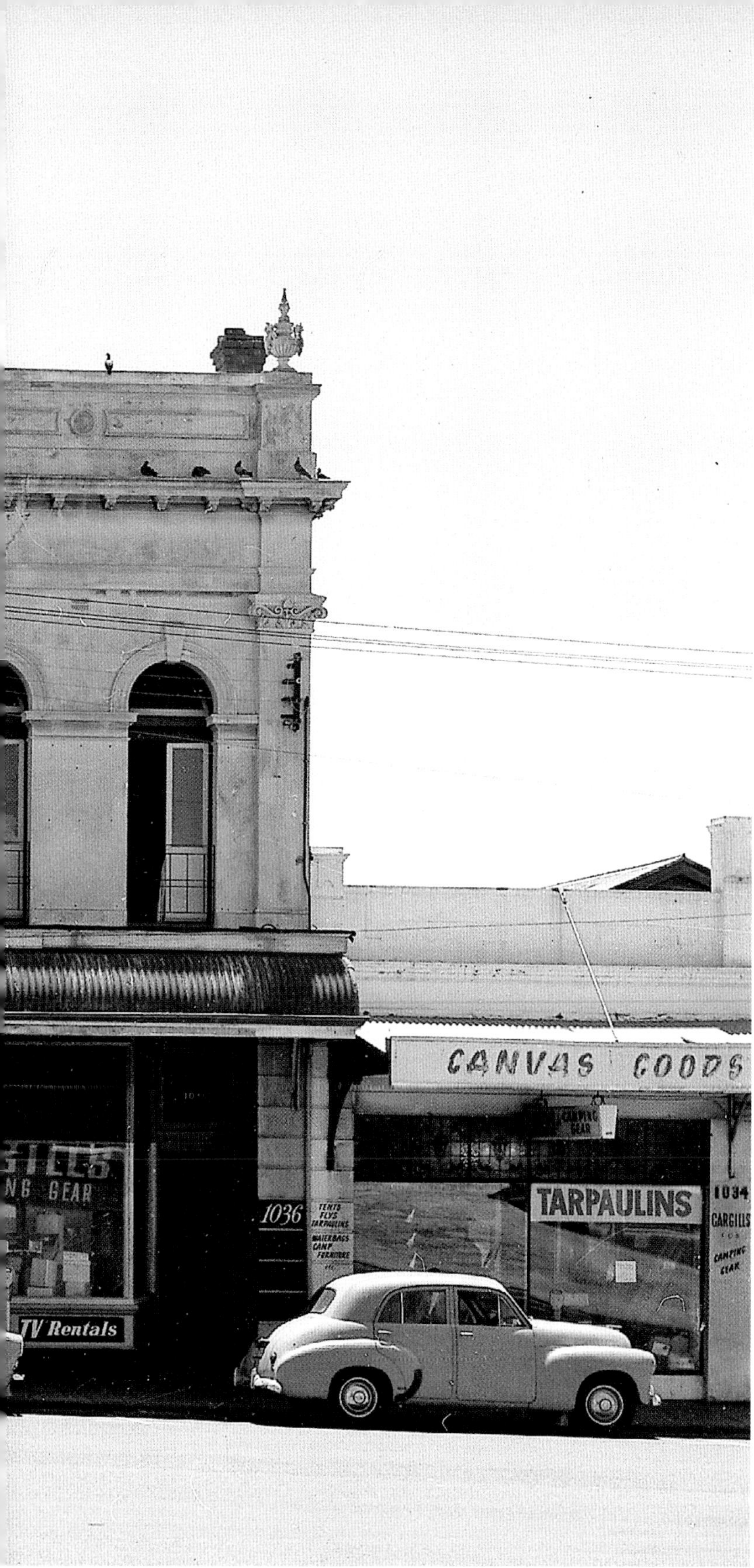


## 1040 Hay Street 1964

**LEFT:** Until 1909, 1040 Hay Street appears in the Wise's Street Directory as a vacant lot. By the 1910 edition the rather fine commercial premises, seen in this photograph, had been built and occupied by a hairdresser and tobacconist, with their respective proprietors living above their shops. Three years later it became a boot maker's shop and continued in this capacity until the 1930s, when it was listed as 'mixed businesses'.

By 1966, when it was demolished, the building contained a general store, Chinese restaurant and a hardware store.

## Doyle's 1964

**FOLLOWING PAGE:** George Street in West Perth suffered greatly when the construction of the first section of the Mitchell Freeway began in 1967. Most of the buildings on the eastern side of the street were demolished.

One of the victims of these demolitions was the ANZ Bank building on the north-east corner of the junction of George and Wellington streets. Built in the 1920s to serve the growing population and businesses in West Perth, the bank vacated the building in the 1950s, after which the building was a retail shop until its demise.

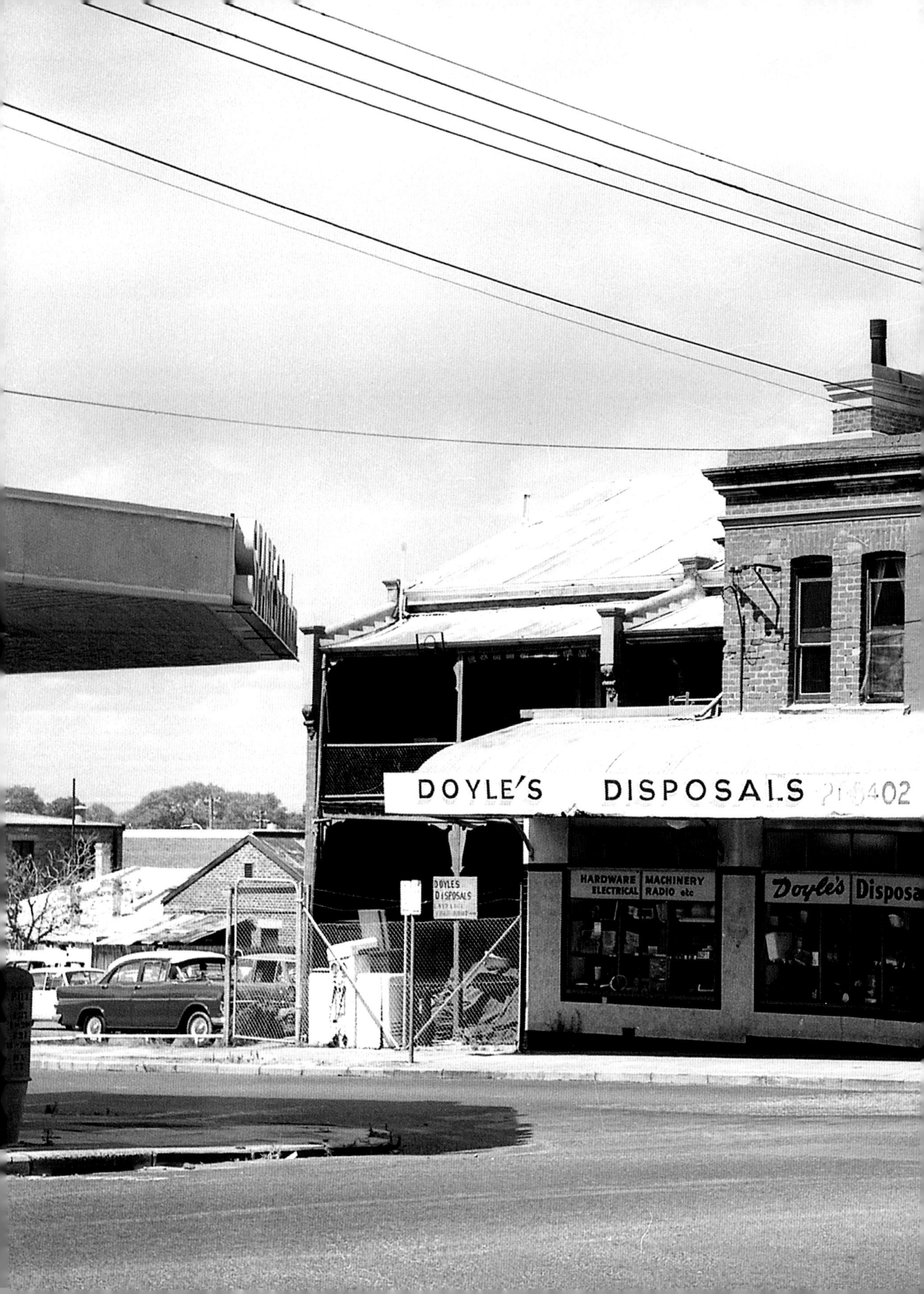
DOYLE'S DISPOSALS
HARDWARE MACHINERY ELECTRICAL RADIO etc
Doyle's Disposa
DOYLES DISPOSALS

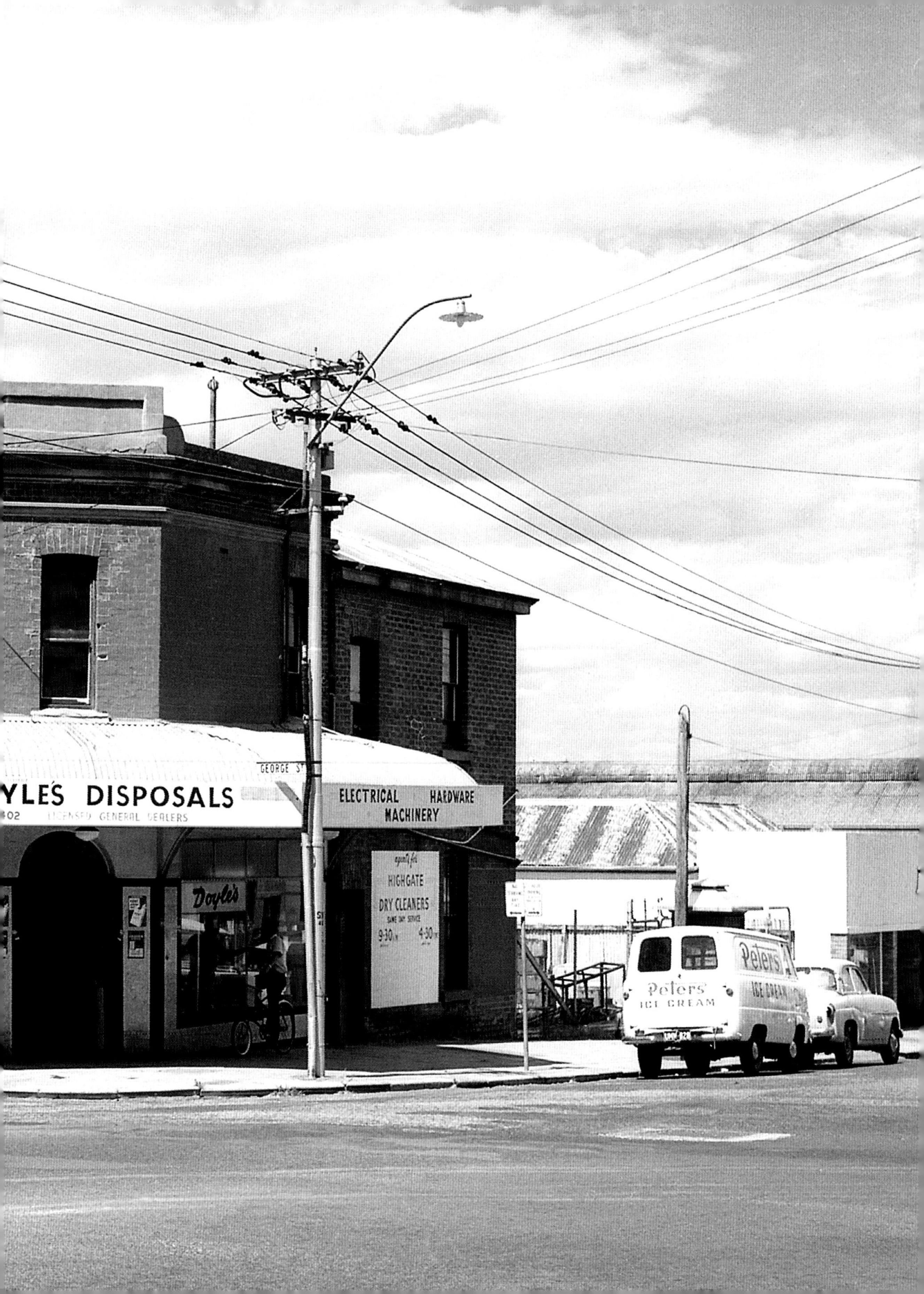
YLE'S DISPOSALS
LICENSED GENERAL DEALERS
GEORGE ST
ELECTRICAL HARDWARE
MACHINERY
HIGHGATE
DRY CLEANERS
Doyle's
Peters
ICE CREAM

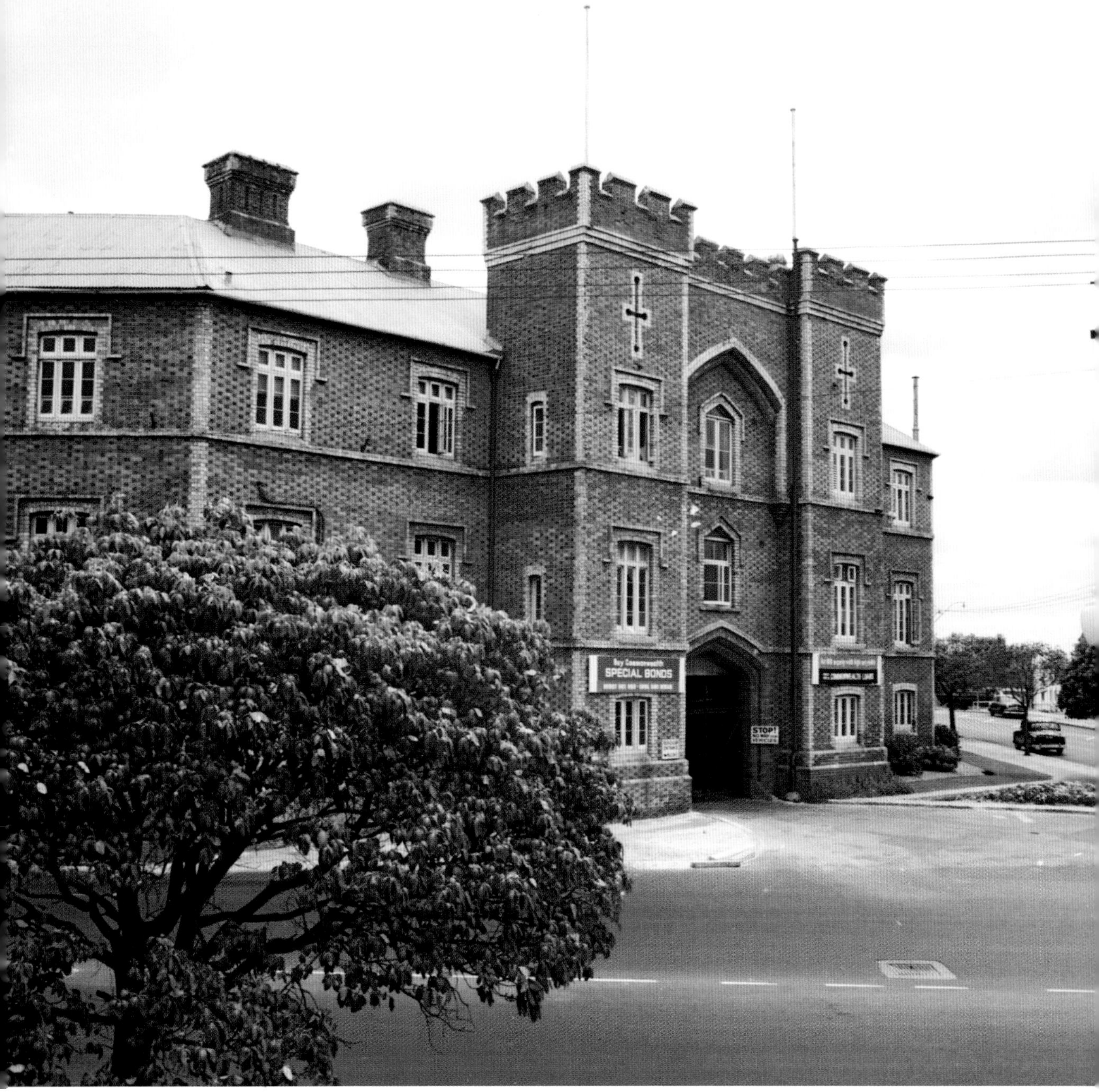


## Pensioner Barracks 1966 and 1967

The introduction of convicts in 1850 to augment the local labour force also brought the personnel required to supervise and guard the prisoners. The Enrolled Pensioner Force travelled on the convict ships as guards. On arrival in Western Australia they were offered a choice of 10 acres of land with which to make a living, or the opportunity to continue work as guards. For those who continued as guards, accommodation was required and so the Pensioner Barracks was designed by architect Richard Roach Jewell and constructed mainly by convict labour. The first families moved into their two-roomed apartments in 1866.

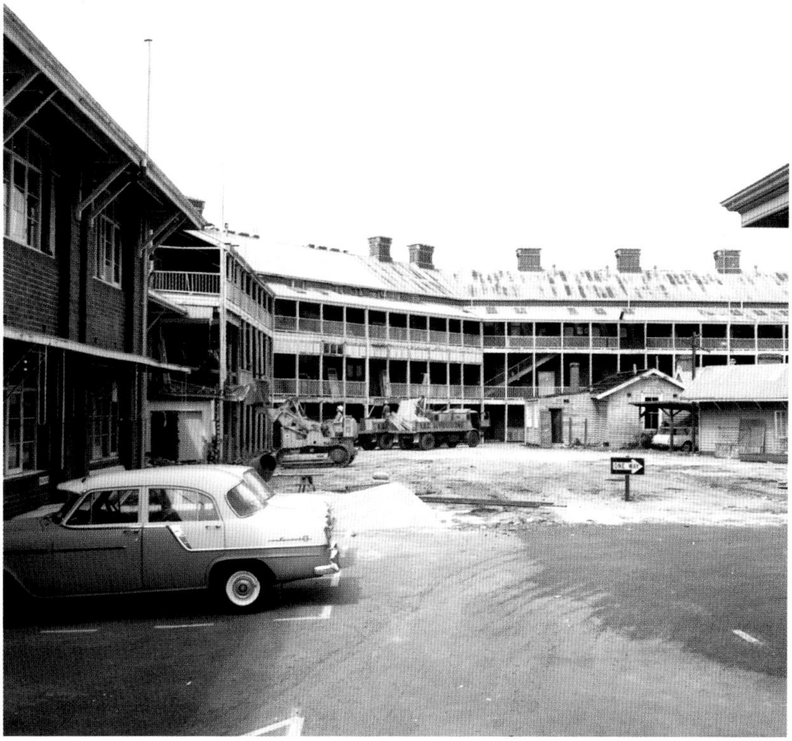

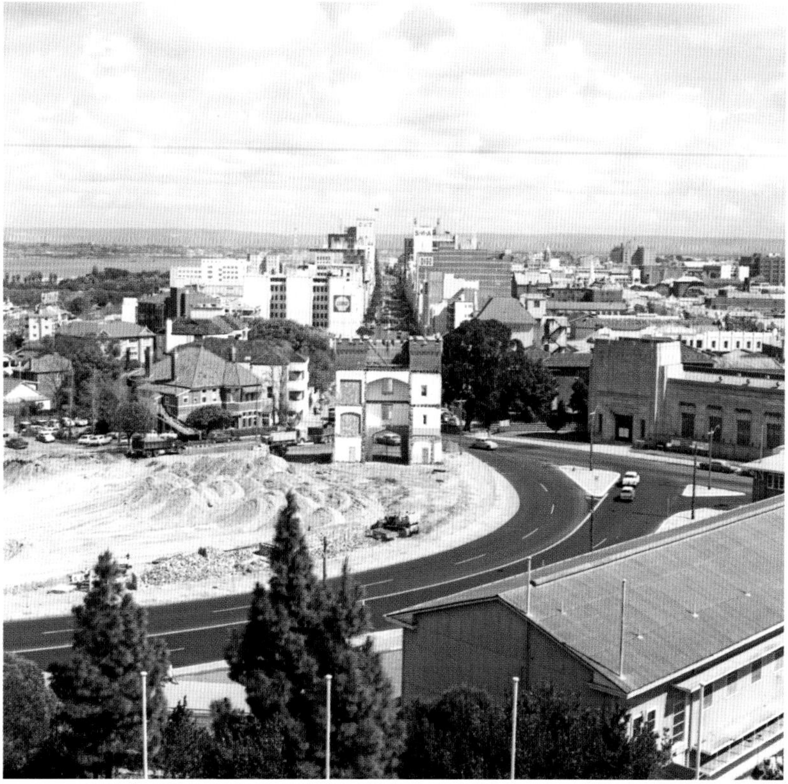

**ABOVE LEFT:** Transportation only lasted for 18 years, but during that time almost 1,200 guards, plus their families, came to live in Western Australia. The force was disbanded in 1887 and the Barracks slowly converted into government offices.

In 1960 the government announced the barracks was to be demolished to make way for the Kwinana Freeway.

**LEFT:** The threat of destruction produced a public outcry and the Royal Western Australian Historical Society formed the Barracks Defence Council to save the building. Despite this, demolition commenced and two bays of the building were reduced to rubble. Attention then turned to saving the gatehouse arch. After several polls to gauge public opinion, all of which were conclusively in favour of retention, a free vote was taken in Parliament and a motion to demolish the arch was defeated by eight votes. This small victory leaves us with an unoccupied building – Perth's 'Arc De Triomphe' – defiantly standing in front of Parliament House.

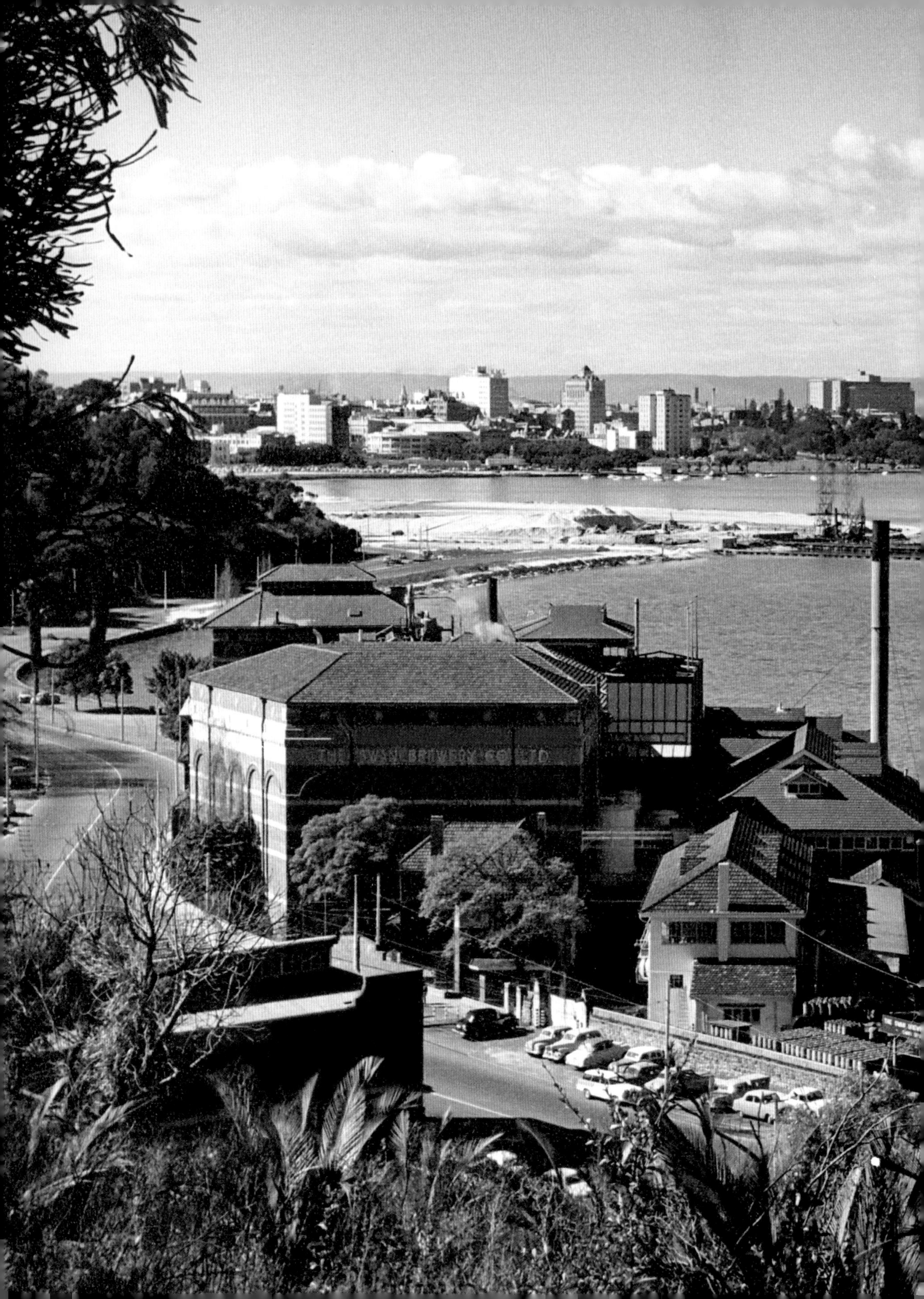

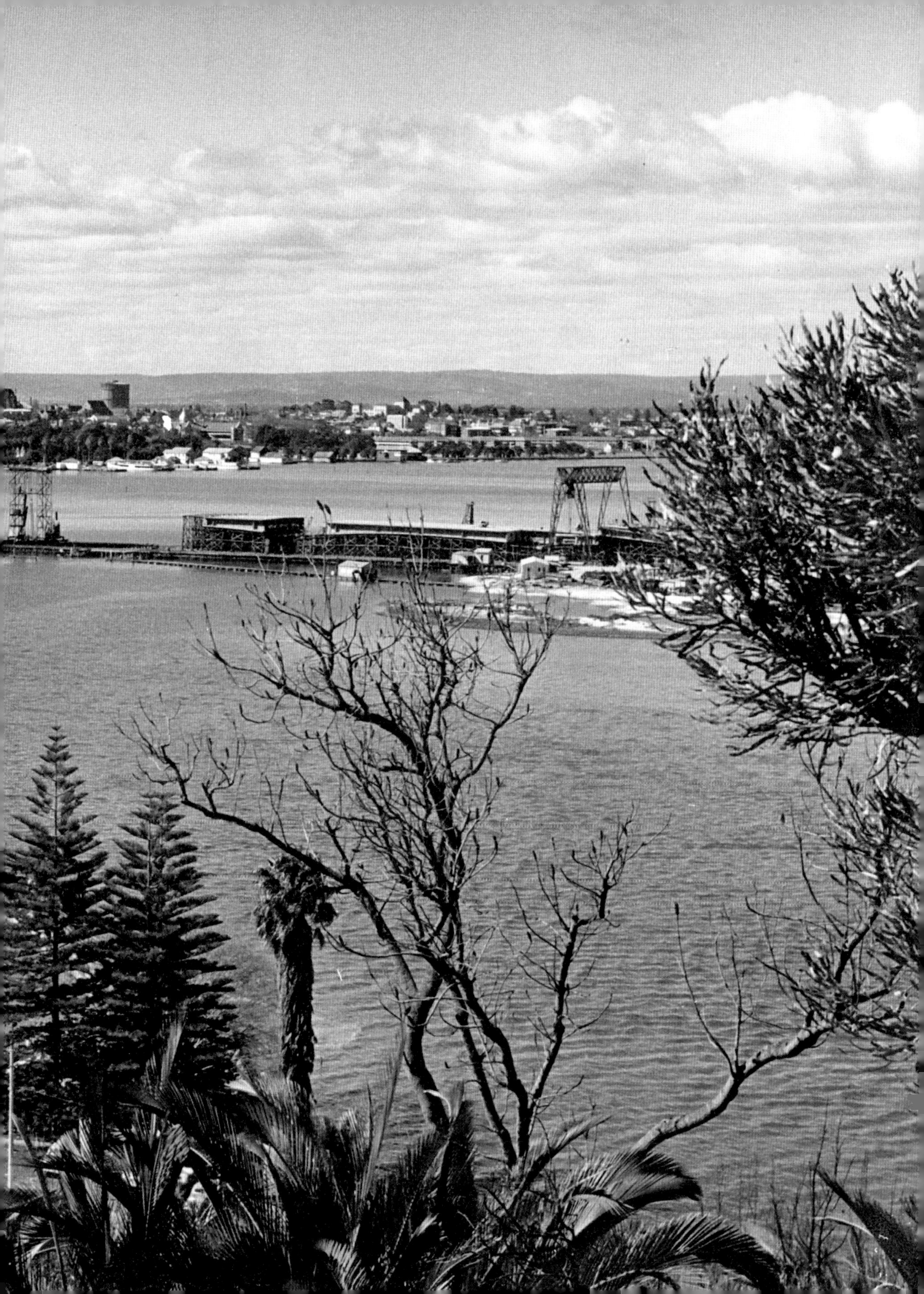

## The Narrows Bridge 1958 and 1959

**PREVIOUS PAGE, RIGHT AND BELOW:** These photos are selected from the very large number of photographs Ernie was commissioned to take by the City of Perth Council in 1958 and 1959 chronicling the construction and opening of the first Narrows Bridge.

From the earliest days of the Swan River Colony, suggestions for bridging the river at the Narrows were suggested, but generally dismissed. 'A scheme so ridiculous and extravagant that it could never be entertained for one moment, save by the most inveterate theorist', scoffed the editor of the Perth Gazette in 1849.

It was not until the 1930s that bridging the Narrows became a serious proposal and even then drew public protest that a bridge would spoil the view to and from the city. World War II then intervened, following which the prediction that the population south of the river would grow to over 100,000 in the ensuing years created a more urgent need for a new river crossing. Eventually, work on a new bridge spanning the Narrows and connecting the northern and southern suburbs began in 1954. There was much public consternation over the choice of site as it was felt the bridge would ruin picturesque views. Veteran campaigner Bessie Rischbieth protested by wading ankle-deep into the river and standing defiantly in front of the diggers.

The six-lane bridge was claimed to be the largest precast, pre-stressed concrete bridge in the world, forming part of the new, 4-kilometre Kwinana Freeway. The last river pile was driven home in November 1958, and the final concrete beam lowered into position in June 1959.

During the construction it was announced the bridge would be known as 'Golden West Bridge'. This caused much amusement amongst the public and as a result, the name was quietly jettisoned. The bridge cost £1.5 million, and was officially opened by Governor Sir Charles Gairdner who was the first person to drive across on 13 November 1959.

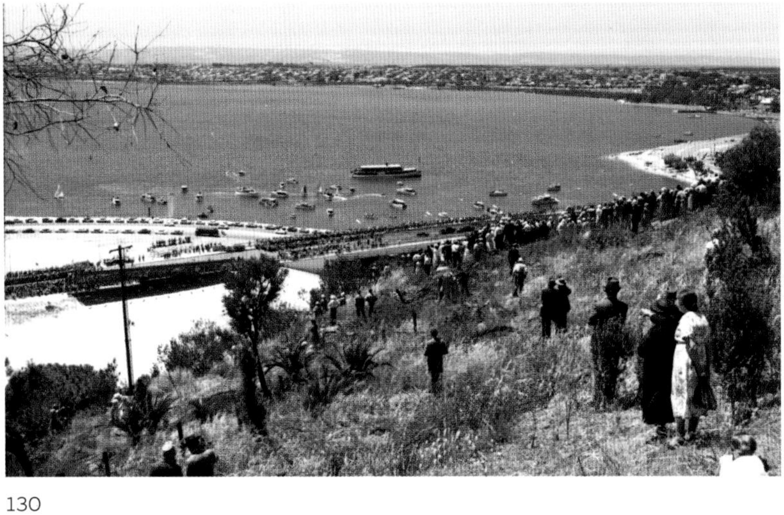

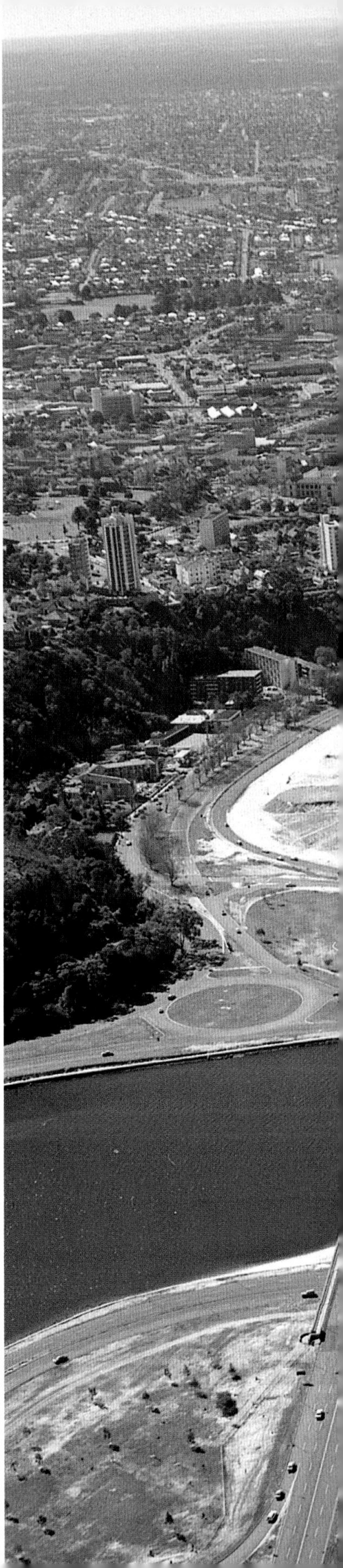

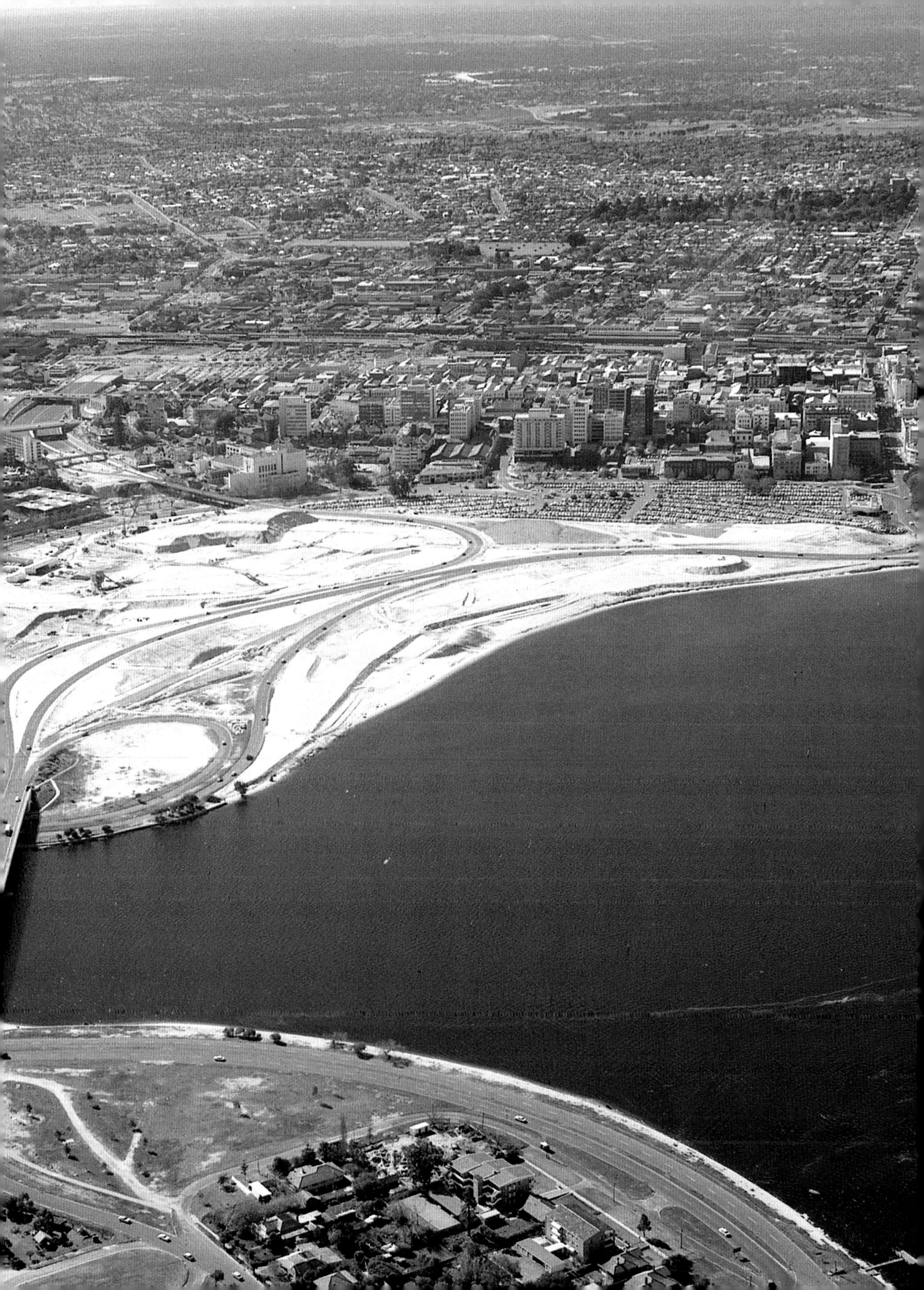

# 4

# Out of Town

The Perth suburbs did not escape Ernie's attention and he delighted in capturing on film both old and new scenes from areas other than the city centre. This chapter reminds us that the metropolitan area has many captivating places, some of which can now only been seen in these photographic records.

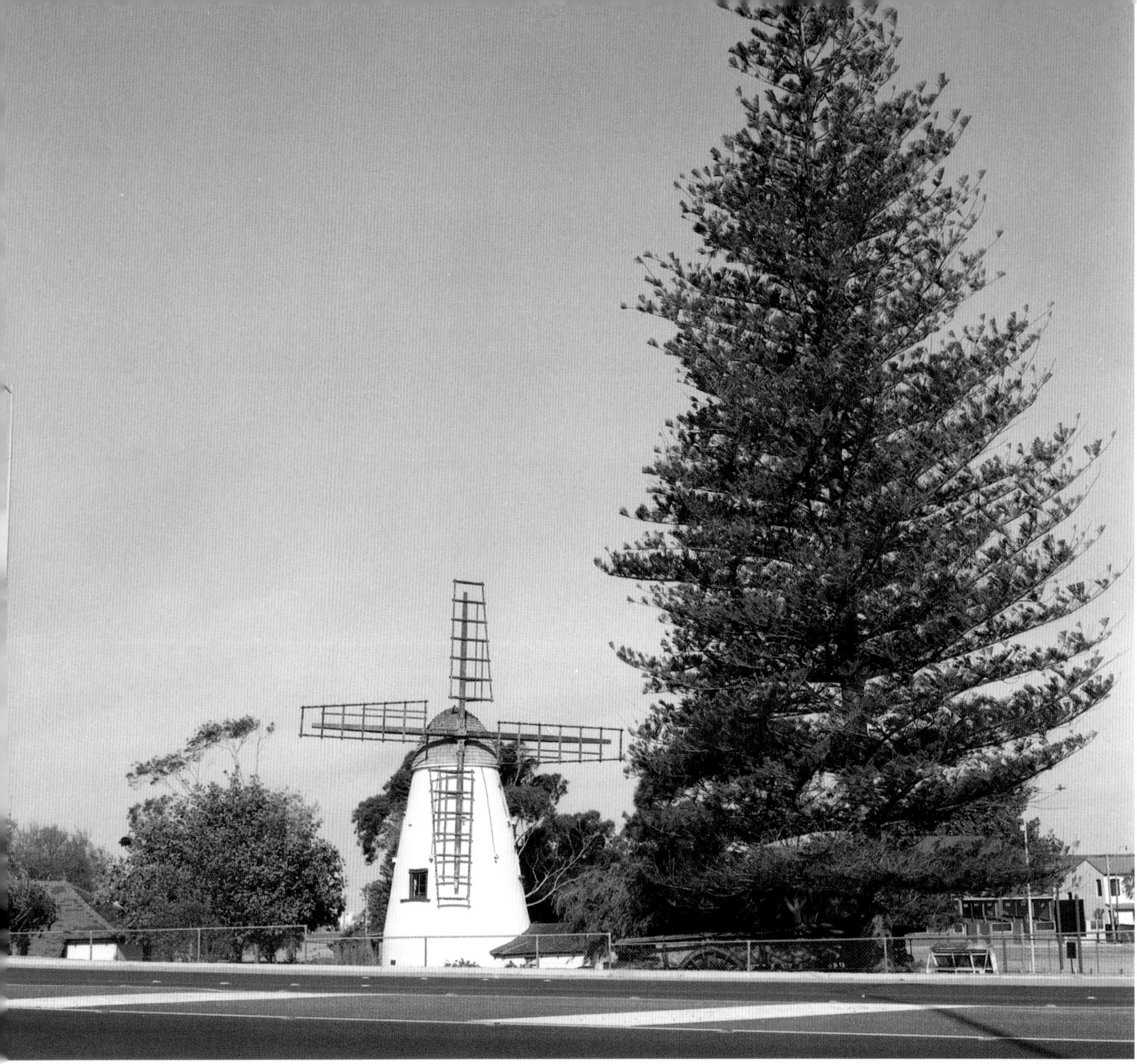

## The Old Mill, South Perth 1982

William Shenton built a windmill in South Perth because he considered it easily accessible to Perth. When it opened in 1837, Henry Reveley, whose own water mill in Perth had failed dismally, peevishly remarked that it was 'a miserable toy, which will never do much'.

Sadly, Reveley was right and even though a new owner converted it to steam power in the 1850s, it closed as not viable, simply because the river made access to Perth more difficult than Shenton had imagined.

After a number of different uses, including as a residence, a wine saloon and a poultry farm, it was vested with the City of South Perth to commemorate the centenary of the founding of South Perth. Fully restored, the mill passed into the care of the National Trust in 1992. In more recent times an extensive restoration returned the Old Mill to a close approximation of its original appearance, though in a modern setting close to the freeway.

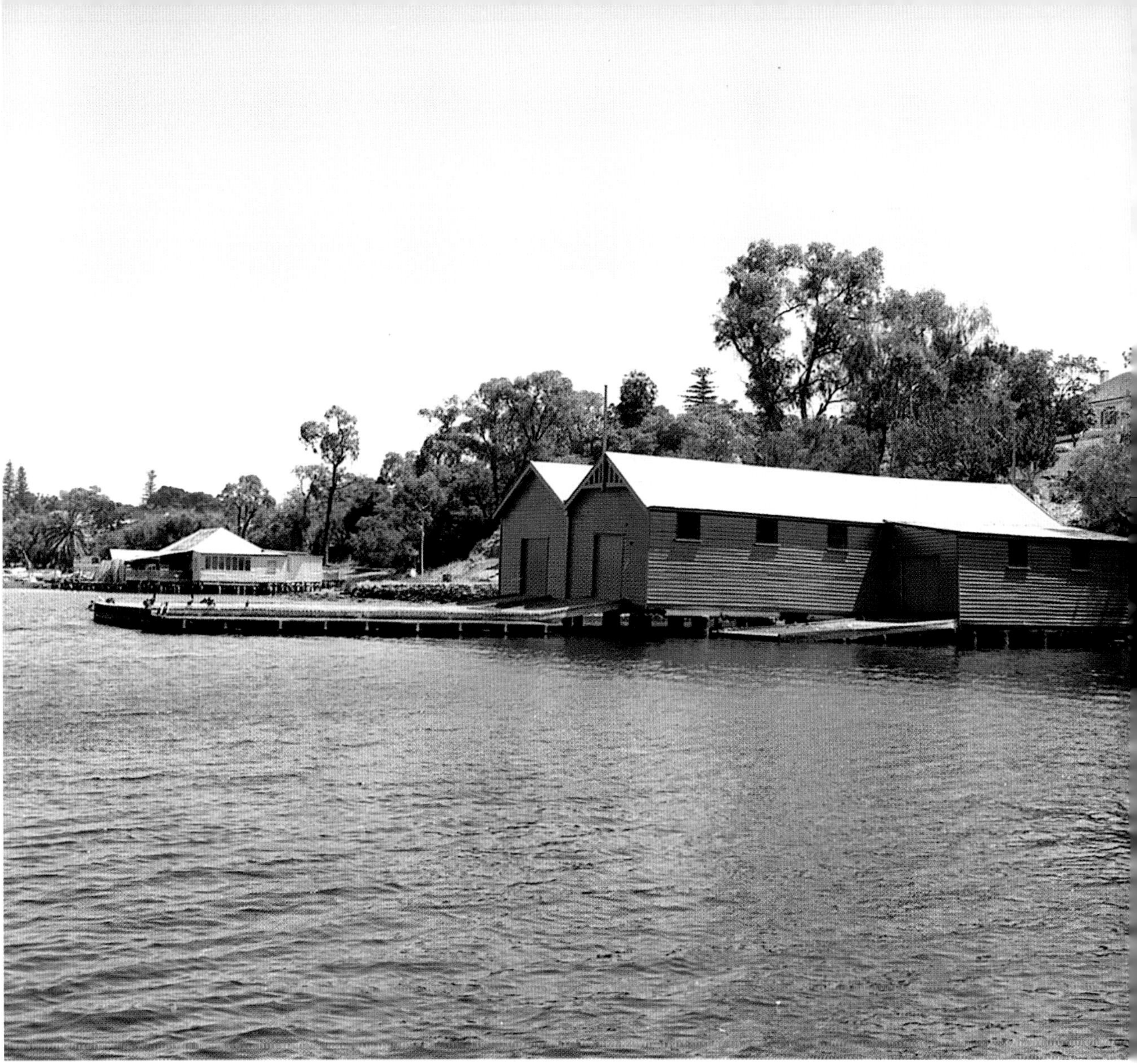

## **Scotch College Boatshed** 1977

Scotch College Boatshed is situated on the spectacularly beautiful section of the Swan River at Freshwater Bay. The introduction of competitive rowing at local private school, Scotch College, gave need for a boatshed on the river. After a protracted fundraising campaign, the College gained permission from the Peppermint Grove Roads Board to erect one of only a small number of private boatsheds allowed on that section of the Bay foreshore.

Designed by the local architectural firm of Hobbs, Smith & Forbes, the original shed consisted of: a main boat room housing the one racing eight and the two fours; a large dressing room with showers; and a lean-to for the training 'pleasure boat'. The complex was opened by the Governor, Sir Harry Barron during a lavish ceremony, in November 1914.

Sadly, the boatshed was the scene of a fatal shark attack in 1923, when a Scotch College student was bitten whilst swimming near the shed.

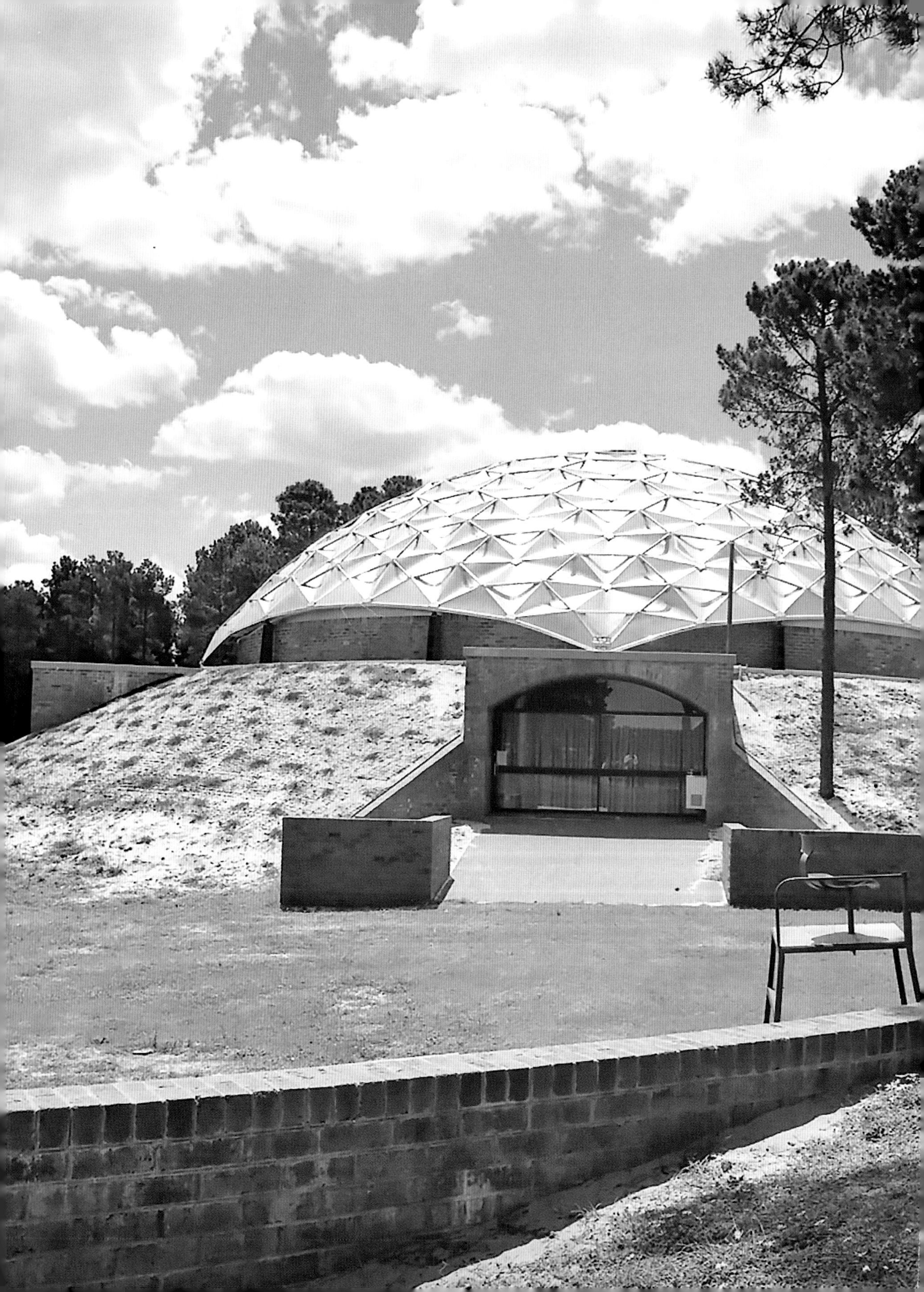

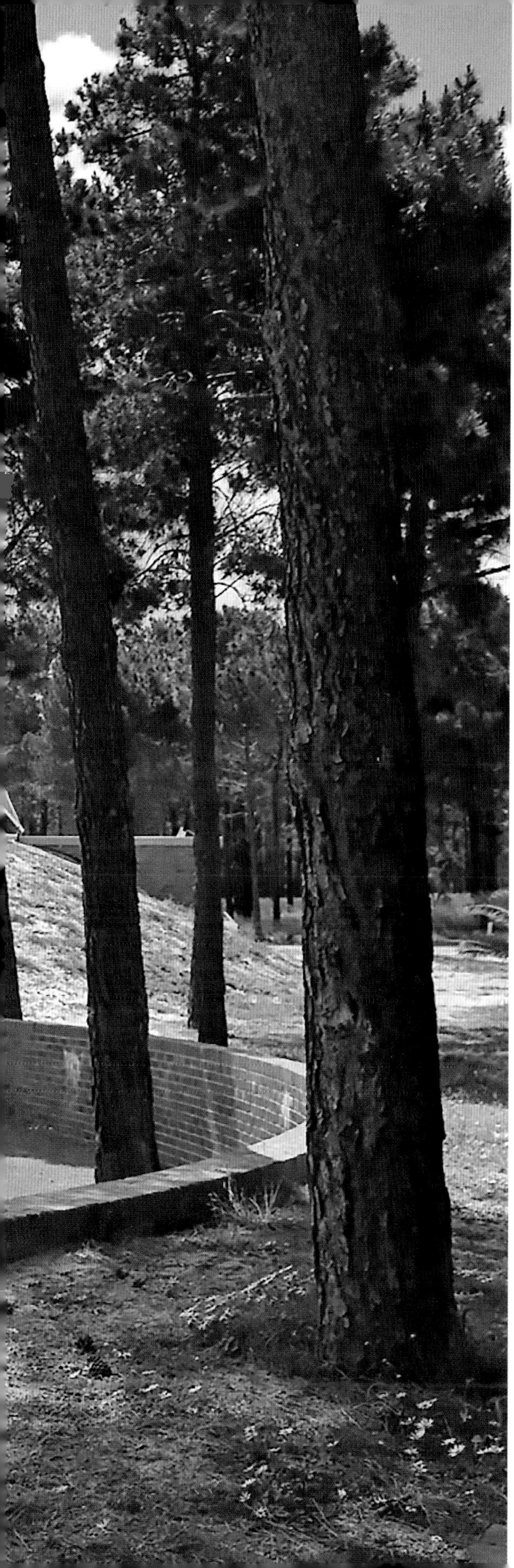

## Geodesic Dome, Curtin University

c.1970

**LEFT:** The geodesic dome is situated on the campus of Curtin University in Bentley. It represents the transformative role the university played in architectural education by responding to the major technological advances of the 1960s and 70s in design and building techniques.

The dome, which is part of the Curtin Stadium Complex, was designed by Graham Harler. A former student of the university, Harler was instrumental in organising the 1966 Australian Architecture Students' Association convention at Curtin University. This convention was attended by American architect Buckminster Fuller and inspired him to design the world-renowned geodesic dome for the Montreal Expo in 1967. The Curtin dome followed soon after as a more diminutive version.

## Post-War Housing 1966

**FOLLOWING PAGE:** Following World War II, it was estimated that about 250 300,000 new homes would be needed in and around Perth to keep up with the ever-growing population. Besides those returning from military service, a Federal Government Assisted Passage Migration Scheme as part of their 'Populate or Perish' policy added to the housing need.

Despite a lack of materials and skilled labour, new estates began to spring up around Floreat Park, Scarborough, Applecross and other suburbs created during the first Gold Rush era.

House designs of the era tended to be simple and utilitarian not only because of a lack of materials or money but also because, until 1952, house size was limited by legislation. By 1954 most Australian homes had only five rooms, but the bathroom had migrated indoors and there was space for a family car in the yard.

Photographed in 1966, these houses on the border of Wembley and Floreat are typical of this post-war housing boom.

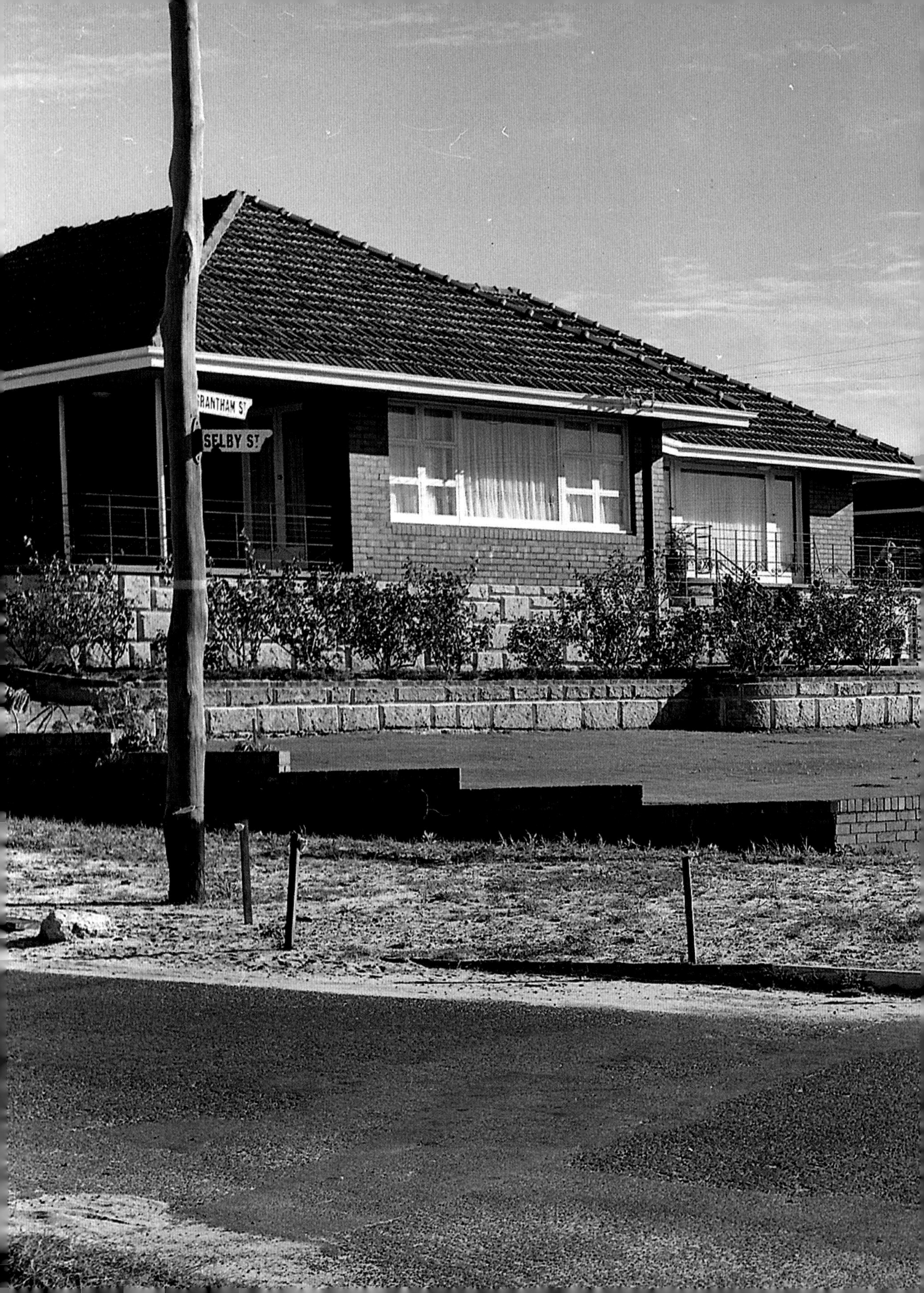

GRANTHAM ST
SELBY ST

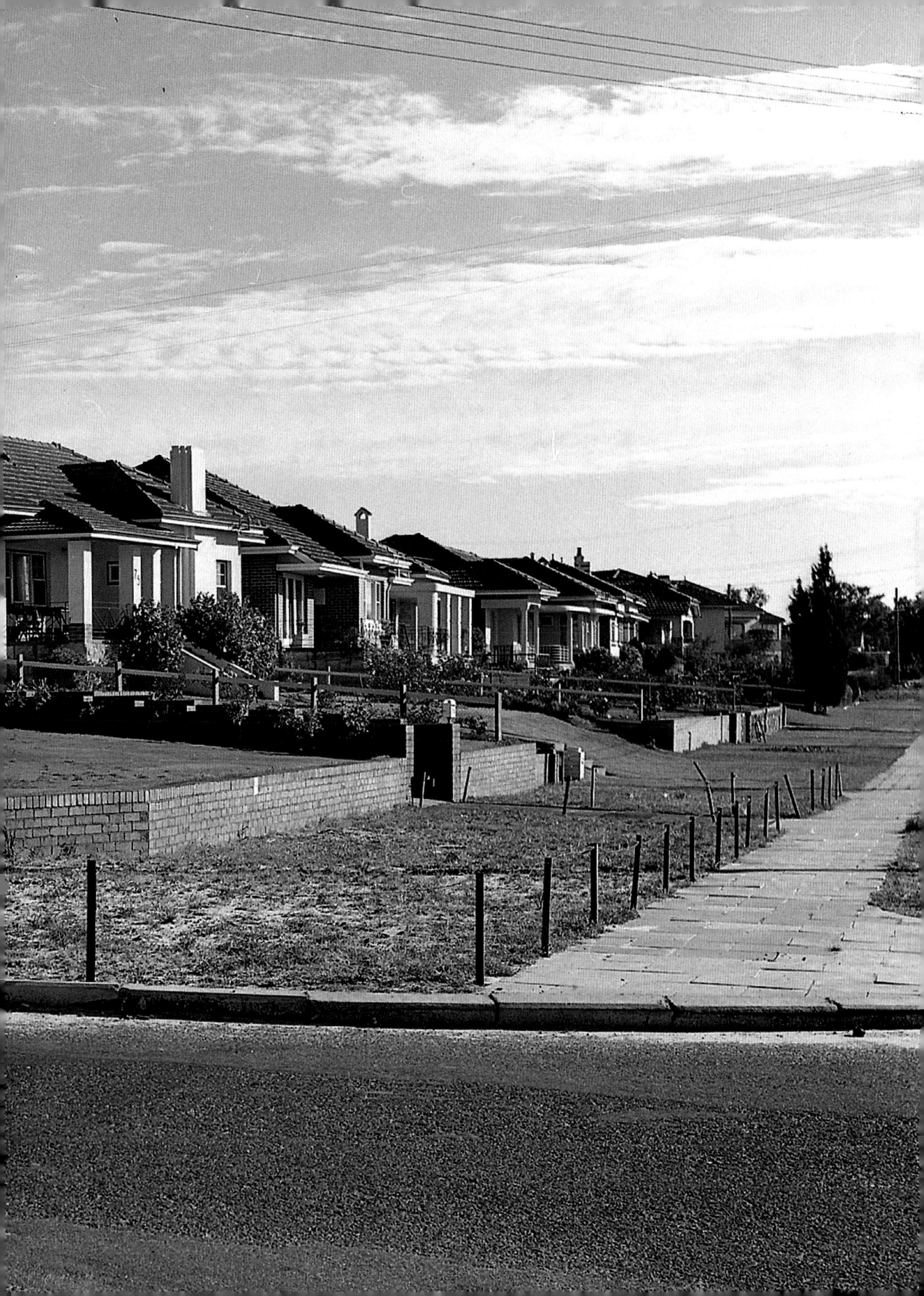

## St John of God Hospital, Subiaco 1982

The Congregation of the Sisters of St John of God was founded in Wexford, Ireland, in 1871. Inspired by the work of their patron saint St John of God, they nursed those in poverty.

In 1895, a group of eight Sisters arrived in Perth at the invitation of Bishop Matthew Gibney to help care for the sick and began visiting them in their homes. Three years later, the Sisters opened a convent, hospital and school in Subiaco.

Initially, a temporary wooden hospital was built on the 7-acre site, but this was replaced in 1898 by a suite of buildings, including a chapel, convent and the man hospital, all designed by the architectural firm of Cavanagh & Cavanagh, who were the favoured architects for the Catholic Church in Western Australia for many years. After the opening ceremony, attended by over 200 people, the West Australian reported, 'The site is an exceptionally healthy one, and as the grounds surrounding will never be built on, the hospital will always receive the benefit of the sea breezes.'

The hospital building was demolished in 1983 to make way for a much larger and up-to-date hospital and the Chapel was demolished 22 years later. The only remaining remnant of the old hospital is a stained glass window to the memory of the McAuliffe family, which is now located in the undercover entrance to the hospital.

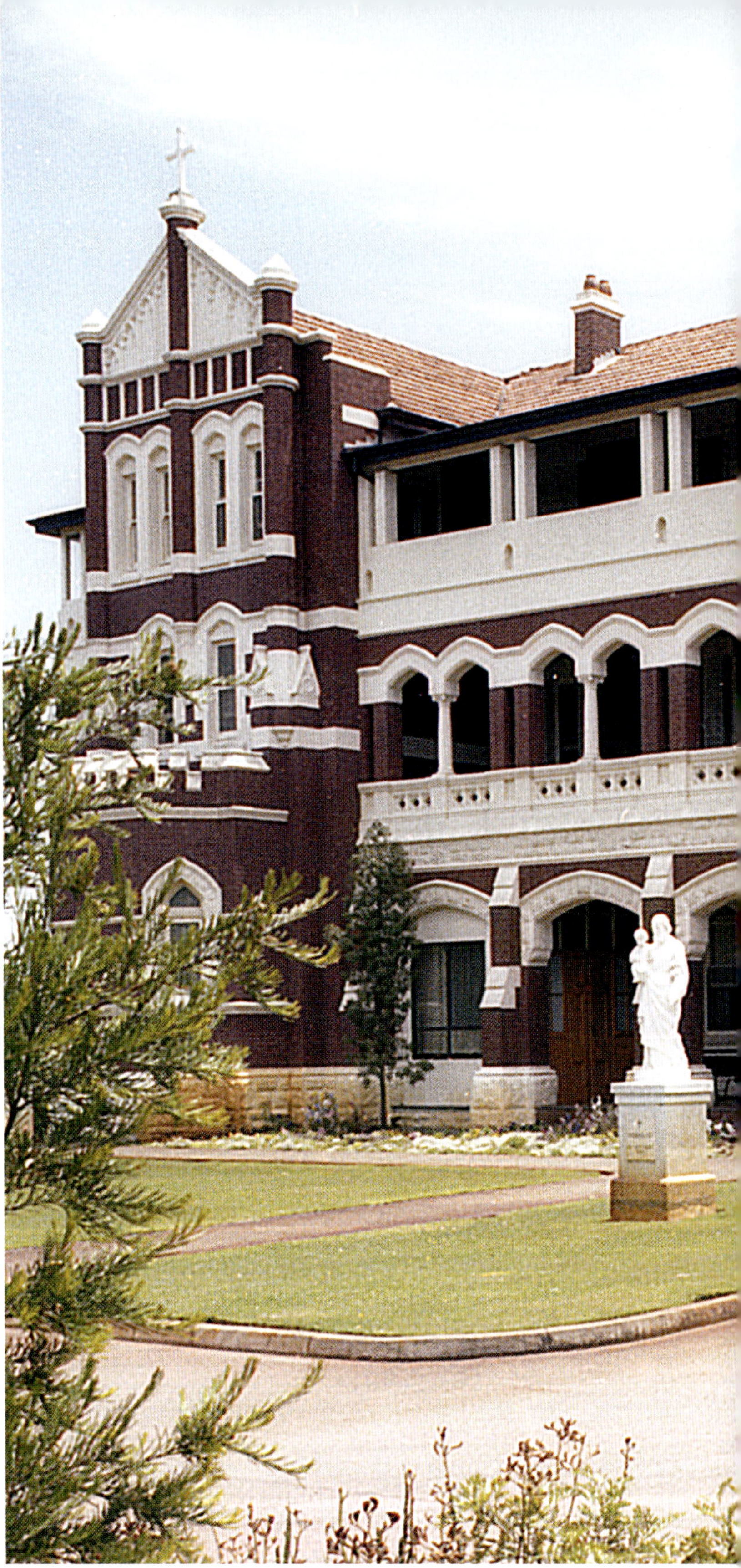

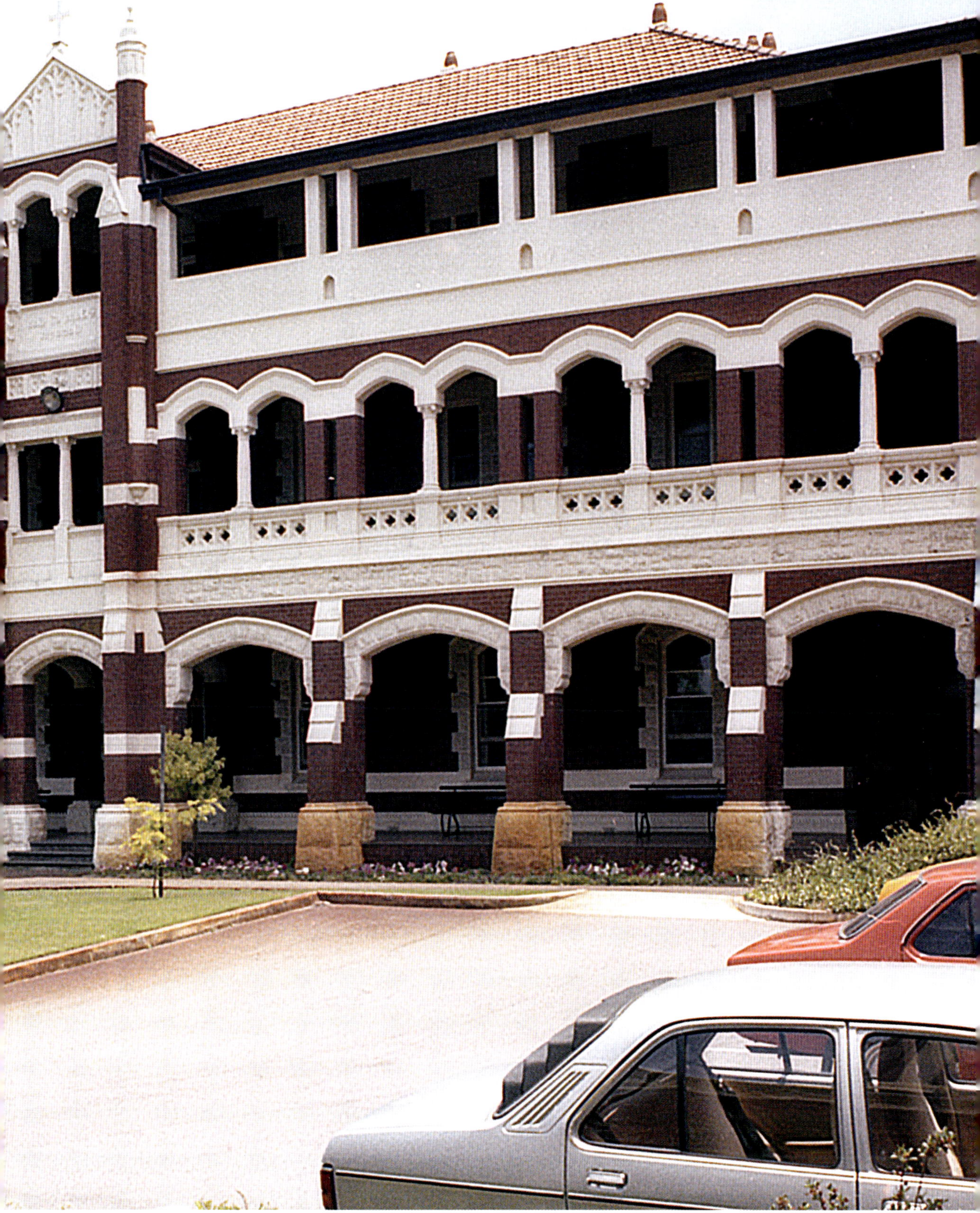

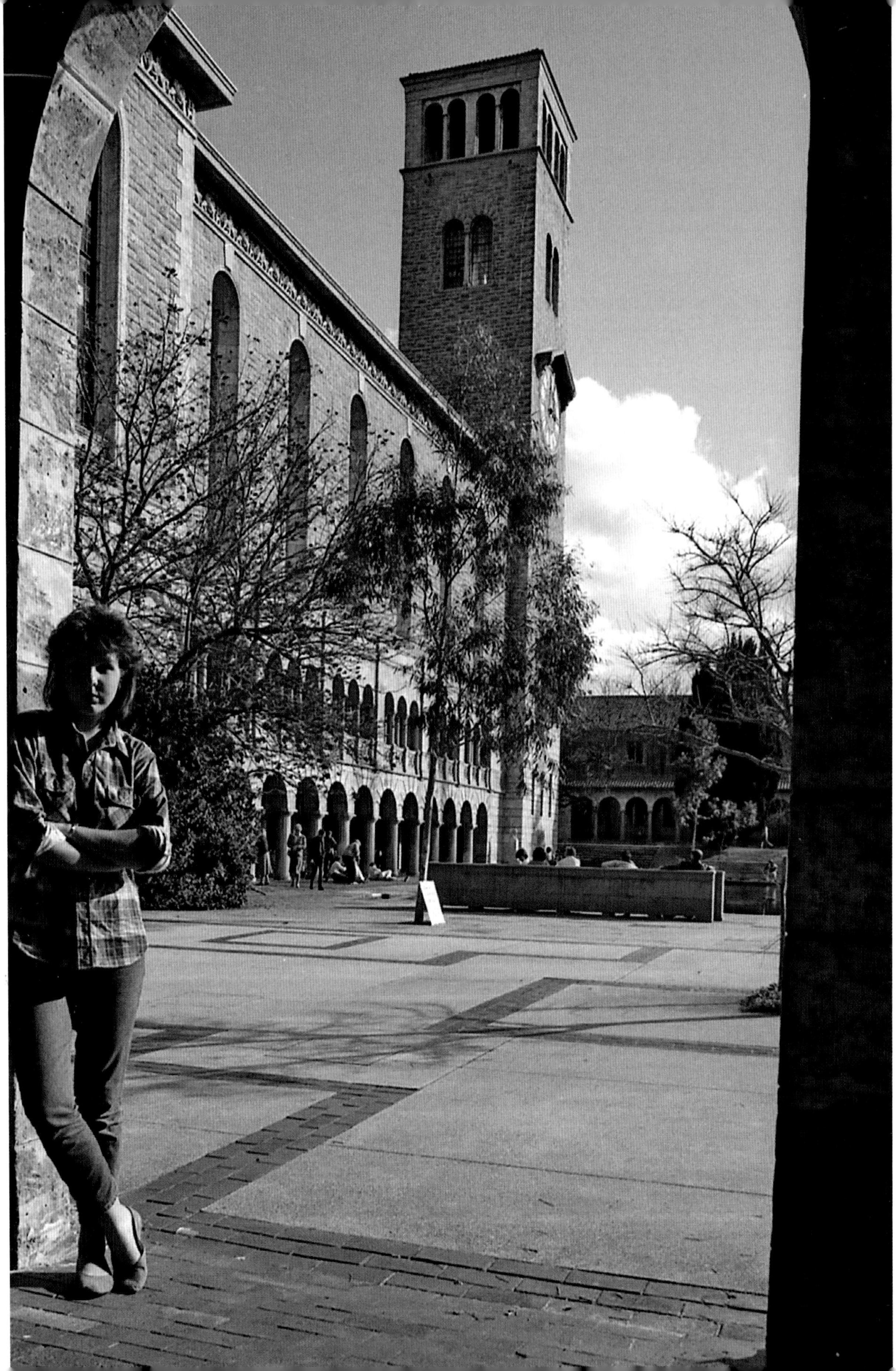

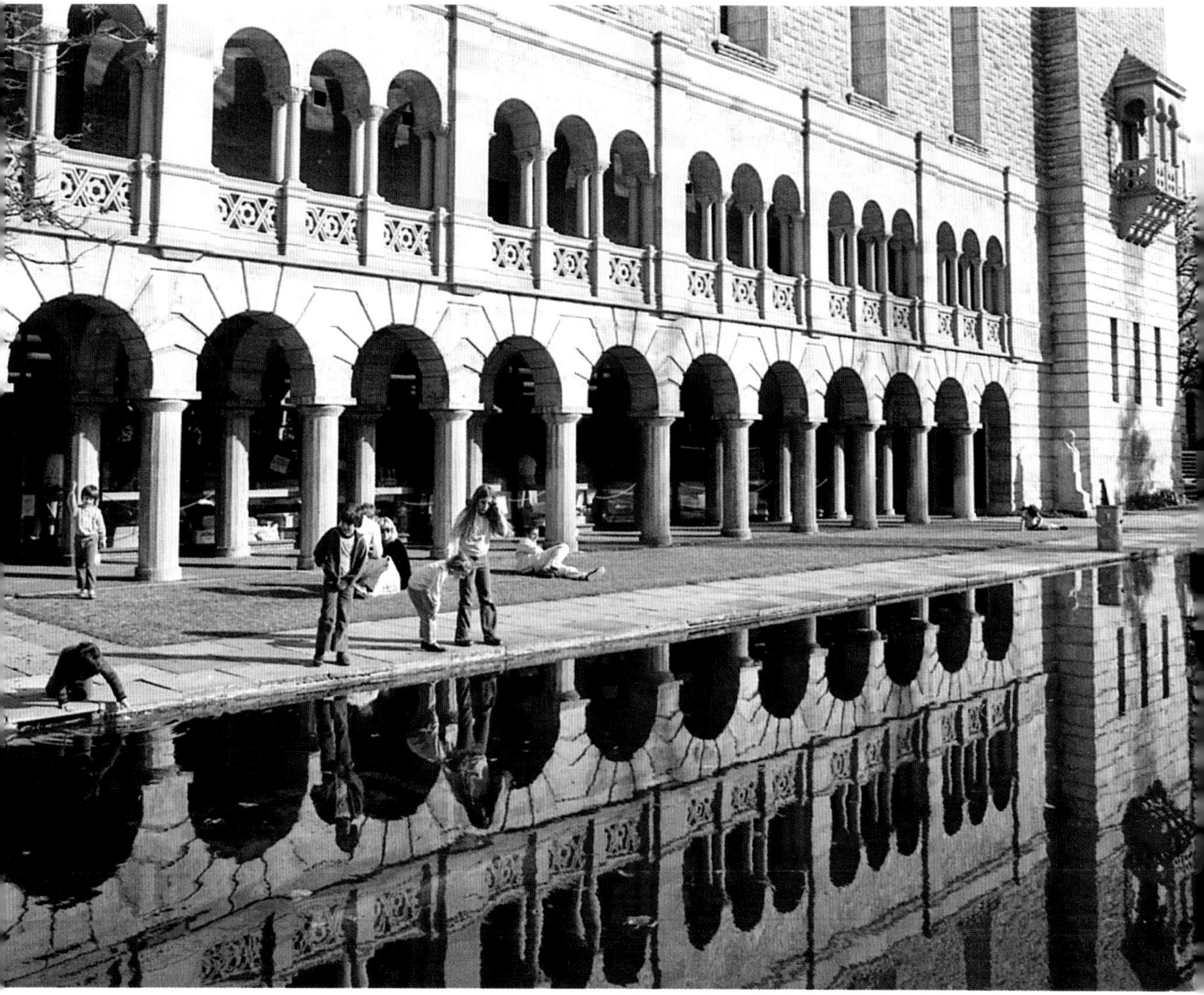

## Winthrop Hall, UWA c.1980

The University of Western Australia was incorporated in 1911. Two years later, teaching began in temporary buildings located in Irwin Street, Perth, with the university moving to its permanent campus in Crawley in the early 1930s.

The Hackett Memorial buildings, built between 1926 and 1932, form an impressive nucleus for the university campus and a fitting memorial to the University's first Chancellor, Sir John Winthrop Hackett, whose unexpectedly large bequest funded their construction.

The crowning glory of the Memorial Buildings is the Winthrop Hall. Opened in April, 1932, the building was described by its architect, Rodney Alsop, who said, 'Renaissance is the only definite term that can be given to the style of the Building'.

As these two atmospheric autumnal photographs show, the building and its surroundings would not be out of place in a piazza in Renaissance Tuscany.

# About the Author

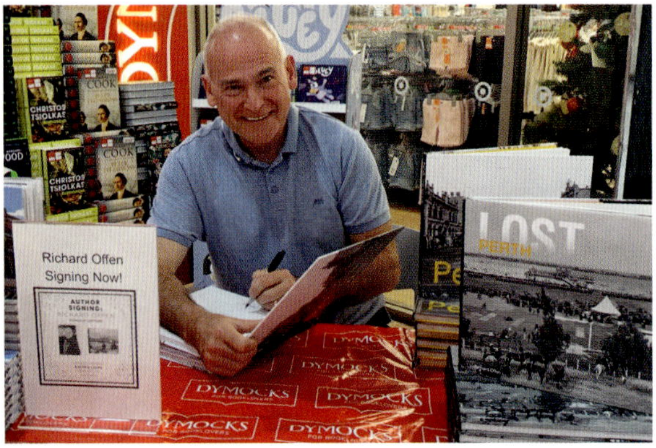


**Richard Offen** spent nearly 15 years on the staff of the UK National Trust. He immigrated to Perth, Western Australia, in 2005 to become the inaugural director of Heritage Perth, a post he held until retiring in 2017. During that time he became a regular speaker and broadcaster, promoting the history and heritage of Western Australia.

In semi-retirement, Richard now spends his time as an author and broadcaster, still having regular slots on radio stations ABC Perth and 6PR Talkback Radio. He has written two titles for Pavilion Books 'Perth Then and Now' and 'Lost Perth'. More recently he has penned two school histories; 'A Place to Grow' – A Centenary History of St Mary's Anglican Girls' School and 'The School in the Bush', charting the 50-year history of Bunbury Cathedral Grammar School.

An avid bell ringer since the age of eight, Richard has been the Captain of Ringers at Canterbury Cathedral and Perth's iconic Bell Tower. In 1976, he was appointed to the Canterbury Diocesan Advisory Committee for the Care of Churches, acting as their bells advisor for 13 years. He is now the Convenor of the Australia and New Zealand Association of Bell Ringers Bells Advisory Panel.

Richard is also a Councillor on the Heritage Council of Western Australia, and President of both the Royal Western Australian Historical Society and the Friends of Battye Library.

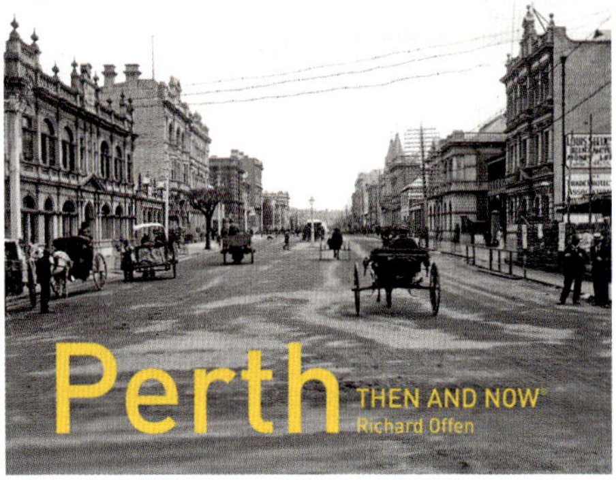


ISBN: 9781910904909

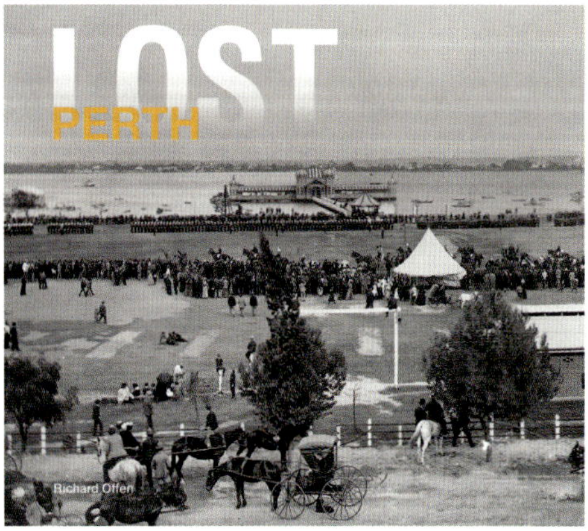


ISBN: 9781911595601